JAPANESE FINANCIAL GROWTH

Japanese Financial Growth

Edited by
Charles A. E. Goodhart
Norman Sosnow Professor of Banking
The London School of Economics and Political Science

and

George Sutija
Professor of International Business
Florida International University

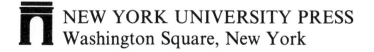
NEW YORK UNIVERSITY PRESS
Washington Square, New York

First published in the U.S.A. in 1990 by
NEW YORK UNIVERSITY PRESS
Washington Square
New York, N.Y. 10003

Printed in Great Britain

Library of Congress Cataloging-in-Publication Data
Japanese financial growth/ edited by Charles A. E. Goodhart and George
  Sutija.
        p.   cm.
    Papers presented at the International Conference on Japanese Financial Growth,
held in London in Oct. 1988.
    ISBN 0-8147-3035-3
    1. Finance—Japan—Congresses.   2. Banks and banking—Japan
—Congresses. 3. Banks and banking, Japanese—Congresses.
4. Monetary policy—Japan—Congresses.   5. Investments, Japanese
—Congresses.   6. Banking law—Japan—Congresses.   I. Goodhart, C.
A. E. (Charles Albert Eric)   II. Sutija, George, 1926–   .
III. International Conference on Japanese Financial Growth (1988:
London, England)
HG187.J3J35   1990
332′.0952—dc20   90–3148
                                                                      CIP

Contents

List of Tables

List of Figures

Preface

This book is a collection of papers presented at the International Conference on Japanese Financial Growth. This was the fifth conference organised by the Permanent Advisory Committee on Eurodollars (PACE) in co-operation with the London School of Economics Financial Markets Group, held in London in October 1988.

Industrial expansion within a country has always been accompanied by financial development. So it was, perhaps, only to be expected that the rise to international prominence of Japanese industry would be accompanied by an associated rapid growth of Japanese financial power, both domestically and internationally. But the scale of this latter expansion has been awesome. Most of the largest banks in the world, as measured by the value of deposits, are now Japanese. Japanese banks are the largest players in the international Euromarkets. The equity market in Tokyo is the largest in the world, not only bigger than the New York Stock Exchange, but dwarfing all the European equity markets combined. Japan is the biggest international creditor and disposes of the largest annual capital outflows. So the context of the global capital market, focused on the three centres, Tokyo, London and New York, will be largely influenced by the developments that shape the future pattern of Japanese banking and securities markets. In order to understand the present forces affecting financial markets around the world, and even more so to be able to forecast their likely changing pattern, it will be necessary to have a clear vision of the main factors conditioning both the present state of, and likely future changes in, Japan's financial services sector. Assembled for this Conference, speakers and discussants, was a group of experts from Japan, Europe and the United States, who provided guidance not only on the general subject of Japanese financial development, but also on the question of how its likely future patterns may affect the wider global capital market.

The editors would like to express their gratitude to the Bank of England, Bank of America, The Industrial Bank of Japan, Stadsparkasse, Cologne and London International Financial Futures Exchange for their generous financial support of the conference. We also express our appreciation to Tim Farmiloe, our editor, and Keith Povey, editorial consultant and Robert Allan Schwarzreich, doctoral candidate, for their assistance in preparation of this volume. To our colleagues, speakers at the conference and members of PACE, the editors express their deep sense of friendship and desire for future meetings and collaborations.

CHARLES A. E. GOODHART
GEORGE SUTIJA

Notes on the Contributors

Robert Z. Aliber is Professor of International Finance at the University of Chicago. He was formerly Senior Economic Advisor to the Department of State, and a staff economist for the Committee for Economic Development and the Commission on Money and Credit. He has written extensively on exchange rates, gold and international financial relations. His publications include: *The International Monetary Game, Monetary Reform and Inflation, National Monetary Policies and the International Financial System, Corporate Profits and Exchange Risk* and *Reconstruction of International Monetary Arrangement.*

Jenny Corbett has been Lecturer (Nissan Institute) on the Economic and Social Development of Japan at Oxford University since 1983. Her most recent research interests have been concerned with monetary policy in Japan and with an international comparison of Japanese corporate finance. From 1981 to 1983 she was a visiting researcher at the Economic Planning Agency of Japan and spent six weeks at the Bank of Japan in 1986.

Richard Dale is Professor of International Banking at Southampton University. He has been the Editor-in-Chief of the Financial Times Financial Regulation Report since 1986. He was an executive with Cripps Warburg, and later with NM Rothschild and Sons Ltd. He was awarded an ESRC research grant to study the relationship between banking and securities markets in specified major financial centres. He spent two years at the Brookings Institution as a Rockefeller Foundation fellow.

Gunter Dufey is Professor of Multinational Business and Finance at the Graduate School of Business Administration, University of Michigan. He has been visiting professor and lecturer at several universities in the United States, Europe and Asia. He served as a consultant to the US Departments of Treasury and Commerce, as well as to multinational companies. He is the author of several books and many articles in the field of multinational business and finance.

Robert A. Feldman is an Economist with the International Monetary Fund. He was formerly associated with the Chase Manhattan Bank,

Federal Reserve Bank of New York, Bank of Japan, and the Nomura Research Institute. His *Japanese Financial Markets* and other publications on Japanese banking and finance are well known in the field.

John Forsyth was educated at Cambridge and joined Morgan Grenfell in 1968. He was appointed Chief Economist in 1973, and made a Director in 1979. He has had extensive experience in the capital market activities of Morgan Grenfell, and was appointed a Group Director in 1988. He has been a member of the Council of the Royal Institute of International Affairs since 1983.

Charles A. E. Goodhart is Norman Sosnow Professor of Banking at the London School of Economics and Political Science. He was a chief adviser at the Bank of England. He taught at Cambridge University and at the London School of Economics in the field of monetary economics. He was, briefly, an economic adviser in the Department of Economic Affairs in London. He is the author of *Money, Information and Uncertainty*, and other books and articles, mostly on monetary economics and monetary history. He is widely known for his pioneering study on the relationship between macroeconomic developments and political popularity and he is the famous author of the 'Goodhart Law': any statistical regularity, notably in the monetary area, will break down when pressure is placed upon it for control purposes.

Maximilian Hall has been Lecturer in Economics at Loughborough University since 1977, delivering a large number of lectures on topics mainly concerned with money, banking and financial affairs at conferences and universities both at home and abroad. He has written several books on monetary policy and the regulation of banks and security houses, and is currently involved in several research projects. One of these concerns financial regulation in Japan, His most recent publication is *The City Revolution*.

James E. Hodder is Associate Professor of Industrial Engineering and Engineering Management at Stanford University, where he has been on the faculty since 1978. In addition to Japanese corporate finance, his research interests are in the general areas of international and domestic corporate finance, as well as international plant location. His most recent research dealing with corporate finance in Japan is contained in a current paper entitled 'Capital Structure and Cost of Capital in the United States and Japan'.

Dietmar K. R. Klein is Director of the international banking section of the Deutsche Bundesbank, and has been associated with the Bank for over twenty years. He is also Chairman of the OECD's Expert Group on Banking, which is a Working Group of the OECD Committee on Financial Markets. He has participated in the work of various international commitees and working groups, including the Bank for International Settlements, the International Monetary Fund and the World Bank. He has published extensively in the field of international banking.

Hiroshi Nakaso became Assistant Representative in Europe of the Bank of Japan in 1984, and is in charge of planning monetary policy at the Bank's Head Office. In 1980 he was seconded by the Bank of Japan to the Ministry of International Trade and Industry as an economist, and in 1982 returned to the Head Office to take charge of guiding the fund management of commercial banks.

Ariyoshi Okumura is the Managaing Director (Research and Information) of the Industrial Bank of Japan. He joined the Bank in 1955 and became Director and General Manager of the International Finance Research Department in 1985. He is a member of, amongst others, the Trilateral Commission and the Industrial Structure Council of the Ministry of International Trade and Industry.

Hirohiko Okumura is Chief Economist with Nomura Research Institute. He worked as an economist at the Bank of Japan and was Chief Economist for the NRI and NCC Co., Ltd. He was Visiting Lecturer at the University of Tokyo. He has published many articles and books on Japan's economy, finance, and on monetary policy. He was awarded a public finance fellowship by the Institute of Fiscal and Monetary Policy of the Japanese Ministry of Finance.

Peter Oppenheimer is a Fellow in Economics at Christ Church, Oxford. He was formerly on the staff of the Bank for International Settlements, and was visiting Professor at the London School of Business. He serves on the Council of the Trade Policy Research Centre in London, and is a director of two investment trusts. He also acts as a consultant to international organisations and business firms, and has published extensively in the field of international economies and public policy.

Kumiharu Shigehara entered the Bank of Japan in 1962, having graduated from the University of Tokyo. In 1970 he joined the OECD and in 1972 was appointed as Head of the Monetary Studies Division. In 1987 he was appointed as Deputy Director of the Institute of Monetary and Economic Studies of the Bank of Japan, and also became a Director of the General Economics Branch of the OECD in that year. He has published a number of books, including one on Japanese monetary policy, and another on economic fluctuations and stabilisation policies, as well as several articles for Japanese economic journals.

George Sutija is a professor of International Business at Florida International University. He was Director of the International Banking Center and Associate Dean at the College of Business Administration. He was formerly a Representative and Program Officer for the Ford Foundation in Latin America. He has published in the field of international banking and management.

Yoshio Suzuki joined the Bank of Japan in 1955, after graduating from the University of Tokyo. He became Executive Director of the bank in 1988. He was a member of the Tax Research committee of the Japanese government from 1984 to 1987, and has published a number of books on monetary policy and the Japanese financial system.

Alexander K. Swoboda is Professor of International Economics at the Graduate Institute of International Studies in Geneva, Professor of Economics at the University of Geneva, and the Director of the International Center for Monetary and Banking Studies. He is a leading specialist on international and financial problems, about which he has published numerous articles and edited several books. His research has been on both the theoretical and applied level. It has centred on macroeconomics, international finance, international adjustment theory, and the econometrics of the international transmission of inflation. He is also a well known analyst of Eurocurrency markets and of international banking issues. He is a member of the governing board of the Swiss Economic Association and was a member of the Academic Panel of the Group of Thirty.

Henry S. Terrell is Senior Economist and former Chief of the International Banking Section, Division of International Finance at the Board of Governors of the Federal Reserve System. He has been associated with the Board for the last fifteen years. He was Visiting Professor of the Fletcher School of Tufts University. He has published extensively in the field of international finances and international banking.

Adrian E. Tschoegl works for the Swiss Bank Corporation (SBCI) as a macroeconomist in Tokyo. Prior to joining SBCI he was a visiting scholar at the Bank of Japan's Institute for Monetary and Economic Studies. He was an Assistant Professor at the University of Michigan's business school for seven years, where he taught international finance, trade and business. He has published numerous monographs and articles on international banking, Japanese finance, gold prices and international trade.

C. Maxwell Watson began his career with the Bank of England in 1969, working on European and then Middle East financial affairs. He was later seconded by the Bank of England to the International Department of the investment bank S.G. Warburg and Co. From 1977 to 1979 he was Secretary of the European Communities Group of Bank Supervisory Authorities and acted as Joint Secretary of the first International Conference of Bank supervisors. He took up the post of Chief of the International Capital Markets Division of the International Monetary Fund in 1983, and now advises on the co-ordination of countries' external financing. He is a fellow of the British Institute of Bankers.

Robin Webster joined the Bank of England in 1966 and subsequently worked in the Chief Cashier's Office of the Overseas Department and Economic Intelligence Department. In 1983 he was seconded as Advisor on monetary affairs to the Bahrain Monetary Agency, and returned to the International Division to become Assistant Advisor on Japanese affairs in 1985.

1 The Future of Japanese Banking

Robert A. Feldman

Japanese banks today face many adaptations and opportunities. The adaptations are necessitated by the financial consequences of fundamental forces on the real side of the Japanese and world economies; the opportunities arise from the new types of asset and liability transformations that will inevitably be part of the adaptation process. Many of the fundamental forces can be identified today. Less clear, however, is the way these forces will affect demand and supply for different types of financial instruments. Even less clear are the opportunities that these demand and supply changes will provide for innovation, arbitrage, risk-sharing and transformation of asset characteristics.

This paper attempts to peer into the financial future from the perspective of the Japanese banking industry. What are the fundamental forces that will affect banks? How will these forces affect the supplies of deposits, Certificates of Deposit (CDs), debentures and equity funding? How will they affect demand for loans, asset prices and liquidity? How will they affect risk-sharing mechanisms and the ability to bundle risk, return, and other asset characteristics attractively? Once answers, however tentative, to these questions have been suggested, a more detailed look at recent trends in the Japanese banking sector is given. The purpose is to see whether recent trends suggest that Japanese banks will succeed in adapting and profiting from the new opportunities.

FUNDAMENTAL FORCES

Many fundamental forces will affect the environment for the financial industry and Japanese banking over the coming decade. A number have similar implications for the type of intermediation that financial institutions will be called upon to do. In some cases, however, intermediation will not be sufficient; transformation of characteristics will be necessary as well, for example, among maturities, currencies, regions or contingencies. To examine the details of prospective forces is to reveal what changes are likely in the characteristics of instruments, what adjustments will have to be made in the financial industry, and what banks will have to do in order to fit in.

The Six Forces

Demographics

Of all the fundamental forces affecting Japan now and over the next decade, perhaps the most fundamental will be demographic. Even today, life expectancy for men at age 65 is 15 years, and for women 19 years. To bear the full burden of living expenses for the elderly, public pensions alone will not suffice, despite recent revisions of the public pension system. Nor can the public medical insurance system bear the full burden of the expected increase in medical costs. Although some of the adjustment to aging of the population will clearly come from further changes in the retirement system (for example, later retirement ages), others will just as clearly cause preferences for private financial assets to shift toward longer-term assets, with health and longevity contingencies.

Another demographic factor of perhaps equal importance is the participation of women in the labour force. What is to be done with the income earned by women, especially housewives working part-time? Will it be saved or spent? If saved, on what conditions? It could well be that, if the money so earned is seen by families as marginal or impermanent, a larger proportion will be saved. Moreover, as would be normal for an increase in total wealth, a larger share of such savings would seem likely to go into return-sensitive assets, or into assets that answer the specific contingency needs of two-earner families, for instance, for disability insurance that protects family living standards in case of accidents.

World trade and development

A second fundamental force affecting Japanese financial markets will be trends in world trade and development; particularly important will be the regional locus of growth and investment. Among the most exciting prospects are those posed by the common internal market in Europe. Although European funding will be available for the many takeover bids and investment projects that are expected as this new Europe takes shape, the powerful incentives for risk-sharing and for incorporating Japanese industrial and electronic prowess into European facilities will provide opportunities for Japanese financing as well. In Asia, the opportunities are also attractive. In China, recent changes in economic policy suggest many good prospects for Japan, although most of these are likely to be in infrastructure projects, that is, projects which are high in return, but long in maturity and subject to large exchange rate risks. India as well has moved towards greater openness to foreign investment; as production costs rise in the Newly Industrialised Economies (NIEs), Japanese investment could well take advantage of the well educated workforce and large internal market in India, subject to exchange risks and perhaps less policy stability than in some countries. In North America, technological dynamism is likely to continue to attract Japanese investment, and Japanese financing with it; this financing, however, would appear likely to be of a shorter-term nature, and less subject to exchange rate risk than that in developing countries, given the new export orientation of North American industry.

Fiscal consolidation

Among the fundamental forces that brought financial market changes in Japan and the world as a whole in the 1970s and 1980s, one of the most important was fiscal deficits. In Japan, the accumulation of deficit financing bonds on bank balance sheets formed the foundation for the liberalisation of interest rates and the blurring of distinctions among financial institutions that occurred.[1] In the world economy, the financing needs brought by the large fiscal deficits in the United States were a major force for deepening markets that hedge currency risk and in broadening participation in international portfolios to new institutions, for example, Japanese insurance companies.

The corner appears to have been turned in controlling fiscal deficits, although continued efforts are needed and success is by no means certain. In Japan, in particular, the recent period of more rapid growth has raised tax revenue while stronger discipline has held down current spending, with the result of lower general government deficits. Privatisation programmes have reduced the public sector borrowing requirement further. Even though there remain fiscal problems such as the high debt to gross national product (GNP) ratio and high share of interest payments in current spending, the intense pressure for innovation in financial markets due to a flood of government bond flotations appears to have abated.

Certain aspects of the fiscal situation suggest, however, that government bond flotations, especially of long-term bonds, may rise again. Current spending priorities emphasise social infrastructure projects and foreign aid expenditures; traditionally, such spending has been funded more heavily through the fiscal investment and loan programme, which in turn has obtained a majority of its funding from postal savings. If recent changes in tax laws or other factors reduce the underlying supply of funding to the postal savings system, then a reversion to bond financing would be an obvious alternative. In any case, it would appear that the maturity structure of government liabilities would need to lengthen, in order to reduce the risks associated with longer pay-off periods of the domestic and foreign investment activities that the Japanese government is undertaking.

Electronics

The electronics revolution has, of course, been one of the key factors underlying rapid innovations in financial markets. The fall of transactions costs attributable to better computers and software has allowed new combinations of assets (such as *sogo* accounts at Japanese banks), improved arbitrage possibilities and better information tracking in order to reduce risk. No end to this revolution is in sight. A crucial question is whether the continuation will stabilise or disturb.

Although a final judgement is impossible, some observations may be made. The first relates to the connection of lower transactions costs and the completeness of markets. To the extent that lower costs allow trading of more types of assets among more types of agents, one would expect more stability. If, however, regulatory or other distortions allow some markets to be highly integrated while others are isolated, risks would become more concentrated and markets less stable. A second observation relates to system risk. To the extent that lower costs mean faster clearing of payments with lower float, one would expect less system risk. If, however, communication among local computerised payments systems turns out to be more difficult than currently envisioned, then system risk might rise. A third observation relates to market concentration. To the extent that centralised processing on supercomputers brings economies of scale, the optimal size of financial institutions may rise. If, however, a combination of localised processing and networking among smaller computers turns out to be lower in cost, then the optimal size of institutions may fall.

Energy

The impact of the energy sector on the financial sector was starkly demonstrated by the fluctuations of energy prices (both up and down) in the 1970s and 1980s (Frydl, 1982). It would be incautious to assume that current low energy prices are permanent, or that the financial sector would be immune from influence if they are not. Indeed, the energy sector has shown some signs of acting according to a cobweb model of very long periodicity. Other developments, such as the greenhouse effect, will complicate the decisions that must be made in order to secure safe and sure energy sources.

The implications of energy sector prospects for the financial sector would appear to be threefold. First, sudden needs for recycling may recur, and portfolios and practices will have to be flexible enough to accommodate such needs. Second, the huge risks associated with developing alternative energy sources will have to be shared efficiently. And third, the correlated nature of shocks both within the energy sector and between energy and other sectors will have to be taken into account as financial institutions choose their portfolios. In short, assets in the energy sector would appear to be headed towards higher risk, longer maturity, and greater correlation among themselves and with other assets.

Consumerism

As Japan has grown wealthier, attitudes towards saving and borrowing have also changed, and a more liberal view of borrowing has emerged. This would be expected in the theory of consumption, because higher wealth means less serious consequences for utility when adverse shocks change the prospects for meeting liabilities. But another factor may be of equal importance: the shift of political power in Japan towards urban areas, and the resulting reduction of certain distortions. This factor is visible in certain pro-consumer movements in economic policy, such as a stricter attitude towards the agricultural sector and reductions in protectionism. The effect of this movement, if it continues, will be a gain in real income for urban areas and a loss for rural ones. The financial sector, particularly the retail segment, will be affected by such changes if there are differences in propensities to save between these areas or in the form such savings take. For example, land prices and the value of collateral could change substantially, creating lending opportunities in urban areas and forcing cutbacks in rural ones.

Implications of the Six Forces

Not all of these forces have identical implications for the balance sheet structure of financial institutions, but some tendencies do emerge. One is that both demand and supply of longer-term assets would appear likely to grow: demand because of the aging of the population, and supply because of both infrastructure needs (at home and abroad) and trends in the energy sector. A second is that contingencies, related, for example, to health of the asset holder, success of an energy or infrastructure project, or land price trends, would appear to take a more important role in financial contracts. A third is that international and cross-currency risks seem likely to grow, because of the international character of many projects and the geographical separation of borrowers and lenders. A fourth is that the importance of retail operations may grow. In short, financial instruments appear likely to become longer, more contingent, more international, and more retail. How will the financial industry, the banking industry, and its regulators adapt to this new environment?

The first adaptation will have to be a lengthening of both assets and liabilities of financial institutions. The individuals and firms will supply funds only on longer terms, and so institutions that cannot accommodate such needs will lose competitiveness; institutions that cannot adjust their asset portfolios will face increased risks. The second adaptation will have to be innovative use of contingencies, coupled with careful analysis of how shocks might force payment of contingencies. This analysis will require a rethinking of the way the law of large numbers – the basis of profitable retail banking – applies in new situations. The third adaptation will have to be a more thorough system of risk analysis and avoidance. Capital adequacy is certainly part of this system, but faster acquisition and processing of information and minute-to-minute evaluation of exposure will also have to improve. Such improvements will be particularly important when both assets and liabilities are longer in maturity, because of the greater fluctuations of face values as interest rates change. The fourth adaptation will have to be creation of a regulatory system that better encourages risk avoidance and that lowers tax and regulatory distortions that can cause unneeded shocks. Moral hazards (for instance, in deposit insurance) and tax neutrality among assets will take on a larger importance. The fifth adaptation will have to be a redistribution of financial industry resources towards urban areas, both on the lending and borrowing sides.

Banks will face some of the most difficult problems in adapting to this new environment, largely because the underlying nature of the largest part of their business remains short-term, non-contingent and domestic. This business will retain a great importance; the integrity of the payments mechanism is of even greater importance in today's interdependent world than before. Thus the key to the prognosis for banks everywhere, and for Japanese banks in particular, is how well they will be able to maintain their role as providers of monetary instruments, which are short-term, non-contingent and domestic, in a world where much of the profit will be in instruments that are long-term, contingent and international.

Moreover not all of the adaptations may be possible within any one institution. Will it be possible, for example, for an institution to become more international and more retail at the same time? This question poses another crucial choice for Japanese banks: should they be supermarkets or boutiques?

THE NEW FINANCIAL ENVIRONMENT

Before considering how these underlying forces have fostered adaptations of banks in particular, it is useful to see the extent to which they have changed the financial environment in general. What innovations have been proposed and implemented? How have systems to reduce and redistribute risk developed? What has happened in areas such as tax neutrality and computer development? Answers to these questions will help to clarify the framework within which Japanese banks must make their decisions.

Innovations

Japanese financial institutions have answered the new underlying demands of their customers with a wide variety of links among institutions and combinations of accounts. For example, most securities companies now have tie-up contracts with banks that allow smooth transfer of funds to and from bank accounts when securities are sold or purchased, in order to reduce transactions costs. Within institutions, formal accounts have been established that mix certain types of assets into a single account, for example, Saitama Bank's recently established 1–3 year account that combines time deposit, government bond holdings, mortgage securities and other paper in a floating mix. And individual innovations continue as well, such as *tokkin* (special investment trusts) that are risky but high yielding and are offered by many institutions. Such innovations have not been trouble-free; in the case of *tokkin*, there have been problems such as the potential for loss accumulation, concentrated management, and difficulties of marshalling information for minute-to-minute decisions about portfolio recomposition.

Some institutions have also created business links that serve the demand for more complete life insurance. Normally, advantageous arrangements such as single premium life insurance contracts would not be available to many potential customers because of the large front-end costs; some banks and life insurance companies have formed tie-ups to lend customers the front-end funds. Life insurance contracts themselves have become more flexible, with provisions in some cases that the value of a term insurance contract at maturity may be converted to pension form. The regulatory structure in the insurance industry has also had to adapt to a more international environment, since the huge funds accumulated by life insurance companies could not be fully used at home; the prudential regulations on the share of assets that can be invested abroad has been raised to non-binding limits (Fukao and Okina, 1988), and more flexibility on the liability side has been introduced by permission for insurance companies to borrow through impact loans.

Health contingencies are also playing a greater role in the design of financial assets. Several banks have begun to offer time deposits that are linked to health insurance contracts, in co-operation with insurance companies. Independently of banks, some new health policies are specifically designed for part-time female workers, indicating the opportunities provided by demographic factors. International differences in disease incidence also suggest possibilities for arbitrage in the design of contingency contracts.

Risk Management

As the financial system has become more complex, risk management has become more important. Older and more familiar risks, such as asset risk, interest rate risk, credit risk and operations risk have increased with the complexity of transactions. Newer and less familiar risks have been added as well, such as sovereign risk, currency risk, contingency risk and covariance risk. Better management of older types of risk and incorporation of newer types into decisions had required all financial institutions to adopt improved risk management procedures. These improvements fall into three categories: better internal controls, better market organisation (which lowers risk by improving asset liquidity) and better supervision.

Internal controls encompass so-called ALM (Asset Liability Management) systems. They typically use a combination of advanced information processing techniques, portfolio composition rules, and discretionary committees that match maturities, interest rate exposures, contingencies, off-balance sheet exposures and so on. The importance of such systems and the imagination required to foresee disasters are pointed out by such recent events as the telephone exchange fire in Tokyo, the Bank of New York computer breakdown, and the Tateho bankruptcy. Development of such ALM systems is of pressing importance in Japan in particular, owing to the decline of the collateral principle in lending.

A more complete set of markets and instruments will be an important contributor to risk avoidance and distribution. Of particular use will be a fuller menu of free-rate instruments of all maturities. The timing of introduction of such instruments is also of interest, because of the risks associated with, for example, an asset portfolio of free-rate, long-maturity instruments based on a liability portfolio of fixed-rate, short-maturity ones. In addition, markets to trade the various types of newly emerging instruments (for instance, commercial paper (CP), mortgage securities, consumer loans and so on) will form an essential source of liquidity for all institutions. Access and trading rules for these markets will have to be developed.

New instruments and markets imply the emergence of new system risks as well, that is, new externalities that must be addressed by public supervision. The critical issue here is moral hazard: how can the government reduce certain types of system risk without increasing others? For example, the rise in wholesale transactions makes the development of one-sided markets more likely, so that larger official intervention may be needed; but an implicit guarantee of government intervention in crises makes risky behaviour in such markets more likely. Long chains of transactions between ultimate borrowers and lenders mean that authorities will have to deal with more intermediaries and consider more sources of possible disturbance. The international aspects of these problems remain perhaps the most daunting, despite the Bank for International Settlements (BIS) capital adequacy guidelines and the Basle Concordat. Japan's financial safety net will have to adapt to these new conditions.

Responding to this situation, the Supervision Department of the Bank of Japan has constructed a risk checklist for Japanese institutions (Shinozawa, 1987). This system focuses on four types of risk: liberalisation risk arising from the different pace of liberalisation in different markets, globalisation risk arising from cross-currency and cross-border operations, securitisation risk arising from dealing in new instruments with immature markets, and electronic data processing (EDP) risk arising from such factors as computer breakdown, crime and long chains of trades. Supervisors are encouraging institutions to analyse more thoroughly where problems might arise and how to respond, to integrate all types of risk into comprehensive ALM systems, and to raise portfolio cushions against adverse shocks.

Branching

Despite advances in electronic information exchange, physical proximity to customers may grow in importance because decision lags have become shorter and providing information has become a more important tool of competition. Branch location is thus likely to grow in importance, with a differentiation among businesses carried out at each location. Decisions will also need to be made concerning what types of transactions to automate and how to regulate placement of cash machines and other facilities. (One can imagine, for example, securities firms wanting to place robot-brokers in *pachinko* parlours, with dial-up videos to provide stock market information.) Assessing the profitability and the risks of following customers will be a major challenge for all institutions, as well as for public authorities.

These assessments are intimately connected with advancements in information processing. Every financial institution will have to devote substantial resources to improvements in this area, and will have to invest huge sums in machinery and software. Designing systems that can interact among institutions raises many questions, for example, those of anti-trust, system risk, economies of scale, and efficiency for the economy as a whole.

Tax Neutrality

Tax distortions have been a critical element in the history of the Japanese financial system, for instance, capital gains taxation, tax-free interest on certain savings accounts, and enforcement differentials among jurisdictions. A consensus has emerged in Japan that such distortions are harmful, because they misallocate financial assets, cause huge fund shifts on rumours of change, and encourage tax evasion. Recent policy changes have attempted to lower such distortions, particularly the abolition of most of the system of tax-free interest earnings (*maruyu*).[2]

The short-term effects of *maruyu* abolition will be felt by all financial institutions, but information is scarce about effects so far. Since *maruyu* was in fact a subsidy to institutions offering accounts to individuals, one would expect that such institutions would be adversely affected. There are, however, distinctions to be made. The postal savings system might at first seem to be at the greatest risk, because enforcement of the old system was weakest there; depositors unable to obtain tax-free accounts might transfer their funds if other characteristics of postal accounts (for example, very long maturities) are not sufficiently attractive. Funds may also flow out of city and local banks; the size of the outflow is harder to assess because of offsetting factors. Tax evasion was a less important reason for *maruyu* accounts at these institutions, owing to traditionally better enforcement, but the short maturities of existing *maruyu* deposits will not brake what outflows occur. Institutions offering longer-term instruments with high yields, for instance, trust banks, long-term credit banks, securities companies, and life insurance companies, stand to gain on balance from *maruyu* abolition, even though tax-free status for some of the instruments they offer (for example, *zaikei* accounts) was removed.

Two longer-term effects of *maruyu* abilition also appear likely. One is that the 'silver market' – deposits of the elderly – will become more competitive. The retention of tax breaks for this age group will remain an important distortion, because their assets preferences differ from those of the population at large. Moreover, as the population ages, the importance of this distortion may grow. Second, the institutions that suffer from *maruyu* abolition will have to compete harder in other areas, and will thus be encouraged to seek regulatory changes that compensate for the loss. Such reactions could ignite further cycles of innovation and deregulation similar to those of the 1970s and 1980s.[3]

ARE JAPANESE BANKS ADAPTING?

It would seem likely, in light of the above, that the new financial environment will challenge institutions to create imaginative innovations, to manage risks more efficiently, to distribute branches better according to their business, to gather and process information at lower costs, and to take advantage of the shift towards tax neutrality. The future of Japanese banking will be decided by how well banks of various types rise to these challenges. Some evidence is already available, in the form of the recent history of their ability to adapt to new market situations. They have taken action concerning liability structure, loan market practices, new business areas, investment management, international markets, capital adequacy, currency expertise development, and so on.

But have these actions been sufficient, or is there more to be done? What roles have been played by competing financial institutions and regulatory authorities? And what do the actions of banks, their competitors, and the authorities suggest about the potential for banks to adapt to the new environment safely and profitably? In each case the details and the implications bear careful study.

Liability Structure

One major change that has occurred on the liability side of the balance sheets of Japanese banks in the last few years is the increase in large-scale, free-rate, interest-sensitive funding. This first major innovation began with the introduction of the certificate of deposit (CD) in the late 1970s, but large-scale time deposits have also been introduced, with progressively lower limits on what is considered large.[4] The benefits of these new liabilities to banks have been substantial, since they have prevented disintermediation. But some problems remain.

Although the CDs are quite liquid, owing to the existence of a deep market, the large-scale time deposits are not. If a bunching of maturities of such large-scale liabilities were to occur, and if several depositors cancelled contracts at maturity, then a bank's liquidity might be threatened. A failure of the law of large numbers could trigger the failure of a bank. Some solutions to this problem come to mind, for example, further reduction in the size of free-rate deposits (so that the benefits of such assets to depositors would not require risk to be borne by banks) or development of a market for large-scale deposits.

Another important change has been a lengthening of Japanese bank liabilities. Even though ordinary banks remain forbidden to accept deposits in excess of two years' maturity, the maturity structure of their other liabilities has lengthened, even while trust banks and long-term credit banks continue to attract longer-term funds. Regulatory changes have allowed smaller banks to float convertible bonds of up to three years' maturity as well, and many have taken advantage of this opportunity. Thus a trend has developed towards diminution of maturity differences among banks, but major differences remain. The long-term credit banks, which retain the sole right to float five year debentures, are in a better situation to adapt to the expected shift of preferences of fund providers towards longer-term instruments.

Some of the difficulties of banks concerning the scale and maturity of their deposits may be overcome by a recent revision of branching regulations. The new regulations allow a denser location of branches and more specialisation, and a branching war has started among major banks in larger cities. So-called 'corporate branches', which will cater specifically to the needs of firms, may now be opened in any number, if located on the third or higher floors of buildings. But the potential for easier branching to help solve liability-side problems of banks will also depend on further deregulation of interest rates and of deposit maturity controls.

Lending Markets

Given the growth of free-rate deposits, one would expect banks to increase free-rate loans as well. This is precisely what has happened in recent years.[5] Free-rate loans are attractive to borrowers because they are an alternative to commercial paper for smaller firms without access to money markets and because compensating deposits are usually not requested.

This trend in loan rate suggests that the prime rate system, particularly the short-term prime rate, may see its importance diminish even further. The short prime rate remains rather artificial, and continues to be tied more closely to the discount rate, which has ceased to be the marginal cost of funding for banks and which is affected by many factors (such as exchange rate developments) that are less important for short-term loans. Pressures for further flexibility in setting loan rates (for example, weaker ties in rate formulae to the short and long prime rates and closer ties to deposit rates, which are the true marginal cost of funds to banks) are likely to build up and to raise the proportion of floating rate loan further over the next few years.[6]

A second important trend in the loan market has been a greater concentration on individuals. Two segments have been highly active –

housing loans and consumer loans. Banks have been active in the housing market, adapting contracts to demographic and tax factors. Some housing loans, for example, can be passed between generations, a feature that is attractive when houses tend to be purchased later in life, and when inheritance tax rates are highly progressive. But competition in the housing loan market will also be intense, as a result of the presence of other institutions, such as housing finance companies and life insurance companies. Even within the banking sector, competition is likely to be intense; regional banks, *sogo* banks, and *shinkin* banks have concentrated more on housing loans than have city banks or long-term credit banks, and are unlikely to surrender this business without a fight. The risks of activity in the housing loan market remain large, and these could be eased by a deeper market in mortgage securities.

Lending to individuals has developed rapidly. One recent innovation is the so-called 'card loans', which are pre-approved credit lines. Such instruments allow significant cost savings for banks because credit approval must only be made once. Conditions on such loans vary from bank to bank, with respect to interest rate (for example, a fixed rate or a link to prime rates) and conditions for obtaining a card (for example, gross assets or net worth). Within the banking industry there remains a difference of opinion on the risk-return characteristics of this business. Some banks wish to lower rates and attract borrowers, on the theory that economies of scale will outweigh the likely diminution in credit quality. Others feel that quality will diminish too rapidly to justify lower rates, and that collateral for such loans, for example, real estate, may not be easy to foreclose or liquidate in case of default. Another question facing banks is whether bank entry into direct consumer credit would jeopardise loans already made to consumer finance companies, which in the past relied heavily on banks for financing.

A third trend in the loan market is a reduction in the distinctions among banks in the maturity of loan portfolios. In the 1960s, city banks tended to have less than one-tenth of loans in long-term assets, while long-term credit banks had more than three-quarters in such loans. In the mid-1970s, some convergence occurred, largely because city banks lent longer as their business diversified into real estate and service sectors. In the 1980s, the city banks have lent longer yet, but the long-term credit banks have actually reduced the share of long-term loans in their portfolios, to about one-half, with the relative waning of their main client, the manufacturing sector.

Robert A. Feldman

New Business Areas

One of the basic principles of the organisation of the financial industry in Japan in the postwar period was the segmentation of markets, the result of which was that bank entry into securities, life insurance, or other business was prescribed. But, as a result of the market pressures of the 1970s and 1980s, the distinctions among institutions began to blur, in both law and fact. Banks began to sell government bonds over-the-counter (*madohan*) in 1984, and securities companies began to lend to customers. In international markets, the overlap has gone much further, with many Japanese banks involved in securities business in the Euromarkets, and securities companies active in traditional banking activities. New institutions, such as credit rating agencies, have made further overlap possible because the credit evaluation role that banks once played *vis-à-vis* their largest borrowers has now been in part usurped, to the benefit of competitors.

One important area of new domestic business for banks is bond dealing in open markets. Banks now account for more than half of the trading in both the Japanese bond market (in which bank dealing began in June 1984) and the bond futures market (which began in October 1985). In order to achieve this position, huge investments in equipment and manpower were necessary, but the result appears to have justified these. Despite this success, bank usage of these markets is far from complete. As of mid-1988, banks were not permitted to intermediate bond futures, could not trade bonds on the Tokyo Stock Exchange, and could not combine bond futures with other instruments in package contracts. Even if these issues are settled, more general issues in the Japanese bond market remain to be resolved. Issue conditions need to be made more flexible, and time-lags in the flotation process need to be reduced. How banks will affect the way these decisions are made is not yet clear, although certain outlines from the experience in other new markets are suggestive.

The CP market, for example, was established with full access by banks, securities companies and other financial institutions. The hybrid character of CPs, which serve borrowers who would normally borrow from banks but are floated in the market like securities, suggests that limiting underwriting and trading to one set of institutions would be disruptive. The critical factor is to maintain the quality of the underlying assets, so that the risk of default and of jeopardising the entire market would be minimised. There are, however, difficulties to be overcome, such as improving delivery and settlement procedures among institutions.

Although initial issues in the CP market were very large, it is difficult to determine whether this success was due to their underlying attractiveness, to testing by firms of the new instrument, or to window dressing at end of financial year 1987. The basis for rate-setting of CPs has been the CD rate for banks, which makes the former rather more expensive than loans, as do the stamp tax of 0.18 to 0.24 per cent (depending on size of the issue) and the risk premium of about 0.25 per cent paid to the underwriter. More flexible maturities would also help the market grow. Furthermore firms may be reluctant to use a market which is still a battlefield between banks and securities companies, for fear of harming relations with one or both sets of institutions.

Another indication of the likely trend in market access rules is provided by the recent recast of the market for private placements. Under pre-1987 rules, such flotations were limited to less than ¥2.0 billion, to purchase by institutional investors, to resale provisions that were restrictive, and to fund-use provisions if the issue exceeded ¥1.0 billion. Moreover, once a firm had issued a public bond, it could not return to the private placement market. Under new rules first proposed in December 1986, issue amount limits would be raised (to ¥10 billion per issue), and the no-return rule would be eliminated. Fund-use and resale restrictions would remain and the general public would not be allowed to purchase the bonds, but all financial institutions, including banks, securities companies and life insurance companies, would be eligible to be lead managers (*assen-in*). A mini-boom in private placements occurred in 1987 as interest rates fell and medium-sized firms sought cheap 7–10 year financing; banks gained not only short-term profits from these flotations but also valuable experience and relationships with clients.

In the trading of Japanese futures, which has been active in government bonds and has begun in equities with a stock index future, the principle of mutual participation has been carried very far. Planning for the Tokyo Financial Futures Market emphasised the benefits of establishing such a market in hedging and dispersing risks, filling a hole in the 24-hour trading of such instruments, and making spot markets more complete. These goals could not be achieved without broad-based access to many types of futures and options contracts. Given provisions of both securities exchange and foreign exchange laws, however, some restrictions on the futures and options markets were necessary: only securities companies may deal in stock futures and options, and only banks may deal in currency spot options. In addition, insurance companies were not allowed to participate in the markets, because the character of the risks that such companies must hedge differs somewhat from those of banks and securities companies. (This ruling, along with the state of the futures and options markets as a whole, will be reviewed in 1990.)

Several issues remain concerning bank participation in these markets. One is the potential for conflict of interest: if banks lend customers funds to participate in these markets but are also market makers, clear conflicts of interest may arise. Second is an issue of regulatory jurisdiction; the Securities Bureau of the Ministry of Finance is to oversee trading in contracts involving securities, while the Banking Bureau and the International Finance Bureau are to oversee trading in contracts involving financial instruments and foreign exchange. If banks become involved in contracts involving both, then regulatory conflicts could occur.

Investment Advice and Management

As portfolios have become more complicated, the need for investment advice has risen. This need may be subdivided into two types, wholesale and retail. On the wholesale side of the business, the clients are pension fund owners, insurance companies or other large institutional investors with very large sums of money and needs for diversification and risk hedging. On the retail side of the business, the clients are individuals or at most small businesses, which are seeking high returns for relatively small amounts of funds for long-term needs such as retirement. The competition for business in these two markets will revolve around which institutions best answer the needs of these clients; the issue is whether economies of scope exist across the two markets. If so, more homogeneity among institutions may develop; if not, more specialisation is likely.

In the market for management of pension funds, much competition has developed. Management of such funds within the welfare pension system is currently restricted to trust banks and life insurance companies, but this restriction has not kept the market isolated; two foreign banks have established trust banks in Japan in order to participate in this business. The very high profitability of institutions engaged in this business in recent years (while partly attributable to low interest rates and the stock market boom) has naturally attracted attention and fostered debate. A similar debate has occurred concerning securities investment trusts (SITs), which currently may be offered only by securities companies. The securities industry has defended its turf on the grounds that competition is already sufficient and that allowing other institutions to offer such accounts would invite conflict of interest. Banks and other potential entrants suggest that the high profits in SITs reflect a monopolistic element, and that more competition would lower costs for ultimate borrowers.

A back door to participation by banks in investment management is provided by investment advisory companies, which provide advice on how to manage assets (and in some cases are permitted total discretion in use of client funds) in return for fees. City banks have been particularly active in establishing such firms, but even trust banks, for instance the Shoko Chukin Bank, and life insurance companies have done likewise. Ties with foreign investment advisors have been critical in some cases in improving the expertise of Japanese firms and in allowing inroads of foreign firms interested in other business areas into Japan. No reliable figures are available on the extent of funds management by such firms, but figures for certain segments suggest that growth has been very rapid.[7]

The retail side of investment advice is also a growth industry. Success in this area depends more, however, on depth in client search and service than on sophisticated management techniques. In pursuing such business, many banks – including local banks, *sogo* banks, and *shinkin* banks – have established consumer finance corners in branches; Sunday consultation hours are even available in some cases. City banks and smaller institutions would seem to have a comparative advantage in this area, given their larger branch networks and relative familiarity in dealing with individuals. It remains to be seen, however, whether information processing techniques – for example, use of computer terminals in the home – might eliminate the advantage that banks appear to have.

International Markets

Despite the extremely active role of Japanese financial institutions, and banks in particular, in international lending, borrowing and trading over the past decade, questions have now arisen as to whether this level of activity will continue. As the Japanese population ages, the savings ratio is apt to fall, reducing the current account surpluses and the need for Japanese financial institutions to recycle funds. The safety of sovereign lending has been tested by the debt crisis. And the growth of Tokyo as an international financial centre may lure back some business now done abroad in order to avoid current regulations or to lower costs.

Japanese banks seem well placed to participate in two of the three regions where major growth is now foreseen over the next decade. In the United States, many Japanese banks are establishing branches in the mid-western states, in the wake of direct investment by Japanese firms in that region. Equity participation in local banks has also been rising. In south-east Asia and China also, investments and loans have followed Japanese investments; in the case of China, ties of several Japanese banks to local investment trust companies have been pursued as well. The recent $6 billion aid/lending agreement between Japan and China will deepen business contacts and give Japanese financial institutions an edge in competing for Chinese business. In Europe, direct advance may be more difficult if a tendency emerges for measures connected with the common internal market to become protectionist. In the financial industry, foreign banks licensed in an EC (European Community) country may not have the opportunity to expand into other EC countries without obtaining further approvals, as domestic EC banks will. However, even if direct financial participation by Japan in a faster growing Europe is hindered by such regulations, indirect participation will be possible through lending to EC banks or development agencies.

An interesting question related to the future of international activities of Japanese banks concerns whether their presence in Euromarkets, particularly in London, will rise or fall over the next few years. This question arises because their current and very substantial presence is rooted not only in the attractions of London but also in the detractions of Tokyo. Over the years London has amassed a formidable set of attractions. The depth of the markets for lending and borrowing has been joined by the absence of deposit insurance premia and reserve requirements, absence of exchange controls, superior communications facilities, a favourable time zone, and a well-known set of laws. In the future, to the extent that Japanese banks expand their international business and increase maturity transformation as the fundamentals suggest they must, London will remain attractive.

But while London developed, Tokyo fiddled. That is, a substantial part of the presence of Japanese institutions in Euromarkets has been due to restrictive regulations or anomalies in business practices in

Tokyo, such as inflexible bond flotation procedures that make it attractive for Japanese investors to go to Europe to buy yen-denominated bonds offered by their own countrymen.[8] It strikes one as odd that London International Financial Futures Exchange (LIFFE) should be ahead of Japanese exchanges in offering futures in Japanese equities. Tokyo is not as far behind as it once was, however.

The two chief improvements in the Tokyo market have been the elimination of restrictive currency regulations and the growth of the domestic money market. These two improvements have allowed huge increases in arbitrage transactions, and have brought interest rates and exchange rates to levels broadly consistent with the law of interest parity.[9] Provisions of the US–Japanese Yen–Dollar agreement, many of which were already under consideration before the agreement was signed, also expanded the menu of instruments available to Japanese investors. The establishment of the Tokyo Offshore Market in December 1986 was another step forward, and allowed better distribution of international lending risks among banks and closer connections of Japanese interest rates with world market rates. A unique advantage of the Tokyo market is its time zone, which allows normal business hours just between the close of the west coast markets in the United States and the opening of markets in south-east Asia.

But there remain many detractions in the Tokyo market. A major detraction is the high taxes on financial institutions, including high profits taxes, the securities turnover law, and stamp taxes. Operational costs can be extremely high, as a result not only of land prices but also of the very high salaries and benefits required to attract skilled foreign specialists to the market. Moreover improvements could be made in the clearing system for bond transactions and in the accounting rules governing dividend and capital gains. And rules governing certain types of flotations can be inconvenient: for example, even though Euroyen CPs can be floated by non-residents of high credit rating, this paper cannot be sold in Japan for two weeks after issue and requires approval by the Ministry of Finance. On balance, it would appear that operation in London or other Euromarkets remains more advantageous in most areas. The trend of the future may be suggested by the recent opening of London branches by some of the smaller Japanese banks, such as the Tokyo Sogo Bank.

Capital Adequacy

The international activities of the banks of all countries over the last decade have exposed them and the financial system to new, more complex and greater risks. Although one defence against these risks is the creation of more complete markets discussed above, an equally important one is having an adequate capital base. Because of historical accounting practices, Japanese banks have often seemed undercapitalised in comparison with banks in other countries; this was justified by the tradition of never letting banks fail (at least in name) and by the large hidden reserves in the form of equities and other assets listed at book value rather than market value. Recent developments, however, have caused a rethinking of capital adequacy in Japan. The more competitive and riskier environment, particularly in international markets, has at least brought the possibility that public bail-out might not always be proper; and stock market fluctuations have cast doubt on whether hidden reserves would indeed be realisable in a crisis.

A first set of new capital requirements for Japanese banks was announced in May 1986. These requirements applied to banks that had an international presence (for example, subsidiaries or branches abroad),[10] and mandated 6 per cent capital coverage of total assets. This set of standards has now been superseded by a set consistent with the guidelines proposed by the BIS in 1988. The new standards have a somewhat stricter definition of capital, include off-balance sheet items, and adopt the risk-asset approach to calculating the denominator, under which certain risk-free assets (such as government bonds) are excluded from the need for capital coverage and other relatively safe assets require only partial coverage. In addition, capital is separated into two tiers, primary capital and secondary capital, with a requirement of at least 4 per cent coverage of primary capital *vis-à-vis* risk-weighted total assets. Secondary capital, which includes 45 per cent of unrealised stock gains and certain special reserves, may not exceed primary capital in reaching the required overall ratio of 8 per cent risk-weighted asset coverage.

Reaction to the new standards in Japanese banking circles has been one of resignation and dismay. Certain commentators have even suggested that a primary goal of the BIS exercise was to reduce Japanese presence in world financial markets, for which blame is laid not so much on foreign pressure as on domestic regulations that have forced so much Japanese business outside Japan.[11] Opinions differ as to how far Japanese banks are away from meeting the new standards and how much capital will have to be raised, but, on the larger point, estimates for all banks for the period to 1992 fall in the range of ¥5 to 7 trillion.[12] More important, however, will be the way banks react in their asset selection behaviour. Some concentration in assets with low risk-asset weights would be expected, but it is not clear that deregulation will allow rapid growth of such business, especially when competing institutions, such as securities companies, are not forced to maintain corresponding capitalisation. Cost cutting is sure to be encouraged, and a closer look at the profitability of individual branches is likely. There is, however, one silver lining to the BIS cloud: bank profits in 1987 were so high that a substantial step towards meeting the new capital ratios could be taken with these earnings.

Payment System Innovations

One of the most interesting features of the electronics revolution in Japan has been the explosive growth in the use of credit and debit cards. In a country in which 90 per cent of the payments have traditionally been made in cash, the potential for cost savings and improved convenience is clear. By law, only banks are allowed to engage in 'exchange transactions', which imply the settlement of debts through transfer of financial assets of fixed face value and absolute liquidity. But the possibilities of electronic banking have called the technological underpinning of this law into question; why, for example, could not debts be settled through exchange of assets of any type on electronic books? The problems of divisibility and settlement risk, which, until recently, were handled most efficiently by cash and deposit transfers, are greatly changed in a world of electronic blips.

The payments system will have to adapt to three features of electronic systems: they are instantaneous; they are easy to access; and they are highly mechanised. The speed of transactions will mean that recourse to suspend payments or to recover funds in case of failure of counterparts in contracts will be more difficult. The ease of access will mean that agents outside the financial sector will be able to provide many of the services on which the integrity of the payments system depends; how to handle regulatory problems in such a situation is far from clear. The high degree of mechanisation will increase the length of chains of transactions, and therefore raise system risk.

One step forward in electronic banking has been the establishment of standards for bank cards by the Japan Bankers Association. Foreign firms, such as VISA and MasterCard, played a critical role in setting these standards, since international use of cards is one of the key benefits that Japanese banks wish to offer their customers. But many issues must be addressed, such as keeping up with technological progress, integrating other financial firms into card networks, integrating the clearing of card-based payments through the Nichigin Net (similar to the Fed Wire in the United States), and settling problems such as the legal status of computer files.

But similar technological problems have been solved in the past. A nationwide cash machine network has recently been established among all city banks with the union of two large independent systems. And the popularity of debit cards, which have a recorded balance from which funds are subtracted when purchases are made, has proven that point-of-sale systems are quite feasible. The key issues for banks are how much in resources they can devote to improving computerisation of the payments system, and how much co-operation among banks, other institutions and authorities is optimal, from the viewpoint of lowering costs and increasing convenience while avoiding excessive system risks.

Foreign Exchange Activities

The likely increase in cross-currency transactions in the future will mean that bank expertise in foreign exchange operations will become more valuable. By law in Japan, only authorised foreign exchange banks (of which there are about 300) may conduct foreign exchange business. Even if this law were repealed, which does not seem likely, other institutions would have difficulty in building up the knowledge needed to conduct such business profitably. This does not mean, however, that any one bank may relax in efforts to develop instruments that are attractive to customers and that reduce the major risks involved in this business; competition among banks will be intense.

Developments will concentrate in three areas: better tracking of foreign exchange exposures within banks, better provision of foreign exchange information and advice to investors, and better accommodation of individuals requiring foreign exchange services. The first will require a sophisticated computer system that allows monitoring of trades on a minute-to-minute basis; many banks have made progress in developing such systems. The second will require competition with established international providers of information such as Reuters; possible competitive edges for Japanese institutions might lie in providing services better tailored to specific needs of clients, for example a Japanese language-based system. Concerning advice, the experience of Japanese banks in hedging foreign exchange risk will have to be packaged and sold to investors. The third will depend on lowering costs and meshing Japanese payments practices with foreign ones, and with increasing convenience such as the yen–dollar cash machine developed by Fujitsu and the Bank of Tokyo.

The Postal Savings System

A problem of particular importance to Japanese banking is what to do about the continuing competition with the Postal Savings System, which has attracted fully one-third of all household deposits in Japan. The postal system has made massive investments in recent years to improve its provision of payments services in competition with banks, and has offered attractive interest rates on types of deposit accounts that are forbidden to ordinary banks.[13] This situation has led to many allegations, including those of unfair competition (because the capital costs and risks of the postal system are in part borne by the taxpayer) and of a bumpy playing-field (because of regulatory laxity by the Ministry of Posts, differences in instruments that may be sold, and so on).

The major issue as of this writing concerns the liberalisation of interest rates on small deposits. Since the rates offered by the postal system are set administratively, banks fear that the post office might use its market power unfairly to reduce bank access to deposits, and thus hurt bank profits, especially when the market rates at which banks must lend are low. The abolition of the *maruyu* system, which is expected to make the postal system all the more eager to keep old deposits and attract new ones, has intensified such concerns.

In the long run, it would seem that the suspicion of unfair competition could be removed only by a full privatisation of the Postal Savings System, but there is by no means a consensus on this step, even though some movement that might lay the groundwork for it (for example, partial rights for the postal system to invest some funds independently of the Ministry of Finance) has been taken. The poor track record of creative solution to differences of opinion about the postal system suggests pessimism as to the speed at which such problems can be resolved, particularly that concerning interest rates on small deposits. Moreover there is increased risk in every delay, because market pressures might develop that would lead to precipitous action by one party or another, which might in turn lead to major fund shifts, and might therefore disturb financial system stability.

CONCLUSION

These details of recent developments in Japanese banking suggest how far Japanese banks have come in adapting to the prospective financial environment – and how far they have to go. This new environment, created by movements of fundamental forces, seems likely to require longer maturities of both assets and liabilities, more international business, more retail business, entry into new business areas (such as securities, insurance and investment advice), more risk reduction through ALM systems and stronger capital bases, broader utilisation of experience in foreign exchange operations, and a less acrid *modus vivendi* with the Postal Savings System. One may summarise progress as follows.

Concerning longer maturities, much progress has been made on the assets side, and some on the liability side; however some banks still face restriction on the maximum maturity of deposits, and this restriction may hamper adaptability in the future. Concerning international business, prospects are bright in the United States and Asia, but question marks hang over expansion in Europe. Concerning retail lending, the major problems seem to be intense domestic competition and the constraints that meeting capital adequacy guidelines places on branch expansion. Concerning new business areas, many barriers have already fallen, although a considerable number remain; trends in new market formation suggest that distinctions among institutions will be as few as possible. Concerning risk reduction, development of ALM systems is proceeding somewhat more slowly than might be hoped, but improvements of capital adequacy are moving along well. Concerning foreign exchange, the situation is bright, as expertise and innovations continue to deter potential competitors from entry. Concerning the Postal Savings System, progress has been slow, and much remains to be done.

In short, the future for Japanese banks looks good (but not perfect) with respect to balance sheet structure and evolution, and promising (but not secure) with respect to risk management.

This prognosis might, of course, be wrong. In closing, it may be of use to examine briefly how it might be wrong. The first question relates to the basic logic of the argument, which goes from fundamentals to a new financial environment to bank adaptations. The fundamentals identified might not be so fundamental after all, and other, unidentified ones may turn up. The linkage between fundamentals and changes in demand and supply for financial instruments might also be subject to question. Moreover the requirements that banks face in adapting may be different from those stated here. A second question relates to an implicit assumption, that is, that no major shock alters the environment. Ruled out by assumption are another and more punishing stock market crash, another great inflation, a deep and worldwide recession, a major shift in geopolitics.

Will these uncertainties subvert the analysis? Is the outlook for Japanese banks bleaker than this cautiously optimistic study suggests? Time alone will tell.

Notes

1. For accounts of this process, see Feldman (1986) and Suzuki (1988).
2. A new *maruyu* system replaced the old one, but the new system is substantially less generous. Tax-free interest earnings are limited to certain accounts of those over 65 years of age, the disabled, and those in certain difficult family situations. Positive identification will also be required to obtain tax-free status for an account, in contrast with the old system, which was riddled with fictitious accounts.
3. See Feldman (1986) for a treatment of such cycles of market pressure and deregulation.
4. As of this writing, time deposits of ¥50 million ($370 000) or more are eligible for free-rate treatment.
5. See Miyuki (1987).
6. Many large corporations are said to favour more flexible loans rate formulae as well, in order to avoid the costs of floating their own commercial paper.
7. See Suzuki (1988) pp. 296–7.
8. For an authoritative statement of this opinion, see Tachi (1988).
9. See Feldman (1986) ch. 8 for a description of the timing of establishment of the interest parity relationship.
10. This definition was somewhat narrower than those originally discussed, but still applied to 35 institutions, including city banks, trust banks, long-term credit banks, some local banks and several central organisations for credit co-operatives.
11. See Tokuda *et al.* (1988).
12. Ibid.
13. The most important of such accounts is the 'fixed amount deposit' (*teigaku chokin*). Such accounts may be opened for maturities as long as ten years with guaranteed interest rates, and funds may be withdrawn without penalty at any time after the first six months.

References

Feldman, Robert Alan (1986) *Japanese Financial Markets: Deficits, Dilemmas and Deregulation* (Cambridge, Mass.: MIT Press).
Frydl, Edward J. (1982) 'The Eurodollar Conundrum', *Federal Reserve Bank of New York Quarterly Bulletin*, Spring.
Fukao, M. and K. Okina (1988) 'Integration of Financial Markets and Balance of Payments Imbalances', Bank of Japan, Institute of Monetary and Economic Studies, mimeo.
Kooro (first name unknown) (1987) 'Togin no Supureddo Yuushi Kyuusoo no Haikei to Shin'i' ('The Background and True Meaning of the Surge in Spread Funding by City Banks'), *Kinyuu Zaisei Jijoo*, 17 August.
Shinosuka, Yutaka (1987) 'Kinyuu Kikan Gyoomu no Kakudai to Risuku Kanri' ('The Expansion of Financial Institution Business and Risk Management'), *Kinyuu Zaisei Jijoo*, 7 December.
Suzuki, Yoshio (ed.) (1988) *The Japanese Financial System* (Oxford University Press).
Tachi, Ryuichiro (1988) 'Henka ni Taioo Dekiru Kinyuu Seido no Hookoo wo Shimesu' ('Showing the Direction of a Financial System that Can Adapt to Change'), *Kinyuu Zaisei Jijoo*, 4 January.
Tokudà, Hiromi *et al.* (1988) 'BIS Kisei no Impakuto to Keiei Kadai' ('The Impact of BIS Regulations and Management Issues'), *Kinyuu Zaisei Jijoo*, 2 May.

COMMENT

Jenny Corbett

Dr Feldman's paper presents an appealing and helpful classification of the main factors driving innovations in areas affecting Japanese banks and of the adaptations which banks have already needed, and will in the future need, to make. His organisation of a very large and difficult set of changes into a format that we can begin to analyse and tackle is extremely helpful.

He postulates six fundamental forces generating change in financial markets affecting banks: demographics; world trade and development; fiscal consolidation; electronics; energy; and consumerism. These factors, he argues, will result in four basic changes in financial markets. There will be increasing importance of longer maturity instruments and of contingent instruments. There will be an increase in international risks and there could be a growth in retail business. The changes will require banks to adapt by lengthening maturities of assets and liabilities, developing contingent instruments and by improving risk analysis and management.

Dr Feldman then considers the progress made by banks so far in the areas of liability structure, loan market practices, new business areas, investment management, international markets, capital adequacy, payments systems innovations, foreign exchange activities and competition with the Postal Savings System.

His central argument is that banks are disadvantaged by the changes he identifies because they imply a movement away from traditional banking business. Therefore the 'key to the prognosis for banks everywhere ... is how well they will be able to maintain their role as providers of monetary instruments, which are short-term, non-contingent and domestic, in a world where much of the profit will be in instruments that are long-term, contingent and international'. That is, in a sense, the prognosis depends on the question: How important will traditional banking business be in the future? And I will come back to that question.

Nevertheless, much of the paper's description of how Japanese banks are adapting concentrates on the ways in which they are moving into the new areas. In this respect Feldman notes:

- a greater sensitivity to risk management systems;
- a lengthening of all banks' liabilities and a reduction in the differences between different types of banks on both the asset and liability side;
- an increase in the share of free-rate assets and liabilities (that is, not under interest rate restrictions);
- an increase in 'retail'-type lending (housing and consumer finance) and tentative moves into the retail sector of investment advice;
- a move by banks into new business of the securities type (bond dealing, CPs, private placements); and
- the spectacular increase in the international activity of Japanese banks.

There are several other important areas of changes in Japanese banking which Feldman raises, but I believe the crux of his argument is that Japanese banks have made good progress in making those adaptations outlined above.

On balance he is 'cautiously optimistic' about Japanese banks' ability to adapt, an attitude based on their good performance so far in balance sheet evolution and improvements in risk management.

In commenting on this structure, I think that there are two very brief comments that I would like to make to start with, but they are really, in a sense, quibbles. One could argue about the completeness of the list of structural changes that he has proposed. On the whole I do not feel that there is very much to be added. I think that, fundamentally, the main features of financial market changes have been captured by his classification, although I would prefer to see a distinction between long-term, gradual changes and short, sharp, shock-type changes. I wonder whether there are differences in the way Japanese banking has adapted to those changes which are long and slow as opposed to those which are sudden shocks.

Secondly, as Feldman himself notes in the paper, one could argue with his causal model linking fundamental changes to financial innovation and then linking those financial market innovations directly to changes in banking practices. In fact I accept his causality. I think that there are other models of financial innovation which put less stress on fundamental economic and technological changes. There are those models of financial innovation which stress a political economy sort of view that financial innovation is the outcome of interest group struggles, and so on. But I would accept the implicit logic of Feldman's argument that fundamental economic factors create the need or the opportunity for innovation but that the specific form that innovation takes is likely to be the result of some inter-group bargaining. Indeed the example that is employed in his paper is the change in savings behaviour and the rise of consumerism, with the likely result of a move towards more urban distribution of financial resources and rising power of consumer interests in Japanese finance.

Turning to my two major points about Feldman's paper, I would say that I certainly agree with his assessment of what are the important changes that have taken place in Japanese banking so far. There is a lengthening of assets and liabilities, although, as he has noted, there is a different pace between different types of banks and some banks face a greater mismatch in their asset and liability structure than others. There is also an important change in the type of business client and the mix of business and individual clients which is being dealt with by banks and, again, a blurring of the distinction between types of banks. Finally, there are the beginnings of the breakdown in the distinction between banks and other types of financial institutions. I am also in agreement with Feldman's basic optimism about Japanese banking prospects, but I would suggest that the optimism should really be based on a rather different set of factors from those which he has suggested.

In a period of rapid financial change it seems increasingly likely that it will be difficult to understand the prospects for different types of institutions if we concentrate only on the characteristics of the assets and liabilities in which they deal. If we treat Japanese banks as institutions which accept mostly short-term deposits from residents and lend mostly short-term to domestic business then it will be true by definition, as Feldman suggests, that traditional Japanese banks will be disadvantaged by current changes.

But if we think in terms of the functions which Japanese banks have performed in the past perhaps we can begin to understand better some of the puzzling features of Japanese banks' apparent success in recent years, and perhaps we can assess two important questions, one of which is posed by Feldman and one of which is missing from his paper.

The first question, which is posed by Feldman, is 'How important will banking business be in the future?' The second question, which is missing from his paper, is 'Do we understand the sources of profitability in Japanese banking?'

To take the second question first. Do we understand the sources (and importance) of profitability in Japanese banking? I think the answer is probably no, but let us review what can be said from the somewhat imperfect data.

1. In the period of rapid growth to the early 1970s the profitability of banks is assumed to have been guaranteed by controlled interest rates and the lack of alternative sources of funds for investment. From the non-Japanese point of view Japanese banks seemed to have an enviable guarantee of both volume and margins. There is, furthermore, evidence that economies of scale were important.
2. But, so far as international comparisons were possible for that period, Japanese banks seemed *not* to be highly profitable by international standards (although they were more profitable than non-financial businesses in Japan).
3. Since the shift to lower growth, Japanese banks' profit ratios have dropped, and are apparently at the lower end of the international distribution.

Therefore the balance sheet shifts, which Feldman describes, do not seem to have brought significant improvements in profits. Furthermore the shift away from the controlled interest rate structure has apparently squeezed margins considerably, so that the gap between the average cost of funds and the average yield on assets is lower in Japan than in major competitor countries.

Some evidence (Iwami, 1988) also suggests that the profitability of international transactions of Japanese banks is even lower than that of domestic transactions, so that the increase in international business is accompanied by a decrease in overall profitability. On this evidence our optimism about Japanese banks does not look well founded; in particular it does not suggest that the adjustments described by Feldman have so far helped the position of the banks.

I suggest that optimism can be restored by turning to the second question, which is posed, but not directly answered, by Feldman – how important will banking business be? – if we pose this question in terms of the functions of Japanese banks rather than the asset and liabilities characteristics stressed by Feldman. In particular, I would stress that the functions of Japanese banks in the past gave them considerable experience in managing risks and handling contingent claims and that that experience will continue to be valuable.

For example, Japanese bankers who backed the motor industry in the 1950s were facing a situation just as risky as high technology venture businesses today. The prospects for the motor industry in Japan in 1952, I would suggest, were nearly as risky as the prospect of some of the businesses that Japanese banks are now asked to support.

Furthermore all banking is in some sense about contingent contracts because of bankruptcy risk. This is particularly true for Japanese banks who take an active role in handling financial distress (and contrary to popular belief are not protected from the risk of client bankruptcy by implicit or explicit government guarantee) and often bear significant losses even when bankruptcy is avoided.

Therefore the view of Japanese banking which I offer is that their past role as the main financial intermediaries in a highly regulated system gave them special importance and experience in collecting information about investment opportunities, monitoring borrowers on behalf of ultimate lenders, and managing contingent assets. In the absence of well-developed financial markets at that time in Japan there were very few other ways in which this information could be communicated.

Thus, even if Japan's financial markets do move further away from loan-type markets to bond-type markets (and we should not exaggerate the degree to which this is happening), the function of information collection, monitoring and management of business contingencies will probably continue to be concentrated in the banking sector because of its past experience. It will be the basis of banks' continuing importance even if the collection of assets and liabilities in their portfolios looks rather different from that of the past.

To summarise briefly, Feldman has presented an illuminating and elegant causal model of changes in financial markets and banking in Japan. His framework provides a very useful map of complex territory and it provides one gauge by which to judge the progress made by Japanese banks. But, in addition, I would raise two questions. How do we reconcile this view with the apparent low profitability of Japanese banking? And secondly, should we not find the source of our optimism about the outlook more in the continuing importance of the functions of Japanese banks as monitors and providers of information than in the pattern of their portfolios?

Reference

Iwami, Toru (1988) 'Internationalization of Japanese Banking; Factors Affecting its Rapid Growth', discussion paper, Research Institute for the Japanese Economy, University of Tokyo, January.

2 Japan's Banking Regulation: Current Policy Issues

Richard Dale

Japan's approach to regulating financial markets differs markedly from that adopted in other major financial centres. In the first place, the Japanese authorities appear to have a strong aversion to financial failures of any kind. On the banking side, there have been no failures involving losses to depositors since the Second World War. The result is that there have been no calls on the country's deposit insurance fund since its inception in 1971. Even so, the insurance fund was substantially strengthened with effect from July 1986.[1] In the securities markets, too, the authorities have tried to avoid losses that could upset market confidence, the most celebrated example being the assistance given by the Bank of Japan to Yamaichi Securities in 1965.

A second distinctive feature of Japan's regulatory regime is the authorities' willingness to intervene informally in situations where market forces are in conflict with official policy objectives. For instance, early in 1988 it was reported that the Ministry of Finance (MOF) had intervened to prevent banks from raising their dividends, the aim being to ensure that higher profits were used to strengthen banks' capital ratios. Banks have also been asked from time to time to restrain their lending, both generally and in relation to particular categories of borrower (notably the property sector). During the October 1987 global stock market crash there were unsubstantiated reports to the effect that MOF had one meeting with the four major brokerage houses and a separate meeting with major institutional investors, in a move to stabilise the Tokyo stock market.[2] In January 1988, evidently concerned about the possibility of another stock market upheaval, the MOF eased the accounting rules applicable to *tokkin* funds (a major investment vehicle for institutional investors) so as to avoid the necessity of recording large unrealised losses on securities holdings. Although such moves may raise eyebrows in the West, the

33

Japanese authorities would no doubt argue that Japan's postwar record of financial stability owes something to official intervention of this kind.

Finally, it is worth pointing out that, whereas the informal guidance provided by the regulatory authorities is distinctively Japanese, the formal regulatory structure governing Tokyo's financial markets is to a large extent a reflection of external influences of various kinds. The legal separation of banking and securities markets is an importation from the United States; the programme of financial deregulation pursued by Japan over the past decade has been prompted by overseas demands that Tokyo should open up its markets; the proposed new capital adequacy rules are, of course, based on the Basle agreement which was originally formulated as an Anglo-American accord; and other current regulatory reforms, such as the attack on insider trading, may be viewed as a reaction to overseas concerns.[3]

These broad observations provide a necessary background for a more detailed consideration of Japan's regulatory regime. The purpose of this paper is to focus exclusively on two aspects of financial regulation which are of particular topical interest: the separation of banking and securities business and the impact on Japanese banks of the new Basle capital adequacy guidelines.

THE SEPARATION OF BANKING AND SECURITIES BUSINESS

Prior to the Second World War there was no prohibition on Japanese banks' securities activities and, although during the 1920s there were widespread bank failures in Japan, banks' securities' business did not play a significant part in the disturbances.[4] In contrast, the operation of US banks' securities affiliates was blamed for the US banking collapse in 1929–33. This led to passage of the Glass-Steagall Act in 1933, which established in the United States a formal legal barrier between banking and securities business. After the Second World War the United States, as an occupying power, imported the main restrictions of the Glass-Steagall Act into Japan, the key provision being Article 65 of Japan's Securities and Exchange Law of 1948. Article 65 in effect states that no bank may underwrite, deal in or publicly offer securities other than government bonds. However, in contrast to the US Glass-Steagall provisions, Japanese banks may purchase and sell securities for their own investment purposes without legal limit. Given this authority,

Japanese banks have acquired major equity investments over the years which collectively amount to nearly 20 per cent of all holdings in the Tokyo stock market.

Article 65 is, then, an alien law, imported from the United States, that has no basis in Japanese financial policies. Accordingly the Japanese authorities have been prepared to accommodate growing market pressures in favour of integration of banking and securities business so long as this can be done without infringing upon the statutory provisions. On the other hand, the fact of separation has created strongly entrenched vested interests, with the securities houses vigorously resisting any incursions into what they have come to regard as their own exclusive business territory. The process of reform has therefore been piecemeal and gradualist, involving reciprocal concessions by banks and securities firms.

The most obvious loophole in Article 65 is that Japanese financial institutions can combine banking and securities business in foreign financial centres where 'universal' banking is allowed. Japanese banks have, for instance, established important securities operations in London and Frankfurt and Japanese securities houses have been successful in obtaining UK banking licences. In order to protect securities houses' domestic client base, the MOF has applied administrative guidance to the effect that Japanese banks' foreign securities subsidiaries should not act as lead managers of publicly offered foreign bonds issued by Japanese companies. However, in April 1988 the MOF indicated that this restriction might be lifted. Meanwhile securities subsidiaries of Japanese banks operating, for instance, in Frankfurt may, under liberalised West German rules, lead-manage Deutschmark denominated foreign bonds issued or guaranteed by the Japanese government, but they may not as yet lead-manage Deutschmark denominated bonds issued by Japanese companies. Nevertheless, judging from the sudden increase in Japanese banks seeking to establish securities subsidiaries in Frankfurt, a relaxation of the MOF rules appears to be anticipated.

As part of the process of reciprocal access to national financial markets Japan has also felt obliged to permit foreign banks to establish securities operations in Japan. In 1986, the MOF began to grant branch licences to securities affiliates of foreign banks, provided that the parent bank held no more than 50 per cent of the equity of the affiliate – the rationale being that a legally independent entity would not be in breach of Article 65. To begin with only banks from universal banking countries were permitted to establish securities operations in this way, but in March 1987 the MOF decided that the same privilege should be accorded to American banks. The situation now, therefore is that foreign banks can undertake securities business in Japan which is not open to Japanese banks themselves and which in the US case cannot be undertaken in the foreign banks' home market.

Nevertheless Japanese banks' access to securities business in the Tokyo market is being gradually increased as a result of a series of policy relaxations by the MOF over the past decade. In 1979, banks were permitted to issue and deal in certificates of deposit; in 1981, the law governing banks' underwriting and distribution of government bonds was clarified, following which the MOF's restrictions in this area were also relaxed to the point where, since August 1987, banks have been permitted to sell government bonds on virtually the same basis as securities houses. In October 1986 the overseas securities subsidiaries of banks were authorised to underwrite and deal in commercial paper issued abroad; and, when Japan's indigenous commercial paper market was established at the end of last year, the paper was classified as a promissory note rather than a security, so to enable banks to compete in the new market on equal terms with the securities houses.

In contrast to these developments, the new regulatory regime for Japan's futures markets, which was finalised earlier this year, reflects a careful application of Article 65.[5] Japanese banks and securities firms have been able to trade government bond futures on the Tokyo stock exchange since 1985. However, under the new plan, the Tokyo exchange is able to offer contracts in foreign government bonds and stock-index futures and a new financial futures market will be established to trade futures and options in interest rates and currencies. Banks will have unlimited access to the financial futures exchange, both on their own account and as brokers; but on the stock exchange they will be limited to trading government bond futures. Securities firms will be permitted to trade freely in stock exchange futures as well as on the financial futures exchange, *except* for spot currency options, the reason for this last exclusion being that the foreign exchange market is the traditional preserve of the banks.

Under the new plan banks and securities houses have equal access to overseas futures and options markets. Specifically both can act as brokers of foreign futures and options to Japanese customers and can trade in foreign spot currency options for their own accounts, but neither may act as brokers in foreign spot currency and stock-index options.

This approach to access to futures and options markets is no more than a distribution of business territory within the framework of the law, following intense lobbying by rival industry groups, and cannot be viewed as an aspect of financial policy. In any event the complex division of functions in the futures and options markets suggests that the Japanese authorities will have to contemplate more radical changes in the regulatory structure if the Article 65 barriers between the banking and securities industries are to be further dismantled. Essentially, there are four alternatives.

First, there is the recent suggestion of the banks to the effect that their overseas securities subsidiaries should be permitted to engage in securities business in Japan in much the same way that foreign banks have been able to establish indirectly held securities branches in Tokyo. Under this arrangement securities houses might in turn be allowed to obtain Japanese banking licences via their overseas banking subsidiaries. Banking and securities business would then be fused within the existing legal framework by a process of 'round-tripping', with banks and securities houses diversifying into each other's home territory by routing business through their overseas operations.[6]

The MOF's recent approval of a Tokyo representative office for Aubrey Lanston, a US government securities primary dealer affiliated with the Industrial Bank of Japan, has been cited by some as a precedent for allowing Japanese banks to conduct domestic securities activities via their overseas securities subsidiaries. However the MOF has argued that Lanston, being a specialised dealer in US government securities, is not classifiable as a securities company under Japanese law. In any event, Lanston's representative office status in Japan allows it only to provide advice and information, with executions being transacted through the New York office.

Secondly, as a second-best reform, the banks have in the past requested that they should at least be able to deal directly with the securities houses and to receive commission on stock exchange transactions, as trust banks already do.[7] Such an arrangement would be permissible under the existing law which expressly permits banks to purchase and sell securities on an agency basis.[8] This, incidentally, is one area where US banks, who already act as agency brokers, can engage in a broader range of securities activities than their Japanese counterparts, despite the similarity of the statutory framework.

A further possibility, within the existing legal framework, would be for the MOF to permit banks to strengthen their existing relationships with securities affiliates. Article 11 of the Anti-Monopoly Law prevents banks from acquiring more than 5 per cent of a non-bank's equity but for financial groups this restriction can be bypassed by means of cross-shareholdings. The leading City banks have already established semi-captive securities houses through group shareholdings and in 1987 it was reported that banks were routinely seconding employees to these affiliated institutions. However the securities industry evidently objected to the strengthening of these bank–securities affiliate relationships and in May 1988 the MOF was reported to have instructed banks to limit the percentage of their groups' ownership of security houses to less than 50 per cent.[9] For instance, under the new guideline the Mitsubishi group has had to lower its shareholding in Ryoko Securities from 75 per cent to under 50 per cent, with effect from June 1988. This is an interesting illustration of the Japanese authorities' approach to regulatory matters, since the 50 per cent rule does not appear to be a legal requirement under Article 65. In any event this is one area in which banks' attempts to expand their securities interests have been firmly rebuffed.

Finally, in preference to non-statutory reforms, the Japanese authorities may be prepared to consider radical changes in the law, particularly if the US Glass-Steagall Act is amended. Article 65 of the Securities and Exchange Law might itself be repealed; or banks might be permitted, through appropriate changes in the Anti-Monopoly Law, to establish wholly owned securities subsidiaries. Alternatively provision might be made for the establishment of financial holding companies (currently prohibited by Article 9 of the Anti-Monopoly Law) which would own both bank and securities subsidiaries.

Significantly, the Finance Ministry's Financial System Research Council (FSRC) is reported to have favoured this last approach in its draft recommendations for reforming Japan's banking system. But the final report, issued in December 1987, omitted any reference to the Article 65 question, apparently because of strong objections from the securities industry. This episode highlights the true nature of the policy dilemma over Article 65: in the Japanese context there is no arguable case for separating banking and securities markets because the two businesses were freely mixed prior to the Second World War without mishap. It is an accident of history that the industries are now formally separated but reunification poses enormous practical difficulties given the strong opposition from those who have a vested interest in the *status quo*.

Placed in a global financial context the existing separation of Japanese banking and securities markets through Article 65 poses broader policy dilemmas, illustrating the difficulties that national regulatory authorities face in trying to accommodate institutions subject to widely differing regulatory regimes.

In the first place, there is the delicate question of reciprocal entry rights to national financial markets. If universal banks are refused entry to the securities markets of countries which uphold the principle of separation this may be construed as discrimination in the applicants banks' country of origin. On the other hand, allowing entry to such diversified institutions (even through specialised subsidiaries) may be viewed as unfair to banks and securities houses in the host country, as well as contrary to national policy.

Similarly, there is the question of whether countries which uphold separation should permit their banks to combine banking and securities business in third markets where there are no separation laws. If national authorities refuse to permit such activities abroad their domestic banks may be increasingly disadvantaged in international wholesale markets. Yet a decision to accommodate this third market loophole throws the whole rationale of the separation policy into doubt. After all, conflicts of interest and financial risks encountered in foreign jurisdictions can feed back to a parent institution in its home market.

Other difficulties may arise where universal banks and specialised institutions co-exist within a tight regulatory framework. For example, in the United Kingdom, the Bank of England has expressed concern over the regulatory advantages enjoyed by specialised security houses originating from countries with domestic separation laws:

Partly as a consequence of these legal separations of functions [between banking and securities activities], a class of strongly capitalized specialist security houses has developed, subject to different and, from a prudential viewpoint, lighter supervision than that applied to banks. Internationally, these are, moreover, sometimes able to engage in activities from which the law debars them domestically. For both these reasons, therefore, they may have, or may be believed to have, an advantage over the commercial banks of other countries which are their main international competitors ...[10]

These problems of regulatory interface have been compounded by the division of responsibilities, in some countries, between securities and bank regulators. This is illustrated by the difficulties that have arisen over the UK authorisation of foreign banks' securities branches operating in London. The UK Securities and Investments Board (SIB), which supervises UK securities firms, initially intended that the home country supervisors of such foreign banks should provide regular and comprehensive financial data to the SIB – in default of which the banks would be required to restructure their UK securities branches into separate securities subsidiaries, with their own dedicated capital monitored by the SIB (or appropriate self-regulatory organisation). However, following strong representations by foreign, including Japanese, banks and their regulators this proposal has been abandoned in favour of a more informal arrangement whereby the foreign regulators will reassure the Bank of England that the banks concerned are financially sound.[11]

The general conclusion, then, on Article 65 is that the continuing separation of banking and securities business in Japan, as in the United States, creates competitive distortions at home and abroad as well as growing problems of regulatory interface *vis-à-vis* the supervisory authorities in universal banking centres.

THE BASLE CAPITAL ADEQUACY RULES

The second regulatory topic to be discussed is the impact on Japanese banks of the recently agreed Basle accord on minimum capital adequacy standards. Under this agreement international banks must achieve a ratio of total capital to risk-weighted assets of 8 per cent by 1992. Tier One or core capital (essentially equity and disclosed reserves) must constitute at least four percentage points of this minimum capital ratio, while Tier Two or supplementary capital is allowable up to an amount equal to the core capital element.

Japanese banks are widely viewed as being vulnerable under the new international requirements because their capital ratios have been falling steadily over a long period in the context of rapid asset growth and a declining return on assets. More recently, the average ratio of equity to total assets of the seven largest Japanese banks is estimated by Salomon Brothers to have declined from just over 2.6 per cent in 1980 to 2.3 per cent in 1986.[12]

However the distinctive feature of Japanese banks' capital structure is their large undisclosed or 'latent' reserves in the form of unrealised gains on securities holdings – investments which, as pointed out above are permitted under Article 65 of the Securities and Exchange Law. The MOF, in its own pre-Basle calculation of regulatory capital, treated 70 per cent of these unrealised profits as eligible capital. On this basis the average capital ratio of the seven largest banks stood at over 8 per cent in 1986 (Salomon estimates). Furthermore, whereas the conventional equity capital ratio of these banks was virtually stable at around 2.25 per cent in the three years 1984 to 1986, the adjusted ratio (incorporating 70 per cent of unrealised securities profits) rose from 5.7 per cent to 8.3 per cent – reflecting the powerful impact on the more broadly defined capital ratio of the extraordinarily buoyant Japanese stock market.[13]

The treatment of unrealised securities profits for capital adequacy purposes was a matter of controversy during the course of negotiations leading up to the Basle accord on minimum capital standards. The compromise finally agreed permits banks to treat as supplementary or Tier Two capital the difference between the book value and market value of their securities holdings – subject to a discount of 55 per cent designed to reflect potential capital gains tax of 50 per cent as well as stock market volatility. The role of these 'latent' reserves is at the centre of the present debate on the implications of the new capital requirements for Japanese banks.

The more general view appears to be that the Basle requirements will weigh more heavily on Japanese banks than on any other national group of major international banks. Therefore Japanese banks will have to rein back their asset growth, which will possibly lead to some reversal of their recent dramatic gains in international markets. However an opposite view has emerged, suggesting that Japanese banks are particularly well placed to meet the new Basle requirements and that they will continue to outperform their US and other foreign competitors.[14] The actual outcome is crucial because Japan's capital adequacy standards have been widely perceived as quite permissive, and it was partly in order to eliminate such potential distortions that the Basle accord on capital adequacy was implemented.

The present position is that the thirteen Japanese City banks as a group have Tier Two capital equivalent to around 4.5 per cent of risk-weighted assets compared with the Basle requirement of 4 per cent by end 1992 (assuming that only the minimum amount of Tier One capital is held).[15] On the other hand, these same banks have a significant deficiency of Tier One capital, which currently stands at around 2.5 per cent of risk-weighted assets compared with the minimum Basle requirement of 4 per cent. This shortfall of Tier One capital has prompted predictions that the City banks will have to raise record amounts of new equity capital between now and 1992, even if they slow their asset growth. For instance, Nomura Securities has predicted that new equity financing by Japanese banks effected by the Basle capital rules will amount to ¥7–8 trillion ($56–64 billion) during the five years to 1992 on the assumption that annual asset growth slows to 7–8 per cent compared with an historic norm of around 13 per cent. On the other hand, if the historic growth rate were to be maintained the new equity requirement would reach ¥9–10 trillion ($72–80 billion).

Quite apart from this trade-off between capital and growth, it is unfortunately quite impossible to assess with any confidence the probable impact of the Basle rules on Japanese banks. This is because the actual outcome depends on the unpredictable response of three sets of players: the banks themselves, the financial markets and the Japanese authorities (effectively the MOF).

So far as the banks are concerned they have various options open to them to strengthen their capital ratios. First, they may shift some of their assets towards low risk-weighted items such as government bonds (0 per cent) and mortgage loans (50 per cent). This is already happening to some extent. Second, they may attempt to widen the spreads on their commercial lending with a view to increasing the average return on assets and raising earnings retentions. This also appears to be occurring in some degree. For instance, the current move by banks to link short-term prime rates to money market rates, rather than to the Bank of Japan's discount rate, and simultaneously to end the present compensatory deposit system, may be viewed as an attempt to raise lending margins. On the other hand, this shift towards 'spread banking' is occurring against a background of weakening demand for bank loans by Japanese companies, reflecting their high liquidity as well as the process of securitisation. It may be, therefore, that banks can only raise their lending margins by taking on greater credit risks – something that is not captured by the Basle capital adequacy framework.

Third, banks may realise some of their existing loans through the process of securitisation (for example, selling repackaged mortgage loans when this is authorised). Fourthly, they may choose to slow their asset growth, particularly in low-margin business such as international inter-bank lending which currently accounts for around one-third of the big five City banks' earning assets. But the split between domestic and international asset growth remains highly uncertain and may depend, for instance, on whether domestic assets are securitised more rapidly than international loans.

Finally, the banks will clearly be focusing on various ways of increasing their core capital other than through increased retentions. In addition to issuing new share capital, such initiatives may include the realisation of undervalued securities holdings, the crucial considerations here being the potential 50 per cent tax liability, the need to preserve existing corporate relationships and the undesirability of depressing share prices. The tax liability may be circumvented by offsetting the capital gain against losses elsewhere in the portfolio, and the other difficulties can in principle be resolved by simultaneously buying back the shares that are sold, as has been done on previous occasions. The life insurance companies have already established a precedent here. They have been able over the two fiscal years 1986/7 and 1987/8 to offset losses on their dollar bond holdings against realised profits on other securities in their portfolios. An example of the buy-back technique was provided recently by Sumitomo Bank. When Ataka Corporation went bankrupt, Sumitomo offset heavy loan losses by selling securities with a low book value and simultaneously buying them back, thereby avoiding any disruption in the stock market.

In theory then, it would be possible for Japanese banks to issue newly authorised forms of supplementary capital, such as convertible bonds and (currently under official review) subordinated debt, thereby freeing a sizeable proportion of the Tier Two capital for switching into core capital via realisation of securities profits. However the MOF would no doubt have a key role in determining the scope for this kind of activity, which might also be viewed critically by foreign banks and their regulators.

The behaviour of the Tokyo stock market also has a crucial bearing on the impact of the new capital requirements on Japanese banks. According to some observers the present level of the market, and particularly the high rating of bank stocks, gives Japanese banks a privileged access to low-cost capital. For instance, in a letter to the Chairman of the Federal Reserve Board, dated 5 May 1988, a group of congressmen pointed out that the common stock of US money centre banks currently sells at less than ten times earnings, while the stock of Japanese banks sells at multiples in excess of thirty times earnings. According to the congressmen, even though US banks may have to raise less capital in absolute terms than Japanese banks in order to comply with the new Basle standards, US banks will be penalised 'because they do not have the same access to reasonably priced capital'. Of course, this disparity in price-earnings multiples between US and Japanese banks presumably reflects the markets' verdict on the relative prospects of the institutions concerned. Nevertheless fluctuations in the Tokyo market will affect not only Japanese banks' access to new capital but also the valuation of 'old capital' (in the form of unrealised profits on securities holdings).

But perhaps the most crucial unknown in the capital adequacy conundrum is the attitude of the MOF. The Ministry has an important discretion, first of all, in interpreting the Basle rules: a draft of the proposed new risk-weightings was circulated in May of 1988 and in general the rules, which are to apply to 31 banks with overseas subsidiaries or branches, apply the lowest risk-weights permissible within the Basle framework. More importantly, the MOF can choose to widen the range of supplementary capital instruments available to Japanese banks. This is an area currently under review. Third, the MOF can, if it wishes, assist the banks by authorising securitisation (and subsequent resale) of existing bank assets such as mortgage loans. Fourth, the whole question of tax treatment of realised gains on banks' securities holdings is crucial, given the potential for shifting Tier Two into Tier One capital. This is another area where the MOF may have a decisive voice, and, indeed, it has been reported that this question, too, is under consideration. Finally, and most important of all, the MOF can be expected to offer guidance on a whole range of matters affecting banks' asset growth, particularly in the most sensitive area of international lending.

Given the uncertain response of the banks, the financial markets and the regulatory authorities, it is not possible to gauge the impact on Japanese banks of the new Basle capital adequacy framework. For instance, it is conceivable that, favoured by a low cost of capital and a large surplus of potentially realisable capital reserves, Japanese banks will be in a position to increase still further their share of international banking markets. Such an outcome would, however, generate considerable international financial tensions. The new Basle arrangements are purportedly designed to ensure greater competitive equality but if the newly levelled playing-field still produces a result in which one side scores too many goals this would be of little comfort to the other players.

The real point, therefore, is surely this: the Japanese authorities are aware of the need to prevent their own banks displacing foreign banks in international markets to an extent that could produce a protectionist response. That, after all, is one reason why the MOF, in May 1986, announced new and more stringent capital requirements for international banks. Since the MOF, as indicated above, has a crucial role in determining how banks respond to the new Basle capital adequacy rules it can be expected to use its discretion to ensure that the banks do in fact restrain their rate of growth to some internationally acceptable level. It is that prospect, rather than the introduction of an allegedly level playing-field in the capital adequacy area, that will tend to even up the scoring power of rival national banking groups.

Notes

1. However, the main reason for strengthening the deposit insurance fund was concern about the increased potential for bank failures in the context of financial deregulation. See 'Maintaining a Sound Financial System in Japan', Shijuro Ogata, Bank of Japan, in Richard Portes and Alexander Swoboda (eds), *Threats to International Financial Stability*, Centre for Economic Policy Research, 1987.
2. See 'The October 1987 Market Break', US Securities and Exchange Commission, February 1988, pp. 11–15.
3. Some of the Japanese authorities' supervisory techniques are also borrowed from the United States. The proposed rating system for banks announced by the Ministry of Finance in 1988 is a case in point. Institutions will be ranked on a scale of 1 to 5 based on five criteria (net worth ratios, asset quality, management control systems, profitability and liquidity). As in the United States, the MOF will base the extent and frequency of bank examinations on the rating of the institutions concerned.
4. The discussion that follows draws on material in Richard Dale, 'Japan's Glass-Steagall "Act"', *Journal of International Banking Law*, vol. 2, no. 3, 1987.
5. See Michael Whitener, 'The Steady Erosion of Japan's "Glass-Steagall"', *International Financial Law Review*, May 1988, pp. 12–13.
6. Yoko Shibata, 'Japan's banks try to enter broking overseas', *Financial Times*, 7 October 1986.
7. 'Bankers ask permission to be discount brokers', *Japan Economic Journal*, 28 June 1986.
8. Article 65 states that 'any bank may purchase and sell securities upon the written order of and solely for the account of clients'.
9. *The Nikkei Financial Daily*, 27 May 1988, p. 1.
10. 'Internationalization of Securities Markets – Current Developments and Implications', speech by Michael Hewitt, Bank of England, before the Group of Thirty Symposium on Equity Markets, London, 15 September 1986.
11. See 'SIB yields on foreign banks', *Financial Times*, 10 August 1988.
12. *The Japanese Banks – At a Crossroads?*, Salomon Brothers, 1 July 1988, p. 33.
13. Ibid.
14. See Neil Osborn and Garry Evans, 'Cooke's Medicine: Kill or Cure?', *Euromoney*, July 1988.
15. The data cited on Japanese banks' Tier One and Tier Two capital is based on 'International Capital Convergence: consequences for Japanese banks and their hidden reserves', IBCA Bank Analysis, May 1988.

COMMENT

Maximilian Hall

Background

A programme of financial liberalisation has been under way for some
time now in Japan but the pace of change has accelerated markedly in
recent years, partly as a result of external pressure. Internal pressures
for change first surfaced around the mid-1970s when the shift from a
'high growth' to a 'low growth' economy necessitated adjustments to
deal with the induced shifts in the flow of funds pattern: corporations
reduced investment and borrowing, households raised their savings
ratio and the government dramatically increased its expenditure,
thereby creating a larger public sector deficit. Bond financing of the
budget deficit, in turn, necessitated an opening-up of the secondary
market and the payment of competitive yields by the government. The
expansion of the secondary bond market, spurred on by a relaxation in
the rules governing banks' sales of government bonds, in turn pro-
moted the expansion of trading in short-term open markets (for
instance, the *gensaki* market) and generated pressures for relaxation if
not abolition of interest rate controls. The appearance of higher and
more volatile inflation rates also played its part by inducing financial
innovation on the part of financial institutions eager to benefit from
higher returns (for example, through the issue of CDs, Money Market
Certificates (MMCs) and *gensaki* market operations) and from the
circumvention of official controls (for instance, through the use of yen-
based foreign currency deposits).

The internationalisation of the real economy and the increase in
cross-border flows which followed the revision of the Foreign
Exchange and Foreign Trade Control Law which took effect in
December 1980 generated pressures for the further internationalisation
of finance. These were reinforced by the exertion of external pressure
on the government to change domestic practices and open up domestic
financial markets to foreign competition (indeed a series of bilateral
talks have been held since 1973 embracing: the 'US–Japan Yen/Dollar
Committee'; the 'UK–Japan Financial Consultations'; the 'Germany–
Japan Financial Consultations'; and, most recently, the 'US–Japan   .
Working Group on Financial Markets'). More generally, the inequi-
ties, distortions and resource misallocation that resulted under the
postwar regime of controls generated ever-increasing demands for

reform, some of which became possible as a result of technological advances in computing and information systems.

This then is the background to the present liberalisation moves which are sweeping through financial markets in Japan, embracing, *inter alia*, deposit rate deregulation, reduced segmentation between institutions (which, traditionally, has segmented long-term from short-term finance, banking from trust business and banking from securities business, and restricted institutions' access to sources of funds), relaxation of collateral requirements, relaxation of maturity controls, the provision to foreign institutions of wider access to the Japanese money and capital markets, the development of a Euro-yen investment and banking market, the introduction of laws designed to stamp out 'insider trading', and an attempt to deepen the short-term capital market.

Given the wide-ranging nature of this reform package, it was obvious that a large number of highly important policy issues would afflict the authorities (notably the Ministry of Finance (MOF) and the Bank of Japan) and so it proved. To single out but a few, the following readily spring to mind:

1. how best to relax the segmentation rules without destabilising the financial system;
2. how best to proceed with deposit rate deregulation, given the dominant position of the Postal Savings Service;
3. how best to implement the principle of reciprocity in financial services; and
4. how best to stamp out 'insider trading'.

Professor Dale has chosen to look at aspect (1) in respect to the reform of Article 65 (or at least the undermining of its intentions) of the Securities and Exchange Law enacted in 1948 and the attempt to raise bank prudential standards through implementation of the recent Basle Committee's 'rules' on capital adequacy assessment. In passing, aspect (3) is also touched upon.

Critique

I enjoyed reading Professor Dale's paper and found myself agreeing with most of the sentiments expressed therein. What I might disagree with, however, is the emphasis laid on certain assertions; this point, I trust, will become clear in the ensuing comment. Breaking down the discussion into two parts, to reflect the author's narrative, I will start with *Article 65*.

He begins his story by comparing Article 65 with its counterpart regulation in the United States, the Glass-Steagall Act. He points out that the two pieces of legislation differ to the extent that, under Article 65, banks are allowed to acquire securities and equities for investment purposes, although the Anti-Monopoly Law limits equity stakes to 5 per cent of an individual company's shares, whereas the Glass-Steagall Act prohibits equity holdings by banks and also restricts their holdings of negotiable securities. It is also interesting to note that the prohibition applying under Article 65 does not apply where a trust contract is involved, nor to dealings in national government bonds, local authority bonds or government guaranteed bonds (although 'administrative guidance', at least until 1975, prohibited all but the underwriting of government bonds). Whilst having its roots in concerns about conflict of interest and the risks of cross-contamination, the Japanese authorities' purpose was also to create a basis for the development of securities companies and to prevent an excess of indirect finance (Suzuki, 1986, p. 40).

Reform, to date, has been both piecemeal and gradualist, as Professor Dale explains. Breaches have resulted from:

1. the concessions granted to foreign institutions in Japan (in 1984, the MOF granted securities licences (more were granted in 1987) to the subsidiaries or affiliates of some foreign banks with branches in Japan, the requirement being that equity stakes in the affiliates were restricted to a maximum of 50 per cent; and in 1985, nine foreign banks were admitted to the trust banking business, thereby allowing them to enjoy privileges denied to Japanese commercial banks);
2. the concessions granted to Japanese banks in respect of their overseas activities (in overseas markets, their securities subsidiaries can underwrite and deal in commercial paper issued abroad and can act as underwriters of bond issues by Japanese corporations, although 'lead manager' position is still reserved for the securities houses according to the 'three bureaux agreement');
3. the authority granted to banks (like securities companies) to underwrite and trade in yen-denominated commercial paper since the inauguration of the market in 1987;
4. the concessions granted to banks under the Banking Law of 1982

which allowed them to engage in securities operations in public bonds, subject to restrictions (which were subsequently relaxed);

5. the decision taken in April 1985 to allow securities firms to make loans collateralised by (local) government bonds and to buy and sell yen-denominated CDs, foreign CDs and commercial paper; and

6. the decision taken in April 1986 to allow securities firms to operate in the yen-based bankers' acceptance (BA) market.

The various options for 'reform', involving 'horse-trading' between the banks and securities houses within the existing regulatory framework and/or reform of Article 65 itself are presented by Professor Dale, as are the problems caused by the continuation of Article 65 for Japan's implementation of reciprocity agreements in financial services.

Reading between the lines, he appears to be advocating reform, if not abolition, of Article 65, because of the competitive distortions created at home and abroad and because of the concomitant difficulties arising at the regulatory interface. What he fails to consider, however, are the supervisory safeguards, for example, to deal with the resultant conflicts of interest and contagion risks, that would become necessary on its reform or abolition. Some kind of cost-benefit analysis is ideally required to 'quantify' the net benefits that deregulation might bring.

Moving on to a consideration of the second part of Professor Dale's paper, namely the *likely impact of the Basle Committee's capital adequacy rules* (confirmed in July 1988) *on Japanese banks* it is difficult to disagree with his conclusion that the actual outcome in terms of the impact on the competitiveness of Japanese banks is indeterminate. For, whilst the 'rules' were certainly designed in part to stunt the growth of those banks enjoying comparatively lenient treatment in respect of capital requirements (which, *ceteris paribus*, allow them to operate on finer margins and hence 'pinch' market share), the actions of the banks, the markets and, above all, the MOF will determine the actual severity of their impact on performance. There is no need to duplicate his analysis here as it would prove difficult to improve upon. However there are a number of other points raised in the paper which merit further consideration.

First of these is the question of the merits of including unrealised gains on securities holdings within 'supplementary capital'. Professor Dale does not indicate his personal view on this, so I feel some clarification is called for. Was the dissension expressed in the Basle Committee's deliberations related to the question of the inclusion of such latent gains in (supplementary) capital or to the extent of their inclusion? In principle, surely, there is little case for their complete exclusion, on the grounds that securities holdings can be realised and used to absorb losses leaving a bank as a 'going concern', the prime qualification of capital according to the Basle Committee. Where the protagonists may have a case, however, is in the determination of the discount to be applied. How was the figure of 55 per cent arrived at? Does it represent objective considerations of potential equity price volatility and notional tax charges or straight political bargaining? If the former, then, it is hoped, the experiences of October 1987, when the world's stock markets 'crashed', were fully taken into account, notwithstanding the outstanding subsequent performance of the Nikkei average; and if the latter, then supervisors have only themselves to blame for the consequences. The second issue I wish to comment upon relates to the banks' possible responses to the potential 'pressures' imposed by the 'new rules'. First, from discussions I had with banks while in Japan in the Spring of 1988, there is a real danger that the banks will take the opportunity, as far as they are allowed, to cut back exposure to less developed countries (LDCs). This must be a cause of concern to those still grappling with the LDC debt problem. Secondly, my discussions led me to take a more optimistic view than Professor Dale about the switch in emphasis away from growth and market share and towards net return on assets and rate of return on capital employed; this had certainly been accepted by all those banks to whom I spoke.

The third and final point I would like to make relates to the degree of discretion allowed national supervisors under the 'rules'. As Professor Dale points out, the scope for discretion is so large that the actions of national supervisors will largely determine the bumpiness of the 'playing-fields' that international banks have to operate on. It is worth recapping on the sources of this discretion. It can arise in the following areas:

1. in the application of risk weights and conversion factors, subject to the *minimum* risk weights prescribed;
2. in the determination of which, and to what degree, items are included in 'supplementary capital', subject to the limits and restrictions laid down by the Basle Committee;
3. in the treatment of banks' holdings of other banks' capital – national supervisors have the discretion to net them off from the banks' own issues in calculating the capital base;

4. in the general approach adopted during the transitional phase (until end-1992); and
5. most importantly, in the specification of the 'target' risk asset ratios (RARs) for individual banks, subject to the minimum ratio prescribed by the Basle Committee.

We already know that the Bank of England, unlike its Japanese counterpart, will take a relatively harsh line in exercising the discretion provided under the rules. For example, it intends applying the rules to all UK banks, and not just those internationally active, by the end of 1988 (the rules provide for a period of grade until 1992); it will exclude all general provisions which reflect lower valuations for assets, notably against LDC debts, from supplementary capital; the 50 per cent risk weight applying to secured mortgage loans will only apply in respect of first mortgages on primary residences; the qualifying criteria applied to the inclusion of subordinated debt in supplementary capital will, in some respects, be harsher than those proposed by the Basle Committee; the Bank will continue to deduct all holdings of other banks' capital from a bank's capital base in computing its RAR; the risk weights applied to some public sector claims will be higher than many supervisors will apply; and, above all, the target RARs set for individual banks are likely to be considerably higher than the minimum 8 per cent prescribed by the Basle Committee.

What this serves to illustrate is that the dawn of 'level playing-fields' remains but a distant dream (although some of the larger bumps have been reduced in size), although prudential standards, at least in respect of capital requirements, are in the process of being raised to levels which do more than reflect the adoption of a 'lowest common denominator' approach to international supervisory convergence. For that at least we can be thankful.

To conclude, then, I believe it inconceivable, given the discretion available to them, that the Japanese authorities will not bow to international pressure and impose capital requirements that will indeed squeeze their internationally active banks. On this, I am pleased to say, Professor Dale and I concur.

Reference

Suzuki, Yoshio (1986) *Money, Finance, and Macroeconomic Performance in Japan* (New Haven, Conn.: Yale University Press).

COMMENT

Henry S. Terrell

Richard Dale has made an interesting contribution to this volume, as I had anticipated, since his earlier book on bank supervision for the Group of Thirty was a standard reference for me for a number of years. My comments will be on Japanese banks, because that has been my principal area of interest.

The following statistics help demonstrate the size and importance of Japanese banks in traditionally defined international banking:

1. Japanese banks currently comprise 16 of the world's 25 largest banks;
2. equity investors look favourably on Japanese banks, valuing their equity at $50–75 billion per bank, on the order of eight to ten times as much as the equity market value for the largest US banks;
3. data published by the Bank for International Settlements indicate that Japanese banks' share of total international bank assets is about 35 per cent, more than twice as large a share as US-based banks which comprise the next largest national grouping;
4. between 1984 and 1987 Japanese banks accounted for about one-half of the estimated total growth of international bank assets; and
5. in the UK and US markets Japanese banks are by far the largest non-indigenous banks (about 50 and 40 per cent of the share of non-local banks respectively).

Therefore, understanding the factors driving the growth of these institutions will help us to understand a lot about the growth of total international bank activity as well as about important players in major banking centres.

The paper presented by Richard Dale makes several useful points about Japanese financial regulation with which I am in general agreement. His paper notes: (1) that Article 65 (Glass-Steagall) is a foreign import with no connection to prewar Japan; (2) that continuation of that statute in a domestic context contains regulatory anomalies when domestic banks are permitted securities affiliations abroad (as US banks are); (3) that Japanese authorities have been reluctant to let any bank fail; (4) that informal guidance plays a large role in banking regulation in Japan; and (5) that it is impossible for an outsider to assess the impact of the Basle agreement on bank capital ratios on further growth of Japanese banks because their future growth will depend upon a variety of factors, including the level of the Tokyo Stock Exchange, the banks' willingness to realise capital gains and to incur tax liabilities on securities (and possibly land holdings) to boost their reported capital, their ability to adjust asset portfolios towards low-risk weighted assets, and upon how the Ministry of Finance interprets and implements the Basle Accord.

What I would like to do in my remarks is to link some of Dale's observations on regulatory policy to my past and present research on Japanese banks and, where possible, to draw implications for regulatory policy.

One important observation is the close similarity in asset growth over time of individual large Japanese banks. In an earlier paper that I wrote with Robert S. Dohner,[1] total asset growth of seven large individual Japanese banks was found to be highly correlated and consequently to respond closely to the same economic and financial variables. US banks, by contrast, tended to be individualistic and idiosyncratic in their asset growth patterns, while banks headquartered in European countries tended to approximate more closely the strong national similarity shown by large individual Japanese banks.[2]

Observers, including Akio Mikuni, a financial consultant, have suggested that a unique Japanese regulatory goal is to preserve the stability of the asset ranking of the large Japanese banks, and that goal is implemented through informal guidance to the banks, a regulatory practice noted by Dale. The data showing the strong similarity of asset growth of large Japanese banks are certainly consistent with that hypothesis regarding regulatory objectives.

A second important observation is the apparent strong impact that Japan's external financial position has on the ability of Japanese banks to grow and compete on a worldwide basis. In a 1979 paper I found a strong correlation between the growth of lending by Japanese banks in the United States and the increase in reported foreign exchange reserves of Japan.[3] The 1988 Dohner–Terrell paper found a close correlation between Japan's current account position and the world-wide total assets of Japanese banks. More recent unpublished research has found a high correlation between a measure of Japan's net foreign wealth and the activities of Japanese banks in both the United States and London. This later finding is particularly interesting because the business orientation of branches of Japanese banks in the United States is largely local, while the activities of Japanese banks in London are largely in non-sterling currencies with non-UK residents.

Finding these statistical relationships is much easier than interpreting them. One interpretation is that customers favour banks whose home country has a strong external position. An alternative explanation for Japanese banks is that regulatory policy on international expansion is a function of Japan's external financial position. (That alternative explanation has been discussed in Andrew Spindler, 1984, *Politics of International Credit*, and Robert Feldman, 1986, *Japanese Financial Markets*.)

A third and more complex alternative is that regulation of domestic Japanese markets, including informal as well as formal controls on interest rates, has shifted Japanese bank intermediation and interbank trading offshore, as worldwide banking markets have integrated faster than Japanese markets have been liberalised. The truth probably contains elements of all three explanations in proportions which are unknown (and probably not constant over time).

A better understanding of the impact of Japan's external position, as well as domestic regulatory policies, on Japanese bank behaviour is important because of the expected future size of Japan's external wealth, and the size and importance of Japanese banks in worldwide markets, including the United States and United Kingdom. Understanding this relationship will help answer, in several years, the question (which Richard Dale and I agree is currently hard to answer) whether the Basle agreement will have slowed the growth of Japanese banks, although the intention of that agreement was to enhance regulatory equality rather than slow growth of any particular group of banks.[4]

A third point I would like to discuss is the notion that Japanese banks may have a lower cost of capital and that that advantage might have helped Japanese banks grow faster. Very high price earnings ratios are often cited as evidence of a lower cost of capital for Japanese banks.

The counterpart to significant differences in cost of capital to comparable firms is significant differences in asset yields to mobile investors. Since some Japanese bank stocks trade in New York, and some US bank stocks trade on the Tokyo Stock Exchange, it would seem fairly easy for investors to arbitrage away major differences in rates of return which would result in comparable capital costs. Therefore it is hard to accept the fact that the cost of capital is significantly lower for Japanese banks.

I agree with the Dale paper that factors other than difference in the cost of capital are operating here and I think more research is needed.

Other factors which could be noted include: (1) holdings of equities in other companies which are carried on the books at acquisition value, (2) holding of stock in companies where the earnings are not fully consolidated in the parent company's reported income statement; and (3) direct and indirect (through stock in other companies) ownership of valuable land in Japan, where long-term rental contracts may have prevented realised rents from catching up with market rental rates. In addition, US companies are allowed to use separate accounting standards for tax (accelerated depreciation) and stockholder (straight-line depreciation) reports while Japanese companies may not. Therefore earnings reported to stockholders of a growing company in Japan where accelerated depreciation is used in both stockholder and tax authority reports are likely to be less than for a similar US company.

This discussion implies that more research is needed to understand why Japanese banks have much higher price/earnings and market/book ratios than US banks, and that it is naive to infer that the cost of capital is significantly lower for Japanese banks than for US banks from data on P/E ratios. Having noted that, let me suggest that one aspect of regulatory policy discussed earlier may at the margin affect the cost of bank capital. If regulatory policy is truly directed towards maintaining relative asset rankings, as well as avoiding bank failures, and thus avoiding cases where shareholders suffer major or total losses, then the potential downside risk to investors in Japanese bank stocks is reduced. This reduction in downside risk may be partially offset by a reduction in upside potential because a well managed efficient bank may be constrained from adding profitable assets to avoid upsetting the ranking structure. To the extent, however, that regulatory policy reduces the *variability* of bank earnings and the possibility of a major loss, it may contribute to some modest advantage in Japanese banks' cost of all funding including capital costs.

I would conclude my comments by making a small criticism about omissions in the Dale paper. The paper, by focusing on Glass-Steagall and the Basle agreement, has limited discussion of liberalisations in Japanese financial markets, such as opening up the market in yen CDs and bankers acceptances, and the opening of the Japan Offshore Market (JOM) in late 1986, all of which have improved the competitiveness of Japan as an international banking centre and the competitiveness of Japanese banks. These liberalisations resulted from market realities as well as external pressures. Japan's role as an international financial centre has been growing rapidly. As of September 1988, banks in Japan had almost $700 billion in external assets, nearly four-fifths as much in gross external assets as banks in London, and more than one and a quarter as much as banking offices domiciled in the United States, including International Banking Facilities (IBFs). The paper would benefit from fuller discussion of these regulatory changes in addition to discussing Glass-Steagall and the Basle agreement.

Notes

*The paper represents the views of the author and should not be interpreted as reflecting those of the Board of Governors or other members of its staff.

1. See Robert S. Dohner and Henry Terrell, 'The Determinants of the Growth of Multinational Banking Organizations: 1972–86', *International Finance Discussion Paper No. 326*, Federal Reserve Board, Washington, DC, June 1988.
2. For example, between 1972 and 1987 the range of the multiples of end period over beginning period assets (measured in dollars converted at current exchange rates) for seven Japanese banks was 12.9 to 14.7, a difference of only 14 per cent. By contrast, for the seven largest US banks, the multiple of 1987 to 1972 assets ranged between 5.8 and 2.2, or 164 per cent. The coefficient of variation (standard deviation divided by the mean) of the asset growth multiplies for the seven large US banks over this period was more than 50 times greater than for the seven large Japanese banks.
3. Henry S. Terrell, 'U.S. Banks in Japan and Japanese Banks in the United States', *Quarterly Review*, Federal Reserve Bank of San Francisco, Summer 1979, pp. 18–30.
4. One technical way in which the question could be answered would be to look at how well a Dohner–Terrell-type model based on economic factors estimated in a pre-1987 period predicted post-Basle agreement growth for Japanese and other banks and, in particular, whether it would 'overpredict' Japanese bank asset growth after 1987. The Dohner–Terrell model based on economic factors in the 1972–82 period *overpredicted* US bank asset growth after 1982, which is consistent with the view that pressure by regulators on US banks to increase capital ratios slowed asset growth.

COMMENT

C. Maxwell Watson

Professor Dale restricted himself, consciously, to two issues of immediate regulatory importance to Japanese and foreign institutions: the

Article 65 debate and the impact of the Basle capital adequacy framework. Rather than review again the ground covered in his interesting assessments, I would like to focus mainly on some longer-term questions that are relevant and which were touched on at the outset of his remarks. He reflected on the interaction between external influences and the regulatory structure governing Tokyo's financial markets. He also mentioned the Japanese authorities' aversion to financial failures, and the relationship between market forces and official policy objectives – and he speculated that 'Japan's postwar record of financial stability owes something to official intervention of this kind'. In doing so, he raised questions about the regulation of financial markets that are not only of interest in relation to Japan but relate to the broader development of the capital market system. Let me try to expand a little on the comments he made and, in so doing, indicate some points of agreement and disagreement concerning his conclusions.

Regulation and Financial Growth in Japan

Sources of Financial Growth

Given the constraining regulatory framework Professor Dale alluded to, how is it that the growth of Japanese institutions in international markets has been so impressive?

Hard as it is to remember now, the Japanese financial markets were trammelled, up to the late 1970s, not only by an intricate network of domestic regulations but by an extensive foreign exchange control law, which insulated the domestic markets from banks' international transactions. It is striking that, when one compares them to other countries' international banks, Japanese institutions' wholly offshore transactions still show up in international banking statistics as enormously more important relative to foreign business channelled through Tokyo.

A major influence on the way Japanese financial activities have developed during the past decade has been the sequence in which the external and domestic regulatory systems were relaxed. Partly because of capital account developments, exchange controls were dismantled first, and in a sequence of moves that affected alternately inflows and outflows. By the mid-1980s, this evolution left Japanese banks and securities houses with very few such restraints on foreign transactions.

In due course, external factors also had an impact on domestic market regulation – for example, the liberalisation of insurance companies' portfolio rules to allow greater holdings of foreign securities. Moreover domestic policy developments in areas other than regulation (for instance, the shortening maturity of government debt) have tended to break down rigidities such as interest rate ceilings. No doubt foreign pressure for deregulation has been most effective in areas where economic developments in Japan – and domestic competition policy – have also been strongly supportive of change.

The pace of domestic liberalisation has none the less been more gradual than external deregulation. In part, this slower pace reflected prudence. But there was also a need to weigh the objective of greater competition, on the one hand, with the case for fiscal restraint, on the other, since a number of financial reforms had budgetary implications. And there was the complication of reconciling the established interests of different industry groups, including the Postal Savings System and various other specialised financial institutions – areas in which continuing progress has been seen as essential to achieve the optimal allocation of savings.

Given the extensive overseas playing-field open to Japanese banks and securities houses, this difference in speed between external and domestic deregulation offered enormous scope for ingenuity and innovation. It is, I think, commonplace to say that the huge interbank flows between Japan and other financial centres have been due in part to the clearing of transactions in ways that minimise costs, including those arising from regulation – a process recognised in many countries' financial markets and benignly termed 'regulatory arbitrage'. The prevalence of secured transactions on the Japanese interbank market, and the prohibition on issuance by City banks of long-term fixed-rate debentures, are examples of rigidities which may have led to 'round-tripping' to the Euro-dollar market and swap-related funding.

Moreover, in the scope of their business activities, Japanese banks and securities houses – as Professor Dale points out – were free in foreign markets to experiment both with new products and with each other's products (as were US institutions). He rightly notes that various new forms of 'round-tripping' could in future further erode the banking/securities barrier.

Apart from regulatory factors, there are a variety of important reasons to explain why the international operations of Japanese financial institutions grew especially rapidly. First, in earlier years, commodity scarcity led to heavy Japanese foreign investment in certain developing countries, and more lately protectionism and trade rigidities in other industrial countries have been forcing the pace of Japanese overseas direct investment: where Japanese equity finance has gone, loan finance has accompanied it. Second, long-run demographic trends, among other factors, have strongly influenced the huge build-up of savings in Japan and thus the current account surplus. Third, and increasingly over time, it has been the underlying strength of Japanese industry and commerce, and the emergence of Tokyo as one of three poles in the global commercial system, that have been driving international financial expansion and underpinning the key role of Japanese banks and securities houses in world markets. These basic factors almost certainly outweigh any regulatory advantages or obstacles.

Implications for the Future

This picture suggests that, owing both to special factors and more fundamental and traditional ones, Tokyo will exercise a crucial influence over the allocation of world savings in the coming decades: savings of Japanese residents – very largely generated in and managed by the private sector – and of the international community. Tokyo has naturally developed, as did London and New York before it, as a turntable for international capital. While private portfolio preferences will be the key determinant of this process, such an evolution none the less places considerable responsibility on the Japanese authorities. The signals and incentives they create through the evolving regulatory structure can play an important role in influencing the efficiency with which these savings support international economic activity. Regulations and prudential approaches that both encourage sound management and are reflective of risk-adjusted returns on financial assets appear essential in this regard. If regulations are not reflective of such returns, it is likely that 'efficient' markets will either arbitrage away the effectiveness of the regulations or magnify a market distortion.

The Basle capital adequacy guidelines reflect such concerns, although I think treatment of sovereign risk could be read as sending some arbitrary signals, and I agree with Professor Dale that it is difficult to predict in which ways the Japanese banks will respond to these guidelines. To the extent that interbank books are swollen by circular flows, that is indeed an obvious place to cut – but the capital savings from such cuts have deliberately been designed to be marginal (they bear only one-fifth the risk weight of full commercial risk). One point I would more strongly stress is the potential to increase earnings by cutting costs and tightly controlling overhead. Overall, a stronger emphasis on risk-related returns in new business is surely the common thread of most possible reactions, including a desire to maintain high stock prices. And it is quite a predictable evolution when institutions have achieved significant penetration in new markets.

A specific issue of interest is the way in which Japanese savings respond to the risks and opportunities offered by third-world economies. Japanese banks have been conscientious supporters of the international debt strategy; the prudential and fiscal regimes applied to them need to differentiate countries correspondingly, and to evolve over time in ways that reflect the growing availability of a 'menu' of financing options. The Japanese authorities have indicated their interest in seeing more market-based debt reduction techniques developed in the framework of the debt strategy. Moreover, through the Eximbank and other agencies, the Japanese authorities are among the most active in channelling and catalysing financial flows to countries pursuing internationally-endorsed policy programmes.

An increasing number of developing economies may also prove open to direct investment. In the 1970s, many of these countries drew instead on debt finance to avoid foreign ownership of firms; but such borrowing has been shown also to entail significant domestic constraints. Through a well-judged opening to direct investment, countries stand to benefit greatly from the transfer of capital and expertise.

With regard to all long-term flows, both loan and equity finance, the institutional framework in Japan, and official signals, will be important. Of course, the most important influence over Japanese capital flows to developing countries is likely to be the policies pursued over time in those countries themselves, together with an orderly sorting out of their existing indebtedness.

Challenges for the Future

What are the challenges regulatory authorities face in the period ahead, and how far can we see the way that economic and market developments point towards possible progress? Let me touch on two sets of issues in particular.

Microprudential Challenges

First, I agree entirely with Professor Dale on the difficulties that national authorities face in supervising different kinds of financial institutions which may offer increasingly substitutable products. He touched on the issue of competitive equality between securities and banking institutions. Closely related is the issue of comprehensive supervision over such intermediaries' hybrid activities at home and abroad. As in many countries, one could have added other intermediaries to this list – insurance companies, specialised financial institutions, and a range of others.

For the banking sector, the weighted risk asset ratio – appraised on a consolidated basis – has developed as the consensus instrument for supervising the solvency of international banks. Even in the banking industry, however, this tool centrally addresses credit risk only; market risks and liquidity risks are dealt with frequently on an *ad hoc* basis. In the securities industry, other techniques (such as 'haircuts') have evolved as a way of marking down asset values in light of market risk. The analogies between these approaches are clear. But only in the relatively recent past, and especially in the United Kingdom, has progress truly been achieved in placing these techniques within a consistent framework. Given the importance of overseas activities and of consolidated supervision, this issue needs addressing even in countries such as Japan and the United States where a domestic separation of banking and securities companies exists.

There may also be natural limits to the effectiveness of supervision and regulation. We are faced in the financial services sector with an increasingly 'mature' and competitive industry, all of whose practitioners are working with variants on one range of products: conditional promises to pay. The opening-up of the financial system redistributes risk: it offers new and ingenious ways of incurring old risks, but also previously unavailable ways of hedging risks. With ingenuity, market operators can craft increasingly sophisticated instruments whose risk management characteristics regulators will have to run to catch up with. This, perhaps – rather than their external origin – is the persuasive reason explaining why various barriers in Japan may come to be adapted in due course.

Macroprudential Challenges

A separate, increasingly difficult question is going to face regulators, and especially central banks, in all the industrial countries: what parts of these financial markets need to be supported? There has been extensive experience and research in the areas of investor protection and deposit insurance, and possibilities such as co-insurance can be explored. But, in addition, there are broader questions of macroprudential concern. In which sectors could international failure entail systemic risk? How far must the authorities stand ready to inject liquidity into institutions or markets lest part of the wholesale funding markets or payments network break down? Can contagion be prevented within a group by having separate subsidiaries, or is a 'banking name' always engaged? And what are the moral hazards that might arise if wide-scale support came to be assumed, especially in the case of the larger institutions?

I am not arguing that the risk of failures should be taken lightly. We know the costs of a major financial market failure, and the record of Japan is enviable in this regard. There are times when governments need to intervene swiftly and convincingly to avoid these costs of failures. At the same time, the costs of intervening to forestall failure – by open-market or open-mouth operations – while less tangible are, I think, no less real. In most industrial countries during the past decade, with liberalisation, deregulation and privatisation, the hand of government over markets has lifted; but there is a question whether, or with what implications, the hand of government support *under* the financial markets, in the form of implicit guarantees, may have extended further in many industrial countries.

To that question there can be several reassuring answers: authorities have been responsive to the strong public concern that governments should not inappropriately take over the risks of financial institutions. The strengthening of supervision – in Japan and elsewhere – on a market-related basis is important. And Japanese banks certainly have been allowed to experience losses on their loan portfolios. Moreover the protection of interbank deposits in international banks has itself not necessarily implied protection of management or equity stakeholders. As with deposit insurance, so with systemic support: offsetting signals or actions at the prudential level are possible. And in a mature industry, with a more competitive environment, takeovers may offer discipline analogous to financial failures.

More broadly, macroprudential policy and the macroeconomic setting interact in their influence on systemic risk. One can identify potential problems in this regard – and opportunities. First, the problems. In a world of unstable financial policies, and hence nervous financial markets, it may be much more difficult for the authorities to take the risk of selectively allowing institutions to fail, given concerns about contagion. And let us suppose for a moment that it proved difficult to arrest (let alone roll back) the drift towards a restricted trade system, yet the movement to liberalise and integrate capital markets persisted – giving rise to what has been described cruelly as an 'inverted Bretton Woods system' of restricted trade and free capital. It would be bad enough to rely solely on capital flows to equalise factor returns across countries. It would be even more problematic if the capital market system were itself distorted by varying degrees of implicit guarantee.

By contrast, in a world of stable financial policies, robust markets and open trade, financial market authorities can both risk more failures and minimise the impact of capital distortions. Already there is much less expectation that inflation will bail out imprudent lenders. And progress in policy co-ordination among major countries has been promising. Thinking back to Dale's comments about aversion to financial failures and 'intervention in market situations', these are issues that may challenge not just the Japanese authorities, but perhaps all the industrial countries' supervisory authorities in the years ahead.

I have tried in my remarks to emphasise the complex interaction of regulations and more basic economic trends, and the important limits on what can be achieved by regulation. Part of our modern mythology is the mystical influence of banking regulators to impede or accelerate the movements of financial markets. Good regulation is essential; but it is easy to overestimate – or to hide behind – the power of the regulator. To adapt what Richard Dale said: one needs to focus on the skill of the players and the strength of the wind as well as the lines and bumps on the playing-field.

3 Monetary Policy in Japan

Yoshio Suzuki

MONEY AND MACROECONOMIC PERFORMANCE UNDER THE FLOATING EXCHANGE RATE REGIME

Gradual Decline of Monetary Growth as a Stabilisation Policy

One main feature of the macroeconomic performance of Japan since the shift to floating exchange rates has been the reduction in the variability of inflation and growth. Figure 3.1 outlines this particular feature very clearly. This figure shows the growth rate of money stock, together with that of nominal and real GNP over the years 1956–88, in terms of quarterly data *vis-à-vis* the same quarter of the previous year. Because the Bank of Japan switched to a policy of focusing attention on M2 + CDs in 1975, this indicator of the money stock is used in the figure. The following aspects of macro performance may be read from it.

In the period 1956–73, in which real growth was very high, the money stock saw large fluctuations in growth rates. Because, under a fixed exchange rate system, tight monetary policy had to be adopted at times of balance of payments crises, money growth fell to as low as 15 per cent; but, when balance of payments problems ended, loose monetary policy allowed money growth to rise to as much as 25 per cent. Nominal GNP growth followed largely the same pattern once lags of several quarters are allowed for, thus suggesting that the causal relationship flowed from the money stock to nominal GNP. Moreover these fluctuations in the growth rate of nominal GNP accompanied fluctuations in the growth rate of real GNP and inflation as seen in the GNP deflator. (The movements of inflation as seen in the GNP deflator are shown in Figure 3.1 as the difference between the growth rate of nominal GNP and that of real GNP.) As a result, the discretionary changes in monetary policy in response to balance of payments brought large changes in monetary growth and great instability to both the real growth rate and the inflation rate, even though they still enabled average high growth of about 10 per cent, along with average inflation of about 6 per cent.

65

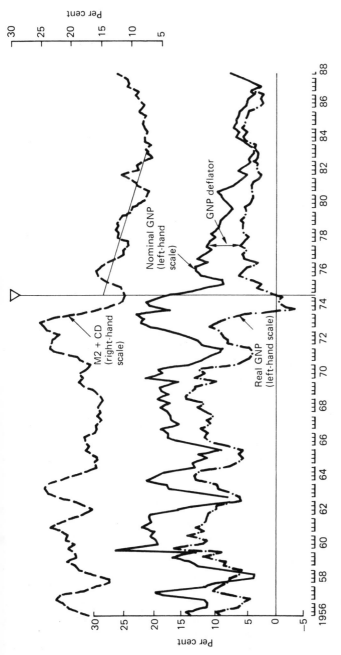

Figure 3.1   Money stock and GNP (nominal and real) in Japan

Notes: 1. Growth rates of money stock and GNP are calculated not against the previous quarter, but against the same quarter in the previous year.

2. 'M2 + CD' data (before 1979/I, 'M2' data) are an average of end-of-month observations. For example, the first quarter is an average of the data at the end of January, February and March.

Let us next look at the macroeconomic performance of Japan from around 1975 after the effects of the shift to floating exchange rates and the effects of the first oil crisis (that is, direct effects) had been exhausted.

Once the Bank of Japan began to focus attention on the money supply as a medium-term indicator from around 1975, the fluctuations in the growth rate of the money stock were reduced, and the deviations from the trend were limited to plus or minus $2\frac{1}{2}$ per cent. Moreover the trend of money growth itself fell during this period from about 15 per cent at the start to 7–8 per cent in 1983–5, that is, until the Plaza Agreement in September 1985. As a result, the nominal growth rate of GNP fell as well.

However the fall in the growth rate of nominal GNP did not have any influence on the growth rate of real GNP, but rather was reflected in a decline in inflation as measured by the GNP deflator. This development is of great importance. With the two exceptions of the period around 1982 and that around 1986, growth over the entire period was very stable and averaged about 5 per cent. The first period of exception was that after the time of the second oil crisis, when double digit inflation required the major industrial countries to co-operate in taking concerted disinflationary policies and thus included the effect of adverse demand shocks from abroad in the form of the simultaneous world recession. The second period of exception is that of the substantial yen appreciation shock after the Plaza Accord.

To summarise, events and experiences since 1975 suggest that lower inflation and a stabilisation of macro performance, that is, stable

Table 3.1 Economic growth rates and inflation rates after introducing the floating exchange rate system

	Real GNP (average annual growth rate)		Consumer price index (average annual inflation rate)		
	1974–9	1980–7	1974–7	1978–81	1982–7
Japan	3.6	3.9	13.0	5.1	1.6
United States	2.6	2.4	8.1	10.7	3.8
Germany	2.3	1.5	5.2	4.6	2.2
France	3.3	1.7	11.1	11.7	6.7
United Kingdom	1.5	1.8	18.1	12.8	5.3

Note: For France and United Kingdom, GDP is used.

inflation rate and economic growth rate, can be achieved by stabilising monetary growth rates and gradually allowing them to decline.

As a result, Japan's recent inflation rates in terms of consumer price index are the lowest and its real growth rates are still the highest among five major countries. This is confirmed by Table 3.1. Since the shift to floating exchange rate system in 1973, Japan's inflation rates have been declining, and in 1982–7 the average inflation rate was 1.6 per cent, the lowest among the five major countries, while Japan's average real growth rates from 1974 to 1987, including the two exceptional periods, averaged slightly less than 4 per cent, which was still the highest among the five countries.

Flexibility of Real Wages and the Supply-Determined Economy

How are we to interpret this experience, that is, a stable high growth rate together with a falling inflation rate? My interpretation is that, except for the aforementioned two deflationary periods, the Japanese economy has been climbing down the vertical long-run Phillips curve, so that stable high growth has been maintained while the inflation rate has been gradually lowered.

This interpretation is based on two assumptions: first, the Japanese economy is close to the classical model in which real wages are flexible enough to always equilibrate demand and supply of labour, so that the economy is always growing on the equilibrium path of full supply capacity (except for the two periods); secondly, Japanese monetary policy after 1975 did not allow major deviation of the actual inflation rate from the expected inflation rate, so that the economy did not deviate from a vertical long-run Phillips curve (except for the two periods).

At this point, it will be useful to explain the background for these two assumptions. First, let us turn to the existence of real wage flexibility, with the result of the economy always being on an equilibrium growth path. In Japan, basic wages are determined on a year-by-year basis during the annual spring offensive. It is not common to have wage contracts that last for two years or more. Besides, bonuses and overtime payments comprise between one-quarter and one-fifth of total annual income in Japan, and this portion of income is much more flexible than the basic wage. Therefore wage adjustment costs during the year are not high. Moreover the wage settlements in the spring offensive have been shown by many empirical studies to reflect not only past and expected inflation but also the demand–supply balance in the labour markets and the state of corporate profits. Because of this flexibility of real wages, it is realistic to hypothesise that the labour market and firms are almost continuously in a state of equilibrium.

In such an economy, the supply capacity in an equilibrium state always determines the growth path. On the contrary, in the Keynesian model, the demand side establishes the growth path because the labour market is usually in a state of disequilibrium and the supply capacity is not fully utilised. Thus the level of aggregate demand controlled by the macroeconomic policies always determines the growth path.

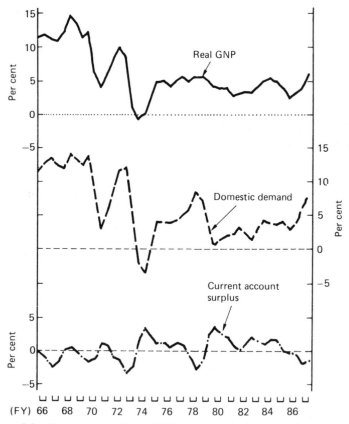

Figure 3.2   Growth rate of real GNP and contribution of each component

Notes: 1. Growth rates and component contributions are year-to-year changes.
   2. Both domestic demand and current account surplus are adjusted for the import of gold bullion to mint coins in commemoration of the Emperor's 60th year of reign.

In the reality of Japan since 1975, which side of the economy has mainly determined that stable growth path? Figure 3.2 suggests the answer. In this figure one can reconfirm that the growth path since 1975 has been stable at about 5 per cent, except for the two periods around 1982 and 1986. Surprisingly, however, the two components of aggregate demand, domestic demand and current account surplus, have not been stable at all since 1975. They have fluctuated as widely as in the pre-1975 period, when the growth rate was quite unstable. Therefore, the factor which makes the difference in stability of the economic growth between the pre-1975 and the post-1975 period does not seem to exist on the demand side. The main reason for the difference seems to be the fact that the Japanese economy had often deviated from equilibrium before 1975, but has been in equilibrium since 1975 except for the aforementioned two periods. The economy in an equilibrium state always follows the stable growth path in line with the stable growth of supply capacity. In such an economy, fluctuation of one component of aggregate demand is cancelled out by fluctuations of the other components. This is the result of the real crowding-out effects since total aggregate demand is always constrained by the stable supply capacity of the economy.

Little Deviation of the Expected from the Actual Inflation Rate

Let me turn to the second assumption, namely that Japanese monetary policy after 1975 did not allow major deviations of the actual from the expected inflation rate.

The monetary targeting implemented by Japan since 1975 has had three major features. First, a broad definition of money (M2 + CDs) has been watched as the most important intermediate target because this monetary aggregate has had the highest correlation with future nominal expenditure and prices. Second, the term over which it is measured is not a week, a month, or even a quarter, but rather an entire year, in the sense that the growth rate of money over the same period of the previous year is used. This is because the value of M2 + CDs in the current quarter exerts influence on nominal expenditure during the following eight quarters. To put this another way, the money supply in any given quarter has only small influence over the nominal income in any particular quarter of the future. This implies that control of the money supply strictly over one month or over one quarter is not very meaningful from the viewpoint of stabilising income expenditure or prices. Third, actual targets are not publicised, but rather forecast values, which refer to the average money stock outstanding relative to the same period of the previous year, are announced for each quarter.

This approach implies that the Bank of Japan implicitly accepts the forecast level of the money supply growth rate. To this extent, the forecast values establish policy information that is of significance to the public. The important point is the trust on the part of the public that the Bank of Japan is controlling the money supply, and that the Bank of Japan has both the ability and the intent to achieve low inflation through such monetary control. As a matter of fact, the expected rate of inflation held by the public has not deviated from the actual low rate of inflation because they expect that, as long as the forecast of money growth remains low to the extent that is shown in Figure 3.1, the inflation rate will also remain low.

TRANSMISSION CHANNELS OF MONETARY POLICY

Interbank Money Rate as an Operating Variable

The questions which still remain to be asked are how the Bank of Japan can control the monetary growth path with such stability as shown in Figure 3.1, and how stable the relationship is between that monetary growth and the macroeconomic performance. Let me now discuss them.

The Bank of Japan controls the money stock through changes in the call and bill rates, which are interbank money rates. The Bank of Japan has never adopted the so-called multiplier approach, whereby the money supply is indirectly controlled by the direct control of the supply of high-powered money through stable multiplier relationships.

To confirm this, we estimated a Vector Auto Regressive (VAR) model of three variables, namely, the money stock (M), high-powered money (H), and the short-term money market rate (r), during the period between the first quarter of 1968 and the fourth quarter of 1987. Table 3.2 reports F-statistics on the hypothesis that there was a causal relationship in the sense of Granger (1969). The results indicate the following:

1. There was unidirectional causality from r to M and from r to H, indicating that the control of the short-term money market rates constitutes the first step in the Bank of Japan's conduct of monetary policy; and

Table 3.2   F-statistics based on three-variable VAR model

dependent \ independent	H	r	M	Causality
H	2.840	6.913*	11.765**	
r	0.418	318.067**	0.728	
M	0.103	6.294**	136.347**	

Notes: H: High-powered money
r: Weighted average of call and bill rates
M: Money stock (M_2 + CDs)
1. Period: from the 1st quarter of 1968 to the 4th quarter of 1987.
2. All variables are percentage increases over the previous quarter.
3. Lag length of the estimated VAR model is selected by the minimum AIC.
4. **(*) indicates that the F-value is significant at 1(5) per cent level.

Source: Bank of Japan, *Economic Statistics Monthly* (seasonally adjusted).

2.   There was unidirectional causality from *M* to *H*, indicating the absence of the multiplier approach in Japan's monetary control.

Let us next consider the process by which changes in the call and bill rates ultimately affect the money stock, by taking as an example the case where the Bank of Japan is attempting to restrain growth in the money stock. Broadly speaking, there are three channels by which changes in the call and bill rates affect the money stock.

First, the increase in the interbank market rates brought about by market operations of the Bank of Japan reduces the marginal profitability of additional loans and increases the profitability of portfolio investments on short-term money market assets for financial institutions. Consequently, financial institutions reduce loans and increase net lendings in the interbank money markets; this follows from the fact that the loan rates of financial institutions are less flexible than the interbank rates, which are in turn based on the official discount rate and regulated deposits rates and by the consideration of the long-term customers' relationship. Moreover, the effect of an increase in interbank rates on the amount of loans of financial institutions through this channel is supplemented by the so-called 'window guidance', a type of moral suasion by the Bank of Japan, which is intended to limit the quarterly increases in the total loan volume of individual financial institutions.

Secondly, an increase in the interbank market rates raises the open money market rates and yields on medium- and long-term government bonds through arbitrage, causing individuals and non-financial firms to make portfolio adjustments away from deposits with regulated interest rates to open market instruments and government bonds whose yields have risen. Financial institutions will thus suffer from outflows of funds in deposits with regulated interest rates. This is a kind of financial disintermediation.

Thirdly, the rise in the general level of interest rates resulting from an increase in interbank rates reduces the expenditures of the private non-financial sector by raising the cost of obtaining funds. Such a reduction in business and household expenditures gives rise to a slow-down in the nominal value of transactions in the economy as a whole and, as a result, reduces the demand for money.

The Effect of Financial Deregulation on the Transmission Channels

Although these three transmission channels still exist today, the further liberalisation of deposit rates since the spring of 1985 has changed the relative importance of each money stock control channel. Important recent liberalisation measures have included the introduction of deposits bearing market-related interest rates (MMCs), relaxation of issuing conditions of CDs, and loosening of restrictions on the interest rates of large denomination time deposits. These measures caused the shift of bank loans from traditional 'prime rate banking', based on regulated interest rates, to 'spread banking', based on market interest rates.

These developments are likely to affect each of the three transmission channels. First, proliferation of 'spread banking' will weaken the restraining effect of a reduction in the marginal profitability of loans on the money stock (the first channel). As a matter of fact, the prime lending rate, which is now linked to the official discount rate and regulated deposit rates, is to be linked soon to the average of market and deposit rates, including deregulated ones. Secondly, further liberalisation of deposit rates will reduce the effect of so-called disintermediation on the money stock (the second channel) by allowing deposit rates to move in parallel with the short-term money market rates. Thirdly, liberalisation of deposit rates and subsequent increases in 'spread banking' in the bank loans market will strengthen the effect of a reduction in the business and household demand for money on the money stock (the third channel).

Therefore the first and the second channels will get weaker and the

Table 3.3   Lagged correlation coefficients between the call rate and the money stock

	Period	Maximum coefficients	Number of lags
Quarterly data[1]	I/1975 IV/1979	− 0.751	− 1
	I/1980 IV/1984	− 0.660	− 2
	I/1985 IV/1987	− 0.480	− 4
Monthly data[2]	01/1975 12/1979	− 0.455	− 3
	01/1980 12/1984	− 0.451	− 5
	01/1985 01/1988	− 0.350	− 18

Notes: 1.   Percentage increases over the previous quarter.
            2.   Percentage increases over the previous month.

Source: Bank of Japan, *Economic Statistics Monthly* (seasonally adjusted).

third will get stronger, and it is impossible to make an *a priori* judgement as to whether the recent liberalisation of deposit rates has weakened the control mechanism of money stock. Cross-correlation analysis indicates, however, that negative correlation between the call rate and the money stock (M2 + CDs) became somewhat smaller and the length of lag longer during the period after 1985, when a series of measures were taken to liberalise deposit rates, as shown in Table 3.3. Of course, there still exists negative correlation between the short-term interest rate and the money stock, and the Bank of Japan will continue to control the money stock by influencing the call and bill rates. Nevertheless one needs to watch very carefully how rapidly the recent financial liberalisation will change the way money stock control is effected in Japan.

Effects of Money Stock on Expenditure and Prices

Let me now turn the discussion to the relationship between the money stock thus controlled and the price level, which is the ultimate objective of the Bank of Japan.

To start with, I will review the relationship between the money stock and real economic activity by the estimation of a VAR model. First, we estimated the VAR model of four variables, namely high-powered money (H), the short-term interest rate (r), the money stock (M) and nominal GNP (Y), during the period from the second quarter of 1967 to the fourth quarter of 1987. The results are shown in Table 3.4. F-statistics indicate unidirectional causality, in the sense of Granger, running from r to M, and then from M to Y, but show no evidence of causality running from H to r, or from H to Y. These results reconfirm the importance of the broad money, not the high-powered money, as an intermediate target.

Next, we estimated a VAR model of five variables, by adding real GNP (y) (in place of nominal GNP (Y)), and GNP deflator (P), to the four-variable VAR model. The results are also shown in Table 3.4. F-statistics indicate the presence of three sets of unidirectional causality, running from r to M, and then from M to P and y. The causality from P to y, the so-called 'deflationary effect of inflation', implies that an increase in M might have two consequences that are largely offsetting, namely an expansionary effect on y and the 'deflationary effect of

Table 3.4   F-statistics based on four- and five-variable models

(a) Four-variable VAR model for H, r, M and Y

dep \ ind	H	r	M	Y	Causality
H	1.808	7.551**	0.719		
r	0.028	248.384**	0.982	2.187	
M	0.143	6.152**	113.770**	0.089	
Y	0.531	1.264	9.232**	3.549*	

(b) Five-variable VAR model for H, r, M, y and P

dep \ ind	H	r	M	y	P	Causality
H	1.063	9.121**	8.095**	0.409	1.957	
r	0.002	191.293**	0.696	0.894	2.331	
M	0.302	5.279**	108.287**	0.247	0.805	
y	0.182	0.163	3.825*	1.028	3.419*	
P	0.173	1.419	7.832**	1.061	21.110**	

Notes: H: High-powered money
          r: Weighted average of call and bill rates
          M: Money stock (M_2 + CDs)
          Y: Nominal GNP
          y: Real GNP
          P: GNP deflator
          **(*) indicates that the F-value is significant at the 1(5) per cent level.

inflation' on *y*. As a result, the effect of an increase in *M* on *y* is uncertain in the long run and thus the long-run Phillips curve is nearly vertical. This is one component of the evidence that, as already discussed above, the Japanese economy can be assumed not to deviate much from the vertical long-run Phillips curve.

Further, let us investigate the recent stability of the demand for money function. Here, as a standard specification, we assume first that the real money stock is determined by the short-term interest rate and real GNP. The result of estimation has yielded a good fit, as shown in Figure 3.3. Using the estimated function to extrapolate, we can satisfactorily trace the actual path of the money stock from the first quarter of 1986 until the fourth quarter of 1986. However the estimated function substantially underforecasts the actual path of the money stock after 1987. Therefore the standard demand for money function does not explain the recent sharp increases in money stock growth.

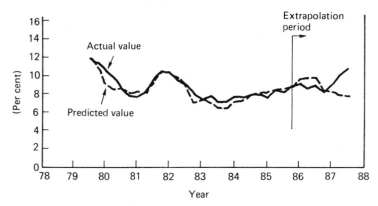

Figure 3.3   Estimation of the money demand function and simulation results
(I)

Notes: 1. Estimated function: period III/78–IV/85
$$\ln(M/P) = -1.3257 + 0.2260 \ln(Y/P) - 0.2732 \ln(1+r)$$
$$\quad\quad\quad (2.1) \quad\quad\quad (4.9)$$
$$\quad\quad\quad + 0.8544 \ln(M/P)_{-1} + \varepsilon$$
$R^2 = 0.999$ $S.E. = 0.00469$
$D.W. = 1.940$ *t*-values in parentheses

M: $M_2 + CD$ (average outstanding, seasonally adjusted)
Y: Nominal GNP
P: GNP deflator
r: Gensaki rate

2. Extrapolation is done as a dynamic simulation beginning in the 4th quarter of 1985.

Next, we estimate an alternatively specified demand for money function by employing the difference between the weighted average of interest rates on individual components of M2 + CDs and the money-market interest rate in place of the money-market interest rate itself. This specification takes into account the possibility that the increased weight of free market instruments in M2 + CDs has reduced the opportunity cost for holding M2 + CDs. According to estimation results, however, the modified version shows little improvement over the standard demand for money function as shown in Figure 3.4. The tv o interpretations seem possible.

First, the underprediction of the money stock might be caused by the shift in the money supply function, rather than money demand function. For example, short-term and long-term interest rates have recently declined to extremely low levels by historical standards and, as

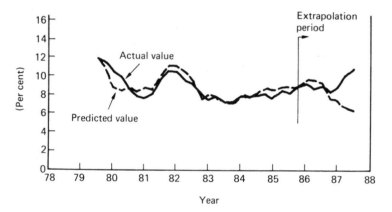

Figure 3.4   Estimation of the money demand function and simulation results
(II)

Notes: 1. Estimated function: period III/78–IV/85
$$\ln(M/P) = -0.9967 + 0.1772 \ln(Y/P) - 0.3741 \ln(1 + c)$$
$$\qquad\qquad\quad (1.5) \qquad\qquad (4.2)$$
$$\qquad\qquad + 0.8815 \ln(M/P)_{-1} + \varepsilon$$
$R^2 = 0.999$ $S.E. = 0.00504$
$D.W. = 1.895$ t-values in parentheses

M: $M_2 + CD$
Y: Nominal GNP
P: GNP deflator
c: Opportunity cost for holding $M_2 + CD$
c: [(Gensaki rate) − (average yield on $M_2 + CD$)]

    2. Extrapolation is done as a dynamic simulation beginning in the 4th quarter of 1985.

a result, the prices of existing assets, such as land and stocks, have increased significantly. Accordingly, the non-financial sector's ability to borrow has risen with the increase in the value of collaterals; the financial sector has increased lending activity. If this interpretation is correct, we have an identification problem. Thus, it is very difficult to know whether the function we are estimating is the 'demand for money' function or the 'supply of money' function, because both functions could be specified in almost the same way.

Another interpretation for the recent sharp increase in the money growth rate in Japan is to take into consideration the stock-motivated demand for money component; namely that is to say, the recent increase in the value of assets might have contributed to the increase in the demand for money. If that is the case, the money demand function which includes the stock of wealth as an additional explanatory variable could solve the problem of the recent underprediction of the money stock.

I would like to reserve my judgement as to which of the two is right. At any rate, the money growth rate is now declining, from the 12 per cent level at the end of 1987 to the 10 per cent level recently reached, as prices of assets such as real estate and bonds have declined.

CONCLUSION

In concluding my remarks, I would like to stress that the Bank of Japan still has some important tasks to accomplish in order to maintain monetary control under worldwide financial integration (so-called 'financial globalisation').

The first task is to determine how to maintain the controllability of short-term money market rates as a whole under the expansion of open domestic markets as well as the Euro-yen market. Because short-term money market rates are ultimately determined by the conditions in the market for high-powered money, which is subject to direct intervention by the Bank of Japan, the controllability of short-term money market rates cannot in principle be weakened through such factors as an increased access to the Euro-yen market. However it is important for the Bank of Japan to develop new operation techniques in the newly-established open markets, such as the CP market, in order to secure the accurate controllability of short-term money market rates as a whole. It is also necessary to enhance the development of the short-term government securities market and the market operation there.

The second task is properly to define the intermediate target for monetary targeting policy. Financial globalisation would present several problems in this respect: (1) it obscures the range of monetary aggregates to be watched; (2) it changes the mechanism of money stock control; and (3) it increases the instability of the demand for money function.

Since 1975, the monetary targeting policy of the Bank of Japan has been conducted successfully, as already discussed and as shown in Figure 3.1. In order to retain the effectiveness of monetary policy under conditions of rapid environmental change in Japan's financial markets, it is necessary to continue to study the mechanisms of money stock control and of transmission from the money stock to real economic variables both in theory and in practice.

Here the effect of the sharp increase in the money growth rate in 1987 upon the rate of inflation and that of the real GNP growth should be carefully watched. As a matter of fact, the real GNP growth over the year jumped to 6.0 per cent in the first half of 1988, as shown in Figure 3.1. Fortunately, however, the inflation rate in terms of GNP deflator remained at 0.5 per cent. In order to avoid the rekindling of inflation, the following conditions on the supply side of the economy should be satisfactorily achieved: domestically, the supply capacity is to increase in parallel with the increase in demand; internationally, the appreciation of the nominal yen rate is to continue so as to offset the inflationary pressures from overseas. Fortunately, we can expect that the dramatic improvement in terms of trade, caused by the tremendous appreciation of the yen since 1985, will have increased the potential growth rate determined by the supply side. The average growth rate in 1988 is now estimated to be about 6 per cent, with the inflation rate as measured by the consumer price index (CPI) remaining at less than 1 per cent.

Finally, we should recognise that, with the progress of financial globalisation, it is a very important task for the Bank of Japan to maintain the stability of financial systems, especially the payment system, in addition to securing the stability of monetary control.

References

Granger, Clive W. J. (1969) 'Investigating Causal Relations by Econometric Models and Cross-Spectral Methods', *Econometrica*, July.

Okina, Kunio (1985) 'Reexamination of the Empirical Study Using Granger Causality: "Causality" between Money Supply and Nominal Income', Bank of Japan, *Monetary and Economic Studies*, vol. 3, no. 3, December.

Roosa, Robert V. (1956) *Federal Reserve Operations in the Money and Government Securities Market* (Federal Reserve Bank of New York, July).

Suzuki, Yoshio (1984) 'Monetary Policy in Japan: Transmission Mechanism and Effectiveness', Bank of Japan, *Monetary and Economic Studies*, vol. 2, no. 2, December.

Suzuki, Yoshio (1986) *Money, Finance, and Macroeconomic Performance in Japan* (New Haven, Conn.: Yale University Press).

Suzuki, Yoshio (1987) 'Financial Restructuring: The Japanese Case', in Federal Reserve Bank of Kansas City (ed.), *Restructuring the Financial System*, August.

Suzuki, Yoshio (ed.) (1987b) *The Japanese Financial System* (Oxford University Press).

Ueda, Kazuo (1988) 'Financial Deregulation and the Demand for Money in Japan', paper presented at the Conference on *Monetary Aggregates and Financial Sector Behavior in Interdependent Economies*, sponsored by the Board of Governors of the Federal Reserve System, May.

COMMENT

Peter Oppenheimer

Dr Suzuki's paper is an exceptionally authoritative one on its subject and an invaluable partial summary of his book on Japanese macroeconomic management and performance. My comments are offered mainly from the viewpoint of a UK reader, occasionally from a wider Organisation for Economic Co-operation and Development (OECD) or global perspective. I do not claim any particular knowledge or expertise on Japan.

I shall follow Dr Suzuki's order in considering first the broader issues of money and macroeconomic performance, and thereafter the more technical and micro issues of monetary control. There is a risk that my remarks will resemble a series of editor's marginal comments of a rather disjointed kind. But Dr Suzuki's paper covers a great deal of ground.

To begin, then, with general questions of Japanese economic performance and policy, I wish to comment on three aspects covered in the paper. The first is the stability of growth since 1975; the second is the functioning of labour markets; and the third is the role and status of the Central Bank in relation to financial markets.

Stability of Growth

As regards the steadiness of growth, without querying the statistical results presented by Dr Suzuki, I would point out that the period he takes is a relatively short one, really no more than a decade. It is also a decade which begins conveniently in 1975 after a nasty bit of instability in 1973–4; and moreover Dr Suzuki insists that you have to make some allowance for 1982 and 1986. So the stability is a qualified one and has to be dressed up a little in order to impress. But that is just a preliminary point. The results presented by Dr Suzuki for Japan show something that can also be demonstrated statistically for the OECD as a whole, namely that the period after 1974 was either more stable or at least no less stable than the period of the 1950s and 1960s ending in 1973–4.

On the face of it, this is a disconcerting result. What about the great economic watershed in the early 1970s after which, as we all know, economic performance in the OECD countries deteriorated sharply? Dr Suzuki's result, in my opinion, does not tell us that the golden age of the 1950s and 1960s was an illusion; or that the economic climate did not deteriorate after 1973. What it tells us is that the stability of growth is not on its own a very interesting or helpful indicator of the economic climate.

In the first place, if growth is averaging 10 per cent a year, one is not too concerned if this involves oscillation between 17 per cent and 5 per cent. By contrast, if the trend rate of growth averages only 3 per cent, even a small oscillation may be worrying. But quite apart from that, numerous other indicators, such as the rate of inflation, measures of social turbulence, protectionist trends in world trade and so on have to be included in order to make a proper assessment of the business climate.

The point is worth stressing, because with a bit of imagination one can see in the numbers put before us by Dr Suzuki the beginnings of some myth creation in 30 or 40 years' time, the myth being that the 1973 watershed never took place and that the so-called golden age of the 1950s and 1960s really was not one. It would be like the effort a few years ago (by Messrs Benjamin and Kochin) to demonstrate that British unemployment in the 1920s was all a matter of voluntary response to the inadvertently generous level of social security income maintenance payments available at that time. As historians we should always, of course, be willing to use the past to shed light on the present. As economists we must beware of using the present to shed darkness on the past.

Incidentally, the suggestion that stability is not an important part of rapid economic growth or of good economic performance generally has been around for a long time. In the 1960s, when many British commentators were obsessed with stop–go, statistical investigations by Tom Wilson and others showed that, for instance, Japanese growth at that time – to which we would all have liked to aspire – was far more unstable than our own. So I am not putting forward anything new.

I have one other comment under this section. Dr Suzuki talks about the spontaneity of Japan's recovery from recession in the 1980s. He indicates that since 1975 the policy of the Bank of Japan emphasised the stabilisation of monetary aggregates. This, in turn, led to price stability and thus recovery of long-term growth was feasible without recourse to stimulative fiscal policy or monetary easing. As seen in Figure 3.1 this was, in fact, the case of 1984–5. I daresay that the Japanese authorities did not engage in stimulative fiscal policy or monetary easing at any time in the first half of the 1980s. But other people did, especially the United States. And to say that the Japanese economy recovered spontaneously without the help of any stimulative fiscal policy is a little disingenuous, since the budget deficit that was being generated on the other side of the Pacific had quite a significant impact on Japanese exports. More generally, I must endorse the comment that the external sector altogether plays a surprisingly modest part in Dr Suzuki's account of Japan's performance.

Functioning of the Labour Market

I turn now to the labour market. European readers cannot fail to be impressed by the flexibility of Japanese real wages to which Dr Suzuki draws attention. It seems to stem in large part not from the way in which the annual Spring Offensive is conducted but from the remarkable fact that in Japan bonuses and overtime payments comprise between one-quarter and one-fifth of total wage income. This appears to guarantee a substantial degree of year-to-year flexibility in earnings. Dr Suzuki might also have mentioned that such flexibility is combined in key sections of Japanese industry with the so-called life-time employment system, an extreme form of implicitly long-term contract giving the employee the greatest possible degree of job security. In other words, there is evidently no need for wage flexibility to be founded upon lack of job security in the American fashion – quite the contrary.

Dr Suzuki refers to the contrast between Keynesian nominal-wage stickiness and classical real-wage flexibility. Keynes himself, unlike some present-day Keynesian economists, did not think real wages inflexible. He insisted only that the real wage was determined by the economic system as a whole and not merely by the pay bargaining process in the labour market. His argument did not incorporate any well worked-out theory of expectations of pay bargainers, and for this reason is subject to question. It would be interesting to learn how Japanese trade unions set their targets for pay bargaining and how much influence they think they have upon real earnings. Is earnings flexibility achieved because of or in spite of the nature of pay bargaining?

Dr Suzuki also emphasises what he calls the equilibrium performance of the economy, the fact that it was apparently moving along an equilibrium growth path for much of the 1970s. The low unemployment rates which Japan maintained throughout the 1970s by contrast with Europe are certainly impressive, and no doubt have something to do with the wage flexibility already noted. But does this signify that the economy was going along an equilibrium growth path? Was there no excess capital capacity, not even in the investment goods sector? Investment did, after all, plunge. We also know that Japanese business can be ruthless in adjusting profit margins downwards as well as upwards. I cannot help thinking that, alongside the noteworthily smooth performance of the labour market, with its maintenance of high employment, there must have been a good deal of turmoil affecting the other factors of production, particularly capital.

The Central Bank and Financial Markets

My third general topic is the central bank's credibility. I was delighted to observe from Dr Suzuki's paper that the Bank of Japan has no truck with the New Classical nonsense about all economic agents possessing identical information. The Bank's approach rests on the maintenance of a healthy degree of monopoly of information. To give everyone the same (incomplete) information is a recipe for financial market instability and not for confidence in the authorities.

None the less, information monopolies may be a less important factor in sustaining the Bank's reputation than consistency between its declared objectives and its policy actions. Such a conclusion is certainly suggested by a comparison of the Bank of Japan with the UK monetary authorities. (The Bank of England on its own does not have the Bank of Japan's autonomy.) The messages put out by UK government spokesmen in the 1980s about priority being given to the reduction of inflation carry much less conviction than comparable statements in Japan, for several reasons.

First, the UK authorities have had immense difficulty in formulating and attaining sensible monetary targets. Secondly, the UK government exaggerated the extent to which its efforts reduced the UK inflation rate in the first half of the 1980s. It overstated the inflation rate which it inherited from the previous administration and it understated the helpful impact of other countries' policies, notably that of the US Federal Reserve, on inflation world-wide. Thirdly, there has been a blatant discrepancy between ministerial speeches proclaiming the elimination of inflation as the prime target of policy and the evident toleration of prices rising at 4, 5 or 6 per cent per annum without firm countermeasures being taken. Limitations on the credibility of the UK authority's anti-inflation stance may be one reason why the weakening of British trade unions and the growing flexibility of labour markets, which have had an excellent effect in improving UK productivity, have had comparatively little success in curbing the rate of increase of money wages.

Effectiveness of Monetary Policy

I now pass briefly from the broad features of Dr Suzuki's paper to two more technical aspects of monetary policy. There is, first, a noteworthy contrast between the confidence expressed by Dr Suzuki in the effectiveness of Japanese monetary policy up to mid-1985 and the much more hesitant stance which he adopts for the period since then. There appear to be three distinct although interconnected reasons for this. These are uncertainty about the money demand function (whether it has shifted once and for all, or whether it is more generally unstable); deregulation of interest rates; and globalisation of financial markets. Assessment of the money demand function is bound up with technical and econometric problems about identification.

Dr Suzuki hints at the idea that we may be seeing not so much a shift in the money demand function as an increase in the amount of financial intermediation per unit (real and nominal) of Japanese GNP. This, if substantiated, is something which Japan shares with other advanced economies. It presumably stems partly from income elasticity and partly from technological factors. It may partly reflect emerging

Japanese comparative advantage in the financial sector. Japanese
banks in particular have become major operators on a global scale. At
the same time, the question may be raised whether growing prominence
of the financial sector at home adequately reflects the preferences of the
Japanese people. Inevitable uncertainty about the future may be
beginning to act as a significant source of market failure, as Tobin
suspects is the case in the United States.[1]

Transmission Mechanisms

My final topic is the transmission mechanisms of monetary policy pre-
1985, that is, in the period of strong policy effectiveness. Dr Suzuki lists
three mechanisms. I suggest that they really come down to two. The
first of the three is a credit rationing mechanism, with financial
institutions reducing client loans in favour of net placements in the
interbank money market. The second is disintermediation, as individuals and non-financial firms shift their liquid asset holdings away
from bank deposits with regulated rates to other instruments. The third
is interest rate effects of the orthodox text-book kind. I do not see that
disintermediation itself constitutes a transmission mechanism in the
sense that it actually points to the way in which expenditure is reduced.
Disintermediation, as its name implies, is a restructuring of financial
flows. If it is induced by tight money and causes a fall in expenditure,
then this comes about either through a portfolio (interest-rate) mechanism or by means of credit rationing. I do not see any third way between
those two and I suspect that disintermediation involves some mixture
of them.
     On that basis, I wonder whether the general tenor of Dr Suzuki's
exposition perhaps understates the historical importance of the rationing side. The Japanese system of moral suasion ('window guidance')
has generally been seen as the chief means by which bank credit is
directed and limited in amount. This relies essentially on rationing.
Britain's experience for most of the postwar period has been similar.
That is, when monetary policy operates directly on domestic spending,
it has done so chiefly through credit rationing, rather than through
interest-rate or wealth effects. The position is now changing to some
extent. In the second half of the 1980s the ratio of debt to UK personal
incomes has risen to far higher levels than before, and credit charges
therefore play a larger role in household budgets. Increases in the
mortgage rate in particular leave households with smaller margins of

discretionary spending on consumer durables, holidays and so forth. It remains to be seen whether widespread loan defaults by the household sector can be avoided. If not, a reversion to greater emphasis on credit rationing may be expected, at least as a temporary reaction.

Outside the household sector the principal transmission mechanism for UK monetary policy since the ending of the Bretton Woods system in the early 1970s has been the exchange rate. This operates not directly on domestic spending but indirectly via the country's international competitiveness and especially via business profit margins. This was most conspicuously the case in 1979–81, when extreme tightness of monetary policy induced a severe recession, mainly through appreciation of sterling.

Conclusion

I therefore conclude by reiterating my endorsement of Adrian Tschoegl's comment below that it is surprising to find so little consideration in Dr Suzuki's paper of the external sector. Tschoegl's comment stressed the foreign-reserve component of the monetary base. I would stress, in this context, two other aspects. One is the yen exchange rate, whose appreciation since 1985 has brought about major adjustments in the productive structure of Japanese manufacturing. Japanese exporters have shifted their component sourcing on a large scale to other East Asian countries such as South Korea, Taiwan and Thailand, so that, while Japanese exports of finished products have remained buoyant, value-added in the Japanese export industries has narrowed sharply.

The other aspect may be seen if Japanese interest rates and external reserves during the 1980s are examined. Their relationship points clearly to the influence of outside interest rates in provoking or permitting changes in Japanese rates. Dr Suzuki has said that with the growing globalisation of markets the Japanese authorities will doubtless have to pay close attention to external factors in future in managing their monetary policy. I find it difficult to believe that they have not already been doing so.

Notes

1.   James Tobin, 'On the Efficiency of the Financial System', *Lloyds Bank
      Review*, 1984; reprinted in Christopher Johnson (ed.), *The Market on
      Trial* (London: 1989). Tobin remarks in his Conclusions:

> I confess to an uneasy Physiocratic suspicion, perhaps unbecoming in
> an academic, that we are throwing more and more of our resources,
> including the cream of our youth, into financial activities remote from
> the production of goods and services, into activities that generate high
> private rewards disproportionate to their social productivity. I suspect
> that the immense power of the computer is being harnessed to this
> 'paper economy', not to do the same transactions more economically
> but to balloon the quantity and variety of financial exchanges. For this
> reason, perhaps, high technology has so far yielded disappointing
> results in economy-wide productivity.

COMMENT

Adrian E. Tschoegl

Basically I am going to discuss very briefly what we might call the
tactical aspect of the Bank of Japan's (BOJ) monetary control. I intend
primarily to provide and discuss information which I hope supplements
Dr Suzuki's contribution and which I think has more to do with money
supply than money demand. Finally I will comment briefly on
exchange rates and inflation.

The Tactical Issue: Interest Rate Seasonality

As far as the short-term or tactical issue is concerned, I would draw
attention to Figure 3.5, which displays the average change in each
month of the year in three-month bill rates. I would argue that the
figure shows a very strong seasonal pattern.

   I think that the BOJ would agree that they in fact manage the three-
month bill rate with an eye to seasonal supply and demand factors. The
interesting point, however, is not that the data exhibit a seasonal
pattern, but that they contrast the BOJ's behaviour with that of the US
Federal Reserve. The Federal Reserve Bank has in its charter the
objective of doing away with regional and temporal differences in
interest rates.

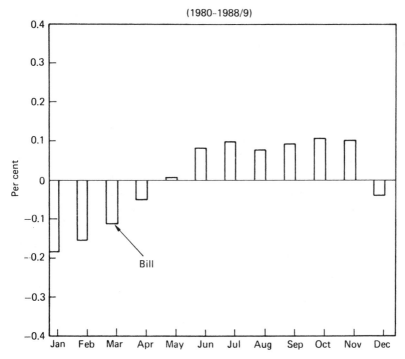

Figure 3.5   Monthly average changes in three-month bill rates

My question, and it is really an open empirical question, relates to the sustainability of a seasonal component in one currency's interest rate when another currency does not exhibit seasonality. I believe that the seasonality component in the Japanese data reflects BOJ money supply management which uses a combination of price effects and quantity clearing to manage the interbank markets. With liberalisation of Japanese interest rates and money markets the seasonal pattern should disappear.

Some Comments on Money Supply

A key issue in the period from 1986 on is not only the change in the money demand function but also the very great increase in money supply. Figure 3.6 shows the year-on-year growth in M2 + CDs in Japan on a monthly basis from 1980 on. There are two issues or possible causes involved in the increase in the growth rate after 1986: one possible cause is deregulation and therefore a shift in the meaning of the various monetary aggregates; another is intervention. I will ignore the money demand function entirely and in particular the question of why there would be a wealth factor in money demand and why this would have changed over time, particularly in the post-1986 period.

Returning to Figure 3.6, the dotted line at the 8 per cent level reflects my sense that the BOJ has a view that about 8–8½ per cent money supply growth has, in the past, been consistent with a non-inflationary rate of growth of the money supply. The combination of 5 per cent real growth plus a 3 per cent rate of decline in velocity would give an 8 per cent target for money supply growth. As can be seen, since early 1987 there has been a quite dramatic deviation from that 8–8½ per cent level.

Now if the recent growth in the money supply is due to deregulation changing what money means, then the 8–8½ per cent level would no longer be an appropriate target. So the questions are: why has deviation from the target occurred; what is the appropriate new target; and does the BOJ have the ability to hit the target?

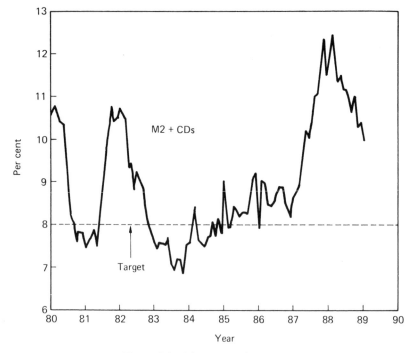

Figure 3.6   Money supply growth

Source: Bank of Japan.

The Development of the Yen/US$ Exchange Rate

Clearly, as far as exchange rates are concerned, one of the key post-1986 events was the Plaza Accord and the post-Plaza Accord Central Bank support for the US dollar. In Figure 3.7 we have graphed the actual ¥/US$ exchange rate since 1976 together with two dotted lines representing the purchasing power parity (PPP), plus or minus 5 per cent.

SBC uses wholesale prices, an econometric procedure and the entire estimation period as a base in order to calculate the PPP rate. I do not want to get into whether the appropriate PPP rate currently is 165 or 180 or 145. What I would like to draw attention to is the pattern of over- and undervaluation.

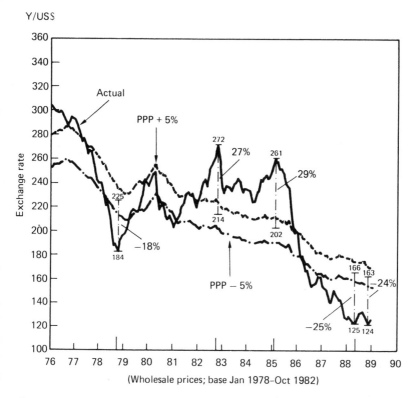

Figure 3.7 Changes in the ¥/US$ foreign exchange rate and purchasing power parity

Source: SBC.

Deviations from PPP and BOJ Exchange Rate Intervention

In Figure 3.8 I have combined the deviations from PPP since 1980 with
the level of Japanese official reserves (in US$), indexed on January
1980. The left-hand scale shows the growth of the official reserves and
the right-hand scale the deviation of the actual ¥/US$ rate from PPP in
yen per US$, given our calculation of the PPP rate.

What I find interesting is that the foreign reserves grew rather
dramatically from about February/March 1986, at about the time that,
on our calculation, the yen moved into undervaluation on a PPP basis.
That is, the steepest rise in the reserves occurred after the yen started to
become undervalued. I think the reason is quite understandable.

When we have co-operation in support of the dollar we have what
amounts to foreign central bank self-defence against too rapid currency
depreciation. I believe we can interpret this as a decision of central
banks in London, Tokyo and Bonn to take losses in their holdings of
foreign official assets rather than losses through unemployment compensation to displaced workers. The governments decided to phase in
adjustment over time rather than face a continued free-fall of the
dollar.

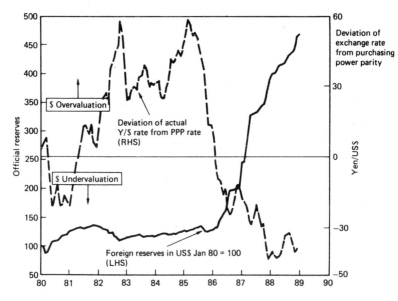

Figure 3.8   Changes in official reserves and deviation from purchasing power
parity

Intervention and the Money Supply

In Figure 3.9 we have year-on-year growth in M2 + CDs overlaid on year-on-year growth in official reserves, both from 1980 on. I would argue that, visually, there appears to be a correlation between growth in official reserves and subsequent money supply growth. Simple statistical tests also suggest a correlation.

Using ordinary least squares (OLS) with year-on-year money supply growth as the dependent variable and year-on-year growth in official reserves lagged 6, 9 and 12 months gives a very nice R-square of 0.88. This would indicate that 88 per cent of the variability in Japanese money supply growth is accounted for by growth in official reserves.

In Figure 3.10 we have actual year-on-year growth in money supply and the predicted (fitted) value from that simple OLS specification. I think that it is fairly evident that there is little left over in money supply growth, particularly in recent years, to be accounted for by sources or factors other than intervention.

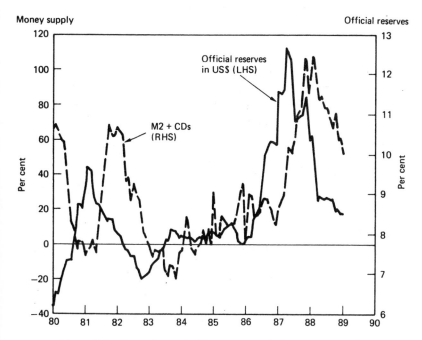

Figure 3.9   Growth in official reserves and the money supply

Source: MOF.

Money supply (M2 + CD)

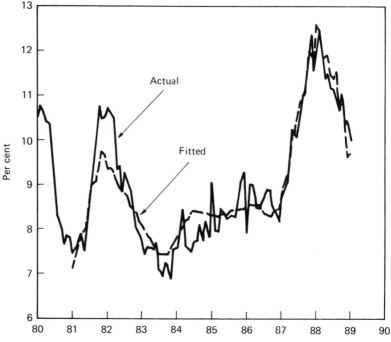

Figure 3.10   Actual and predicted values for money supply growth

Now, admittedly the tests are very sparse and simple. Nevertheless I think we can establish a working hypothesis that the growth of the money supply in the post-1986 period has been almost entirely due to intervention and that deregulation has had very little effect. Deregulation does not appear to have been a major source of money supply growth.

This would suggest that the key factor in money supply growth has been international co-operation. The Bank of Japan, in the absence of co-operation or the need to intervene internationally, is quite capable of hitting the targets in terms of money supply growth. Furthermore the target growth rate, say the traditional 8–8½ per cent, should not be changed very much.

We are still left with many questions, but one that I found most interesting is why intervention had a lagged effect. The process looks like one in which intervention is first sterilised but in which, over time, the sterilisation appears to come undone. As I said at the beginning, I have left out completely any consideration of wealth effects in money demand or why excess liquidity (in the terminology of the market) or excess money supply sometimes feeds into asset prices rather than the general price level.

Exchange Rates and Inflation

The last issue I would like to discuss is exchange rates and prices, or rather inflation. The first point I would like to make is that what we seem to be seeing, if we extrapolate from the fall in the rate of growth of reserves, is a fall in the rate of growth of money supply and thus a step-wise increase in the money supply between 1986 and 1989. This step-wise increase in the money supply should give us a step-wise increase in the price level after some lag period.

If this is so, then from an *ex post* point of view year-on-year growth in the consumer price index will first show a rising trend and then a

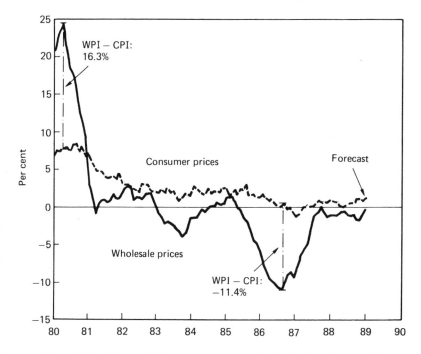

Figure 3.11   The gap between consumer and wholesale price growth

Source: BOJ.

declining trend; but *ex ante* there has been no increase in the rate of inflation. What we will find is simply that the economy moved to a new higher price level but with the rate of growth of prices remaining unchanged.

As far as the relationship of exchange rates to rates of inflation is concerned, I would draw attention to Figure 3.11. I would like to suggest that what we have here is evidence that the exchange rate is actually irrelevant to consumer price inflation. What one can see is a great deal of damping of changes in consumer prices with the variability being taken up within firms. That is, the variability in costs is absorbed by the corporate sector at the margin. Furthermore the dip in wholesale prices in the 1986/7 period is probably due almost entirely to the fall in oil prices.

This should not be interpreted as evidence of something strange in the Japanese distribution system, as I have found the same pattern in Dutch, German and Swiss prices. That is, I have noticed the same tendency to greater variability in wholesale price growth than in consumer price growth. What the figure does suggest is that, as far as the consumer price level is concerned, any exchange rate or terms of trade effects tend to appear more at the margins throughout the value-added chain. These exchange rate and terms of trade effects tend to have a much more limited or attenuated and lagged effect on the consumer price level.

4 Japanese Capital Exports through Portfolio Investment in Foreign Securities

Hirohiko Okumura

CAPITAL EXPORTS THROUGH PORTFOLIO INVESTMENT

As a component of Japan's total capital exports, portfolio investments in foreign securities continue to occupy a major portion. However, in 1987, the relative weight of the private sector's investments in foreign securities declined and this change in the composition of Japanese capital exports was one of the major factors which caused the turmoil in world financial markets. In this context, the future development of Japanese portfolio investment in foreign securities is a public policy issue of great importance. The purpose of this paper is to make clear the recent behaviour of Japanese institutional investors in this field which should have deep relationships with the change in the Japanese financial system.

Japan's capital export in the past few years is characterised by three points. First is that portfolio investments in foreign securities continue to occupy a major portion, while the relative weight of loans remain small. Secondly, direct investment has recently been expanding at a faster clip (see Table 4.1). Thirdly, both external assets and external liabilities display rapid increases (see Table 4.2).

Among these channels of capital exports by private Japanese economic entities, direct investment should take on a greater relative weight in Japan's capital exports in the near future. For example, the difference between the attitude of Japanese and German firms regarding direct investment overseas is readily apparent from the different weights of direct investment in each country's exports of capital: medium-term corporate responses to an increasingly strong mark and yen differ considerably between West Germany and Japan. Many

96

Table 4.1 International capital account transactions in Japan ($ billion)

	1981	1982	1983	1984	1985	1986	1987	Jan–June	July–Dec	1988 Jan–June
Capital-account balance	−1.0	−16.6	−21.3	−36.4	−54.6	−74.6	−41.5	−19.6	−21.9	−35.3
Long-term capital (net)	−9.7	−15.0	−17.7	−49.7	−64.5	−131.5	−136.5	−76.6	−60.0	−51.5
Securities transactions	4.4	2.2	−1.9	−23.6	−43.1	−101.4	−93.9	−59.9	−33.9	−24.5
Foreign securities	−8.8	−9.7	−16.0	−30.8	−59.8	−102.0	−87.8	−58.3	−29.4	−38.0
Domestic securities	13.2	11.9	14.1	7.2	16.7	0.6	−6.1	−1.6	−4.5	13.5
Direct investment (net)	−4.7	−4.1	−3.2	−6.0	−5.9	−14.3	−18.4	−7.2	−11.1	−15.6
Other long-term capital (net)	−9.4	−13.1	−12.6	−20.0	−15.5	−15.8	−24.2	−9.5	−15.0	−11.4
Short-term capital (net)	8.7	−1.6	−3.6	13.2	9.9	56.9	95.6	57.0	38.7	16.2
Banking flows (net)	6.4	0.0	−3.6	17.5	10.8	58.5	71.8	49.1	22.7	17.5
Other short-term flows (net)	2.3	−1.6	0.0	−4.3	−0.9	−1.6	23.9	7.9	16.0	−1.3
Errors and omissions	0.5	4.7	2.1	3.7	4.0	2.5	−3.9	5.7	−9.6	4.0
Changes in net official monetary position (− = improvement)	−4.2	4.9	−1.6	−1.3	1.4	−13.7	−42.2	−29.8	−12.5	−6.5

Source: Calculated by NRI and NCC from The Bank of Japan, *Balance of Payments Monthly*.

Table 4.2 The gap of net external assets between Japan and the US ($ billion)

end of year	1977	1985	1986	1987	1990
Japan					
Ext. assets	80.0	437.7	727.3	1071.6	
Ext. liabilities	58.0	307.8	546.9	830.8	
Net ext. assets	21.9	129.8	180.3	240.7	435.6
US					
Ext. assets	379.1	949.4	1071.4	1167.8	
Ext. liabilities	306.3	1061.3	1340.6	1536.0	
Net ext. assets	72.7	−111.9	−269.2	−368.2	−727.3
Japan − US					
Net ext. assets	−50.8	+241.7	+449.5	+608.9	+1162.9

Notes: 1. Figures to the end of 1987 are actual.
2. Year-end 1990 figures are calculated using the following assumptions. This simulation starts from the strong assumption that the trade imbalances in both Japan and the United States narrow to almost zero by the end of 1990.
2. (a) Interest payments and receipts for both Japan and the United States are calculated by multiplying the previous year's year-end net external assets and net debt by an annual interest rate of 5 per cent.
2. (b) Leaving out the above interest receipts results in the following figures for Japan's current account surplus: 1988, $81 billion; 1989, $45 billion; 1990, $20 billion.
2. (c) Leaving out the above interest payments results in the following figures for the US current account deficit: 1988, $151 billion; 1989, $90 billion; 1990, $40 billion.

Source: NRI and NCC.

German firms count on research and development and trimming of business in unprofitable areas as medium-term management actions that the rising mark has made necessary, but few firms envisage direct investment overseas. Japanese firms count equally on higher spending on research and development, but few count on shifting their main line of business to another area, and a very high percentage plan to expand overseas through direct investment (see Tables 4.3 and 4.4). However, although capital export should continue to expand vigorously, the weight of direct investment will not reach a sizeable proportion as is the case with US capital exports.

This outlook also applies in the case of loans. With no sign of upturn in sight, the growth of loans will most probably remain lacklustre. If opportunities for yen-denominated external loans increase, financial institutions will take on a more positive attitude, expanding their loans. In reality, however, there is no convincing evidence that the yen's internationalisation will progress fast enough to ensure a rapid increase in the yen-denominated loan for the coming four to five years. From this outlook for direct investment and loans, it appears that portfolio investment in foreign securities will continue to be the mainstay of Japan's capital exports.

The other characteristic of Japan's capital export is continued rapid growth of both external assets and external liabilities. This growth depends on two factors: first, whether financial institutions continue short-term foreign currency procurement and short-term and long-term foreign currency management; and secondly, whether non-financial business firms continue positive fund procurement in overseas capital markets.

The first factor may suggest that Japanese financial institutions have grown strong enough to conduct international financial intermediation, and thus this trend will probably continue in the future. However, at the same time, if deregulation becomes more prevalent in Japanese financial markets and if heavier restraints are imposed on the equity capital ratio, such management may be forced to slow down.

The second factor comes from the fact that the development of Japan's domestic bond market is now behind that of the Euro-bond market and the foreign bond market. If fund raising through the issue of bonds of Japan's domestic market becomes possible under the same conditions as the Euro-bond market, thanks to the progress of deregulation on the domestic bond market, then fund raising by non-financial business firms in overseas markets will become less active than now. (See Appendix.)

Table 4.3 Possible courses of action for West German companies in response to a highly valued mark

	All companies (%)		Companies classified according to number of employees (%)				
	weighted[1]	unweighted	(1)	(2)	(3)	(4)	(5)
Entering new fields (non-mergers and acquisitions)	34	37	38	40	38	44	27
Entering new fields (through mergers and acquisitions)	20	16	9	11	14	23	27
Direct foreign investment	17	14	3	9	13	18	24
Liquidation of unprofitable areas	50	48	48	51	43	45	52
Research and development	73	69	39	66	76	79	77

Notes: 1. Weighted according to the number of employees in each bracket (1)–(5):

	number of employees	weight (%)
(1)	20–49	7
(2)	50–199	18
(3)	200–499	16
(4)	500–999	13
(5)	1000+	46

2. Columns do not total to 100% as multiple answers were received.

Source: NRI, IFO Institute for Economic Research. Survey conducted in November 1986. Among the companies participating in IFO's monthly business survey, those industries producing capital goods (automobiles and consumer electronics included) were aimed at in this study. Companies operating in the general machinery, electrical goods, automobiles and chemical sectors were included. A total of 650 companies responded.

Table 4.4 Possible courses of action for Japanese companies if faced by the dollar remaining at around ¥150

	Manufacturing	Materials	Assembling and processing	Others
			(per cent)	
Cost reduction	86.9	85.7	93.7	79.3
Further rationalisation	85.5	88.3	92.4	72.4
Strengthening domestic sales	72.9	75.3	78.5	62.1
Diversification (into service sector)	34.1	31.2	36.7	34.5
Diversification (other than into service sector)	34.1	41.6	34.2	24.1
Developing new products	50.9	53.2	59.5	36.2
Developing higher value-added products	73.4	81.8	79.7	53.4
Switching into a different type of industry	8.4	13.0	6.3	5.2
Strengthening research and development	69.6	74.0	70.9	62.1
Expansion of direct foreign investment	41.1	28.6	55.7	37.9
Using parts from affiliated overseas producers	34.6	13.0	70.9	13.8
Expansion in imports of raw materials	48.1	50.6	53.2	37.9
Expansion in imports of intermediate goods	31.8	20.8	46.8	25.9
Increasing OEM	10.7	3.9	22.8	3.4
Selling foreign products under own brand name	15.0	5.2	22.8	17.2
Other	3.7	5.2	2.5	3.4

Source: Federation of Economic Organizations, survey of affiliated companies conducted in September 1986.

If this is the case, the flow of funds, in which Japanese economic entities raise funds overseas and again manage them overseas, would help slow down the trend of increasing utilisation of the Euro-bond market in the medium term. However, on the other hand, for four to five years to come, the flow of funds will follow a course similar to what it did in the past because international financial intermediation will become more active with the expanded international operations of Japanese financial institutions and with Tokyo's development into an international financial centre.

An important point that should be kept in mind in discussing portfolio investments in foreign securities is that portfolio behaviour differs according to the type of investor (see Figure 4.1 and Tables 4.5– 4.9). In this context, in order to analyse the behaviour of institutional investors more deeply, let us categorise Japanese investors into six economic entities and consider the trend of the relative share of these categorised investors.

First of all, life insurance companies and trust banks have played a key role among private financial institutions. These institutions, which are losing their domestic ground in long-term commercial and industrial loans, focus their portfolio management on the following objectives:

1. high coupon yield; and
2. investment from the point of view of long-term holdings.

Before 1985, it seemed that these institutions were not so sensitive to foreign exchange risk. The reasons were twofold. First was the historical reason, that is, these institutions were still in the accumulation stage of foreign assets, although they could already invest in foreign assets even before the new foreign exchange law was enacted in 1980. Second was the regulatory reason; for example, because there was a monthly ceiling on the maximum net increase of portfolio investments in foreign securities (say, no more than 20 per cent of the increase in total assets) and no carry-over to the next month, each institution tried to avail itself of the monthly allocation to the fullest.

At present, these two reasons are losing force and these institutions have become more sensitive to foreign exchange risk. In fact, they use hedging techniques frequently and the weight of US dollar-denominated securities in their total financial assets is coming down. However a rapid increase of 'new money' in these institutions will continue to support their investment in US dollar-denominated assets for the next

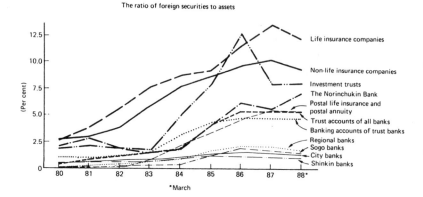

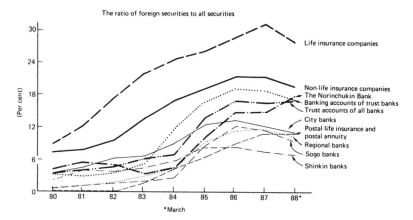

Figure 4.1   The ratio of portfolio investments in foreign securities by financial
institutions in Japan

Sources: The Bank of Japan, *Economic Statistics Monthly*; The Norinchukin Bank,
Monthly Review of Agriculture, Forestry and Fishery Finance; The Investment Trust
Association, *Monthly Report of Investment Trust*.

few years, although they are developing investment techniques aimed at
global diversification and total return-oriented portfolios.

Investment trusts are a second major type of investor, whose
behaviour is different from that of life insurance companies and trust
banks. Investment trusts aim to maximise total return in a relatively
short time-span, say one to two years. In this context, it is natural for
them to change their portfolio composition in terms of outstanding
levels. Actually, in 1987, investment trusts frequently decreased foreign

Table 4.5 Investment in foreign securities, classified by type of financial institution (foreign securities–assets ratio) (per cent)

End of year	1980	1981	1982	1983	1984	1985	1986	1987	1988*
City banks	0.48	0.62	0.80	0.85	1.11	1.44	1.61	1.55	1.34
Regional banks	0.14	0.23	0.42	0.61	0.89	1.70	2.18	2.16	1.87
Sogo banks	0.07	0.16	0.22	0.27	0.40	1.25	1.92	1.76	1.49
Shinkin banks	0.46	0.65	0.61	0.71	0.89	1.22	1.23	1.07	1.00
The Norinchukin Bank	1.83	2.14	1.95	1.46	1.80	4.09	6.26	5.70	7.15
Life insurance companies	2.70	3.87	5.70	7.67	8.76	9.29	11.68	13.73	12.37
Non-life insurance companies	2.75	3.04	3.89	5.95	7.78	8.67	9.76	10.38	9.42
Banking accounts of trust banks	1.05	0.97	1.06	1.51	3.27	4.41	4.86	4.87	4.75
Trust accounts of all banks	0.40	0.79	1.11	1.56	1.99	4.13	5.46	5.46	5.33
Postal life insurance and postal annuity	—	0.01	0.02	0.87	2.24	3.38	4.68	5.57	5.45
Investment trusts	2.09	2.85	1.97	1.74	5.04	7.97	12.77	8.08	8.12
Total (excl. investment trusts)	0.63	0.88	1.19	1.52	1.99	2.88	3.72	4.02	3.74

Note: * March.

Sources: The Bank of Japan, *Economic Statistics Monthly*; The Norinchukin Bank, *Monthly Review of Agriculture, Forestry and Fishery Finance*; The Investment Trusts Association, *Monthly Report of Investment Trust*.

Table 4.6 Level of investment in foreign securities, classified by type of financial institution (¥ billion)

End of year	1980	1981	1982	1983	1984	1985	1986	1987	1988*
City banks	592	808	1 138	1 317	1 891	2 802	3 553	3 888	3 635
Regional banks	96	174	347	540	876	1 837	2 530	2 799	2 562
Sogo banks	21	56	86	111	165	548	888	907	885
Shinkin banks	189	290	294	363	494	721	783	745	706
The Norinchukin Bank	238	313	322	283	379	955	1 624	1 607	2 051
Life insurance companies	681	1 123	1 901	2 927	3 841	4 771	7 306	10 342	9 802
Non-life insurance companies	193	235	336	570	819	1 022	1 375	1 744	1 650
Banking accounts of trust banks	129	135	176	298	783	1 303	1 747	1 902	2 008
Trust accounts of all banks	172	331	559	943	1 435	3 461	6 213	7 871	7 762
Postal life insurance and postal annuity	—	1	4	194	558	946	1 465	1 968	2 009
Investment trusts	126	205	184	245	921	1 592	4 095	3 468	3 749
Total (excl. investment trusts)	2 315	3 470	5 167	7 549	11 247	18 370	27 488	33 778	32 970

Note: * March.

Sources: The Bank of Japan, *Economic Statistics Monthly*; The Norinchukin Bank, *Monthly Review of Agriculture, Forestry and Fishery Finance*; The Investment Trusts Association, *Monthly Report of Investment Trust*.

Table 4.7 Level of total assets, classified by type of financial institution (¥ billion)

End of year	1980	1981	1982	1983	1984	1985	1986	1987	1988*
City banks	122 839	131 242	141 903	155 707	170 185	193 970	220 468	250 989	270 392
Regional banks	68 756	75 758	81 999	89 005	99 020	107 892	116 284	129 406	136 918
Sogo banks	33 007	35 607	38 286	40 909	41 304	44 001	46 236	51 479	52 772
Shinkin banks	40 866	44 413	47 938	51 390	55 400	59 116	63 778	69 753	70 720
The Norinchukin Bank	13 020	14 657	16 499	19 453	21 098	23 341	25 946	28 191	28 680
Life insurance companies	25 292	29 054	33 394	38 142	43 856	51 368	62 532	75 351	79 258
Non-life insurance companies	7 024	7 759	8 643	9 587	10 539	11 792	14 082	16 814	17 524
Banking accounts of trust banks	12 376	13 986	16 664	19 683	23 987	29 591	35 934	39 055	42 320
Trust accounts of all banks	43 250	42 266	50 342	60 489	72 188	83 841	113 726	144 009	145 637
Postal life insurance and postal annuity	14 701	16 959	19 502	22 222	25 003	27 975	31 286	35 306	36 847
Investment trusts	6 051	7 229	9 327	14 088	18 297	19 972	32 075	42 914	46 195
Total (excl. investment trusts)	381 135	411 703	455 174	506 589	562 584	632 891	730 278	840 357	881 068

Note: * March.

Sources: The Bank of Japan, *Economic Statistics Monthly*; The Norinchukin Bank, *Monthly Review of Agriculture, Forestry and Fishery Finance*; The Investment Trusts Association, *Monthly Report of Investment Trust*.

Table 4.8 Investment in foreign securities, classified by type of financial institution (foreign securities–total securities ratio) (per cent)

End of year	1980	1981	1982	1983	1984	1985	1986	1987	1988*
City banks	3.54	4.66	6.42	6.87	9.39	12.68	13.55	12.54	11.21
Regional banks	0.69	1.10	2.08	3.09	4.79	9.47	11.61	11.89	10.44
Sogo banks	0.58	1.19	1.73	2.10	3.07	9.08	12.55	11.66	9.64
Shinkin banks	3.33	4.20	3.88	4.66	6.10	8.66	8.68	7.70	7.23
The Norinchukin Bank	4.30	5.55	5.21	3.80	4.71	10.34	14.84	14.98	18.05
Life insurance companies	8.98	12.38	17.52	22.23	24.88	26.40	28.91	31.35	28.06
Non-life insurance companies	7.42	7.98	9.75	13.71	17.16	19.37	21.52	21.50	19.56
Banking accounts of trust banks	3.26	3.09	3.59	5.39	12.11	16.88	19.26	18.99	17.25
Trust accounts of all banks	2.23	4.07	4.80	6.41	7.27	13.98	17.08	16.71	17.09
Postal life insurance and postal annuity	—	0.02	0.04	1.82	4.58	6.71	9.15	11.18	11.03
Total	3.13	4.21	5.54	7.16	9.48	13.60	16.34	17.01	16.09

Note: * March.

Sources: The Bank of Japan, *Economic Statistics Monthly*; The Norinchukin Bank, *Monthly Review of Agriculture, Forestry and Fishery Finance*; The Investment Trusts Association, *Monthly Report of Investment Trust*.

Table 4.9 Total investment in securities, classified by type of financial institution (¥ billion)

End of year	1980	1981	1982	1983	1984	1985	1986	1987	1988*
City banks	16 719	17 363	17 738	19 168	20 134	22 101	26 219	31 013	32 424
Regional banks	13 891	15 911	16 706	17 485	18 314	19 405	21 796	23 533	24 543
Sogo banks	3 766	4 720	4 965	5 315	5 396	6 038	7 078	7 780	8 146
Shinkin banks	5 670	6 912	7 585	7 799	8 114	8 330	9 022	9 681	9 771
The Norinchukin Bank	5 550	5 646	6 186	7 454	8 069	9 239	10 947	10 729	11 367
Life insurance companies	7 594	9 070	10 857	13 165	15 441	18 077	25 276	32 987	34 933
Non-life insurance companies	2 602	2 949	3 447	4 164	4 776	5 278	6 389	8 114	8 440
Banking accounts of trust banks	3 984	4 394	4 924	5 527	6 469	7 725	9 070	10 019	11 639
Trust accounts of all banks	7 743	8 147	11 662	14 716	19 747	24 765	36 366	47 097	45 430
Postal life insurance and postal annuity	6 465	7 368	9 169	10 625	12 204	14 098	16 006	17 590	18 223
Total	73 988	82 485	93 243	105 421	118 670	135 059	168 173	198 546	204 916

Note: * March.

Sources: The Bank of Japan, *Economic Statistics Monthly*; The Norinchukin Bank, *Monthly Review of Agriculture, Forestry and Fishery Finance;* The Investment Trusts Association, *Monthly Report of Investment Trust.*

assets significantly. Since the period within which the customer cannot liquidate is not long and the fund manager has to disclose performance every day, investment trusts will continue to be the most active investors, in the sense that they are apt to change their portfolio composition frequently (see Table 4.10).

Thirdly, bankers' bank type of institutions have recently become major investors. A typical example is the Norinchukin Bank. The Norinchukin Bank is a central organisation created in 1923 to serve agricultural and forestry financial institutions. Valued at around 10 trillion yen, the amount of securities which the Norinchukin Bank has is the largest among all Japanese private institutions. With loan activity continuing to be slack, operations in securities investments will continue to be given maximum emphasis in the Norinchukin Bank's operations.

Over the next several years the Norinchukin Bank will continue to increase securities investment by 2 trillion yen a year ($15.4 billion at $1.00 = 130 yen). Because of the high volume of this new money, it is natural for the Norinchukin Bank to put more emphasis on investments in US government bonds, a vast market, than it did in the past. In fact, early last year, the Norinchukin Bank intended to increase the share of overseas securities in its total securities from about 15 per cent to about 20 per cent, although subsequently the bank hesitated after the sharp drop in the value of the US dollar. Still, we could say that this bank is in a stage of accumulation of external assets.

Fourth, small and medium-sized financial institutions, like credit unions, also actively invested in foreign assets. These institutions have been losing their share in the loan markets because of the fierce competition posed by the bigger financial institutions, such as city banks. They were successful in keeping their profitability by taking advantage of the up-sloping yield curve and investing their collected short-term deposits in domestic longer-term securities. However, in the first half of the 1980s, interest rates of domestic longer-term securities dropped below the 8 per cent level which these institutions desired to keep. With this background, they preferred to invest in foreign bonds which had higher yields than domestic bonds. The consciousness of currency risk was not so strong at that time. In and after 1985, as the value of the US dollar started to fall, the attitude of these institutions towards portfolio investment in foreign assets became less positive. It will take a long time for these institutions to become active investors in foreign financial assets once again, because at present they are very sensitive to foreign exchange risk.

Table 4.10   Investment in foreign assets by Japanese investment trusts (¥ billion)

Stock		Total assets	Foreign assets	US	Others
1986	7	25 625	2 569	2 398	171
	8	27 706	2 963	2 759	204
	9	28 459	3 020	2 816	204
	10	29 031	3 458	3 201	257
	11	30 170	3 770	3 448	322
	12	32 075	4 095	3 681	414
1987	1	33 016	4 264	3 763	501
	2	34 541	4 380	3 811	569
	3	35 322	4 147	3 427	720
	4	37 022	3 784	3 060	724
	5	39 443	4 006	3 239	767
	6	41 037	4 651	3 816	835
	7	42 485	4 924	4 066	858
	8	43 724	4 719	3 907	812
	9	44 536	4 514	3 726	788
	10	43 643	3 972	3 268	704
	11	42 513	3 720	3 044	676
	12	42 914	3 468	2 800	668
1988	1	44 710	3 650	2 983	667
	2	45 927	3 856	3 185	671
	3	46 195	3 749	3 126	623
	4	47 893	3 670	3 044	626
	5	48 743	3 793	3 188	605
	6	50 518	4 594	3 955	639
	7	51 851	4 968	4 308	660

Flow		Total assets	Foreign assets	US	Others
1986	7	637	−6	−7	1
	8	2 081	394	361	33
	9	753	57	57	0
	10	572	438	385	53
	11	1 139	312	247	65
	12	1 905	325	233	92
1987	1	941	169	82	87
	2	1 525	116	48	68
	3	781	−233	−384	151
	4	1 700	−363	−367	4
	5	2 421	222	179	43
	6	1 594	645	577	68
	7	1 448	273	250	23
	8	1 239	−205	−159	−46
	9	812	−205	−181	−24
	10	−893	−542	−458	−84
	11	−1 130	−252	−224	−28
	12	401	−252	−244	−8
1988	1	1 796	182	183	−1
	2	1 217	206	202	4
	3	268	−107	−59	−48
	4	1 698	−79	−82	3
	5	850	123	144	−21
	6	1 775	801	767	34
	7	1 333	374	353	21

Source: The Investment Trusts Association, *Monthly Report of Investment Trust.*

Fifth, non-financial business companies are also important investors in the foreign markets. They invest in longer-term assets for their shorter-term holding assets and usually choose uncovered purchase when they buy foreign currency assets. This type of investment naturally embraces interest rate risks and currency risks. There are two reasons to explain why they do not like to evade such risks. One is the financial system itself, that is, they are still accustomed to the traditional behaviour which resulted from 'the long-term relationship and implicit contract' type of transactions in the traditional financial system. The other is the active asset management by business companies.

In the case of US multinational companies, there is a policy which dictates that the treasurer's top priority in the management of funds should be either liquidity or safety of assets, and the criterion of high return is secondary. However, in the case of some Japanese companies, there is no such clear policy and, usually, high return is given much more weight than in US companies.

Finally, major commercial banks have also bought a large amount of foreign bonds. However the pattern of investment is somewhat different from that of the above-mentioned entities. A typical example of this investment is the purchase by commercial banks of floating rate notes with money borrowed in the Euro-dollar markets. Developments in the near future will depend on new regulations, such as 'capital adequacy', and also on the shape of the yield curve.

For some economic entities, the present stage is already post 'initial stage'. For example, since 1983, the relative weight of foreign securities in the assets of financial institutions has increased sharply. The percentage of foreign securities in assets of all financial institutions excluding investment trusts grew from 0.6 per cent at the end of 1980 to 1.5 per cent at the end of 1983 and then to 4.0 per cent at the end of 1987. Foreign securities as a ratio of total also expanded from 3.1 per cent at the end of 1980 to 7.1 per cent at the end of 1983 and 17.0 per cent at the end of 1987.

With the rise in the relative weight of foreign securities in their portfolio, it is natural that some institutional investors have begun to pay more attention to foreign exchange risk. Kawai and Okumura concluded as follows:

The relative expected return factors were important in explaining Japanese capital outflow in the first subsample period (Jan. 1982–Dec. 1983) but not in the second subsample period (Jan. 1984–Sept.

1987). Whereas the risk factor played the role of discouraging investment in the second subsample period, this was not the case in the first because the share of foreign assets in the portfolio of major investors was still relatively small and, consequently, the exchange risk factor associated with foreign bond investment was not perceived to be important. As the share of foreign securities in Japanese investors' portfolio rose in the second period, their behavior became increasingly sensitive to exchange risk.[1]

The regression result is summarised as follows:

$$B_t = 2015.9 + 163.6t + 5478.1D2 - [161.0 - 294.6D1]\ (i_t - i_{t*} - e_t)$$
$$(437.7)\quad (17.6)\quad (1806.2)\qquad (113.3)\quad (145.7)$$

$$- [-302.8 + 602.2D1]\ \sigma_t$$
$$(175.9)\quad (255.7)$$

$$R^2 = 0.733,\ RMSE = 1709.8,\ DM = 1.51,$$

[Sample period: January 1982–September 1987]

where numbers in parentheses indicate estimated standard errors of the coefficients, and

B_t = Japanese investment in foreign bonds (in $US million),
$D1 = 0$ for $1982.1 \leqslant t \leqslant 1983.12$ and 1 for $1984.1 \leqslant t$,
$D2 = 1$ for April 1986 and 0 elsewhere (primary dealership dummy),
$i_t - i_{t*} - e_t$ = the Japan–US long-term nominal interest rate differential adjusted for expected rates of change in the exchange rate (per cent),
σ_t = exchange rate volatility (the standard deviation of daily exchange rates, in yen/$US).

More concretely, I would like to point out that, in an environment of volatile exchange rate movements, investors do not participate in portfolio investments in external assets but rather stay on the sideline because it becomes very difficult for them to predict the future developments of exchange rate movements.

The developments in March and the autumn of 1987 substantiate the implication that instability in foreign exchange movements induces vicious circles between foreign exchange rates and the long-term interest rate and also between the long-term interest rate and business activity. One should well understand that monetary authorities could not guide private institutional investors into investing in external assets under these circumstances.

As mentioned above, the present stage of portfolio investment in foreign securities is different from the 'initial stage'. However, neither is the present stage a 'matured stage' in which investors adjust the 'outstanding' level of assets, not just the 'flow' of assets. Japanese institutional investors are still the 'buy and hold' type of investors and all they would like is to change the allocation of 'new money' among financial assets. The reasons for Japanese investors not having adjusted the 'outstanding' level of assets are as follows. First, investors would like to maximise the coupon income in the current period, not the return during the holding period. Secondly, some big investors understand that the absolute amount of foreign assets held is too large, so that to sell a major portion of these assets without causing a sharp decline in the prices of the assets is difficult. Thirdly, the increase in the flow of funds into the contractual-type financial institutions which are the main investors in foreign assets is becoming very considerable as the structural change in financial market has triggered the disintermediation process (see Table 4.11). Portfolio managers of those institutional investors have to ration the 'new money' among assets, including foreign assets. Under these circumstances, it is not surprising to find that fund managers would like to put first priority on the selection of assets for 'new money' and not on the portfolio selection for outstanding assets as a whole. As a fourth reason, the fact that deregulation in financial markets is still under way is important: if financial transactions were completely deregulated, financial institutions would have to compete in terms of explicit factors. The use of explicit factors enforces a change in strategy for Japanese financial institutions. For example, life insurance companies will use their latent profit from stock investment for their dividend payments. And, generally speaking, there will be a tremendous increase in the number of financial institutions which will utilise the Asset Liability Management (ALM) technique. Surely those developments will re-orient portfolio management policy more towards 'outstanding assets'-based adjustment.

As already pointed out, Japanese capital exports have a strong relationship with the development of the internationalisation of the yen and the developments in the deregulation process. If these developments proceed further, then a new pattern of money-flow will emerge, resulting in a different demand for foreign assets.

Table 4.11   Fighting for individual savings in Japan (year-on-year change, March–June 1988)

Gains (¥ billion)		Losses (¥ billion)	
1. Big loan trusts	+ 1 296	1. Small time deposits	− 1 874
2. Large time deposits and MMCs	+ 837	2. Medium-term gov't bond funds	− 730
3. Endowment insurance	+ 800	3. Postal savings	− 131

Note: Interest rate on small time deposits below 50 million yen is controlled by the monetary authority.
Source: NRI and NCC.

At present, Japan's capital export is mostly on a US dollar-denominated basis. With the increased internationalisation of the yen and growing opportunities for yen-dominated capital export, more economic entities will involve themselves in capital export. For example, if opportunities for yen-denominated external loans increase, financial institutions will take on a more positive attitude, expanding their loan operations. Under these developments, one of the characteristics of Japan's capital export, continued rapid growth of both external assets and external liabilities, will diminish.

INTERNATIONALISATION OF THE YEN

In this context, let me explain a little the outlook on the developments of the internationalisation of the yen. International use of the yen began with portfolio investment, but has recently started to include every type of financial transaction. At present, the yen is second only to the US dollar as an international currency for portfolio investment, and is equal to or has surpassed the use of the Deutschmark and Swiss Franc in other private-sector financial transactions. In particular, the weight of the yen in international interbank transactions has grown considerably.

Also, in the area of international funds procurement, the yen's share grew remarkably in the first half of the 1980s. However it would be hard to say that the yen has been used much for transactions between third countries. The yen still has a way to go before it will have the same standing as the US dollar as an international currency.

One requisite for the internationalisation of the yen is its greater use for private-sector trade transactions, but, if the appeal of yen-denominated financial transactions does not increase for trade-related companies, there will be no incentive for increasing the amount of such transactions. In short, an efficient market for yen-denominated financial assets is an indispensable condition. For example, using Tobin's classification, it is necessary to increase (1) information-arbitrage efficiency; (2) fundamental-valuation efficiency; (3) full insurance efficiency; and (4) functional efficiency. Finally, to satisfy these conditions, yen-denominated financial transactions must be completely liberalised, and domestic and international markets for yen-denominated assets must be fully developed.

TOKYO AS AN INTERNATIONAL FINANCIAL CENTRE

Next I would like to examine whether or not Japanese financial markets are fully developed as an international financial centre with the yen as its international currency. In general, for international financial transactions to occur smoothly, the following functions are necessary:

1. The establishment of the type of financial institutions and markets that are conducive to international financial transactions.
2. The establishment of efficient communications and transportation and international service organisations for lawyers and accountants.
3. The ability to collect financial and economic information from around the world, analyse it, and transmit the results back around the world.
4. The instantaneous and accurate reflection of information on various relevant happenings in the world in prices for financial transactions.
5. The international standardisation of taxation and other forms of financial transactions.
6. The ability to trade in English, the common language of the international financial world.

At present, Japan's financial markets trail New York and London in several of these areas. However Japan is furthering the liberalisation of its interest rates, and a bold start has been made, as can be seen in the establishment of money markets such as bankers' acceptance (BA) and commercial paper (CP) markets. Private-sector financial institutions are catching up with the powerful overseas institutions in their capability for developing new products through the efficient formation of shared networks with major economic groups overseas. Strengthening the ability of private-sector financial institutions to collect and analyse information from around the world is still a problem, but here again we can expect progress as, since Japan has become a supplier of capital for the world, collecting information has become much easier.

Judging from what has just been said, it seems that it will not be very long until Japan really takes off as an international financial market. Together with this, it is likely that the yen will internationalise to a level proportionate to the strength of the Japanese economy in the near future. However it is still hard to believe that the yen will take the place of the dollar as the international currency. For example, the dollar is used at present far more than the US economy's weight in the world suggests. The dollar is used extensively in financial and trade transactions between third countries, and international commodities such as oil are generally priced in dollars. It is unlikely that the yen will function to this extent as a medium of exchange or a unit of account in the near future.

In short many changes are necessary if the yen is to replace the dollar and become an international currency in the true sense of the word. A strong economy and developed financial markets by themselves are not enough: Japan's rules for economic transactions should be more oriented towards spot and explicit types of transactions; Japan's presence on the international political scene should increase; and leaders from all areas in various countries should form strong networks with their Japanese counterparts. Five to ten years are necessary for these conditions to be met, after which we could have a full-fledged international currency of the yen.

Thus the internationalisation of the yen and, following from that, the future trend of capital exports, are strongly related to the future development of Japan's capital markets. Because the core of the market's development lies in the corporate bond market, several points necessary for improving it are examined below.

1. In line with the trend towards securitisation and globalisation, Japan's capital markets should continue to achieve the most remarkable growth in the world.
2. However, as Japan is the world's leading creditor nation, her capital markets (as public goods on an international scale) need to be developed and liberalised internationally.

3. To this end, a more competitive market possessing the workings of the market mechanism is required. A more elaborate description of the five points for rectification is given below.

    – *The improvement in the method for issuance of government bonds.* The structure of the government bond market was laid out in the latter half of the 1970s and was more or less completed by the first half of the 1980s. However some points, such as the problem of replacing the present issuance method with public auction and the withholding tax for treasury bills (TBs), were left out. Of these, the former is more pressing. At present, long-term and mid-term government bonds are issued by way of public auction, whereas ten-year bonds are issued through the syndicate for underwriting. I believe all bonds should be issued by way of public auction. In relation to this other interest rates apart from government bonds should be more reflective of the demand–supply situation in the market, free from the so-called interest structure of the past. Hence, in the effort completely to liberalise interest rates, public auction should be operative for all government bonds whose markets, after all, are the centre of the entire financial market. The Ministry of Finance has adhered to the issuance formula for ten-year bonds for fear that shifting to public auction may increase cost. Finally, the authorities have begun to realise the problem and have decided that, starting in fiscal year 1989, the disposition of about 40 per cent of ten-year bonds will be through public auction.

    – *The removal of the factors which obstruct the internationalisation of the primary market.* In order to effect a truly competitive environment in the capital market, there are many liberalisation measures which should be promptly implemented, such as a drastic revision of the trust system; diversification of products; and review of the principle of collaterals and serious use of rating classifications, and so on. As one can see from Table 4.12, costs are pushed up because of the rigidity of the trust system.

    – *The necessity to develop the money market.* The development of the money market is a natural consequence of structural changes. Foreign exchange risk control has become more important as fund management gets more internationalised. The development of the money market will serve to control foreign exchange risk. Japan's money market should commence

Table 4.12   The comparison of all-in cost between domestic (straight) bonds and Euro-yen (straight) bonds, Spring 1988

	Domestic (straight) bonds		Euro-yen (straight) bonds	
Condition Years to maturity	6	12	6	12
Issue amount (¥100 mill)	500	500	500	500
Coupon rate (per cent)	5.0	5.0	5.0	5.0
Issue price (¥)	100	100	100	100
Security	General mortgage	General mortgage	General mortgage	General mortgage
Issuer	Electric power companies	Electric power companies	Electric power companies	Electric power companies
Offering method	Public offer	Public offer	Public offer	Public offer
Initial cost	Underwriting commission: 1.5 Trustee fee: 0.25 per cent	Underwriting commission: 1.6 Trustee fee: 0.25 per cent	Underwriting commission: 1.875 Trustee fee: ¥0–600 000 (negotiated by issue)	Underwriting commission: 2.0 Trustee fee: ¥0–600 000 (negotiated by issue)
(Commission figures in per cent)			Costs shown below for trustee fee of ¥500 000	Costs shown below for trustee fee of ¥500 000
Annual maintenance cost	Trustee fee: 0 Miscellaneous fees	Trustee fee: 0 Miscellaneous fees	Trustee fee: ¥600 000/year or less (negotiated by issue) Costs shown below for trustee fee of ¥500 000	Trustee fee: ¥600 000/year or less (negotiated by issue) Costs shown below for trustee fee of ¥500 000
All-in cost (per cent)	5.50687	5.32976	5.43195	5.28246
Trustee fee (per cent)	0.05633	0.03474	0.00125	0.00107
All-in cost excluding trustee fee (per cent)	5.45054	5.29502	5.43070	5.28139

Source: NRI and NCC.

with the development of the BA and CP markets, followed by the total shift to public auction for ten-year government bonds and a major expansion in TBs.

- *The international standardisation of the tax system.* This is very important, as is shown by the following example. In the event that there is a total shift to public auction for all government bonds, a market for futures contracts maturing on the issuing day is a premise, but, in that case, it is also necessary for parties that are short to borrow bonds in the market for settlement on that day. In this situation, in the United States, repo is ordinarily used as an instrument to borrow bonds for settlement. However, in Japan, the transaction is construed as a trading deal and the tax implication is so heavy as to render the transaction useless. Even with CP, the concomitant stamp duty raises the issue cost, and, because of withholding tax, the marketability of instruments like TB is seriously hampered, making the job of non-residents even more difficult.

- *The international standardisation of transaction procedures in the secondary market.* There are some points in the secondary market which need to be reformed. For example, as far as non-government bonds are concerned, the lack of an active secondary market is an obstacle to the development of the primary market. A reason behind this is the procedural difference in the registration of ownership transfer; that is, whereas this can be effected by the Bank of Japan on the same day for government bonds, for non-government bonds a number of days will be required before the notice of registration change is delivered. Moreover, since non-residents may want to possess the actual certificates, a same-day switch from actual certificates to registration receipts and vice versa is possible at no charge with government bonds, whereas for non-government bonds a certain number of days is required, plus a fee (for example, ¥25 million for ¥10 billion face value). Consequently non-resident transactions are virtually rendered non-existent. In order to solve this problem, the transfer system that applies to government bonds should also be applied to non-government bonds.

CONCLUSION

Medium-term prospects show further internationalisation of the yen, increased financial liberalisation and the possibility of a change in the pattern of capital exports. However, in the short run, the unique pattern of capital exports from Japan, which has been discussed above, should continue, centring on private-sector foreign portfolio investment. Assuming this is the case, I would like to conclude my remarks by summarising the policy implications of Japanese capital exports in the following manner.

It should be emphasised that, although much of the abundant Japanese capital is ready for investment overseas, judging from recent trends of savings and investments in domestic economy, there is some hesitation on the part of private investors to invest in financial assets because of the instability of foreign exchange rates. This leads us to understand that, if some news triggers instability in exchange rates, Japanese net investments in foreign securities will contract, and, on the other hand, if exchange rates are stabilised by measures such as a change of policy, then net investment will turn upward. In fact, these movements have been occurring since March 1987 through to the present day: at first we had a vicious circle, and since February 1988 we have been enjoying a virtuous cycle. The uncertainty prevailing in the foreign exchange market can be calmed, for the time being, by a well-co-ordinated policy of the concerned governments which will give a clear and unequivocal message of determination to solve the problem. But a more fundamental solution boils down to the reduction of the US trade deficit. Time is of the essence and policy makers must act carefully as market forces may not allow the current stability in the financial markets to continue for long.

Appendix   International Flow of Funds in Japanese Residents' Euro-bond Financing

When residents raise funds in the Euro-bond market, restrictions apply to the sale of those issues to domestic investors for the first two to three months after issuance. First, in the case of yen-denominated securities, sales to residents are prohibited for 90 days after issuance according to administrative guidance (sales of dual-currency bonds are prohibited for 180 days). It is thought that these restrictions, which are written on the papers accompanying documents which must be submitted under the foreign-exchange law, are more effective than just administrative guidance once the documents have been submitted. On the other hand, for securities denominated in other currencies, administrative guidance prohibits the sale of more than 50 per cent to domestic investors in the first two to three months after issuance. At present, about 40 per cent of an issue of bonds with warrants, the leading form of bonds denominated in other countries, is sold to residents in the two to three months after issuance.

Following the restricted period, no similar restrictions apply, so there have been cases where nearly 90 per cent of the issue has been bought by residents in the period three to six months after issuance. However, in general, there needs to be a secondary market for Euro-bonds outside Japan, as it is not desirable for issuers to have all of the issue held by Japanese residents.

How issued bonds are traded between residents and non-residents is determined above all by exchange rate trends and the perceived credit risk between domestic and foreign investors. For example, in the case where the Euro-yen rate falls, the weight of residents' holdings decreases, while that of non-residents increases. Japanese investors tend to be less averse to credit risk than non-Japanese, so for those issues with somewhat lower credit ratings, Japanese investors tend to be prominent buyers.

Secondary trading is not very active. This is because financial institutions look unfavourably upon sales to investors who will sell immediately, and also because of the differences in taxes between Japan and other countries, particularly withholding taxes (levied in Japan but not in Europe). Also special target bonds, such as zero-coupon bonds aimed at specific investors, are obviously difficult to trade in the secondary market once sold to the investors concerned. The diagram below depicts the basic relationships and flow of funds when recourse is made to the Euro-bond market.

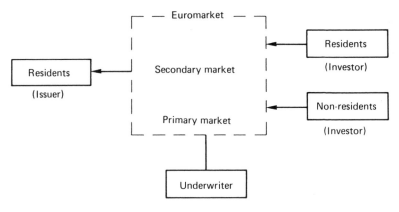

Figure 4A.1 International flow of funds in Japanese residents' Euro-bond financing

Notes

1. Kawai, M. and H. Okumura (1988) 'Japan's Portfolio Investment in Foreign Securities', Japan Center for International Finance (JCIF) Policy Studies Series No. 9 (January).

COMMENT

James E. Hodder

Mr Okumura's paper is wide-ranging. Its main focus is capital exports, with particular emphasis on portfolio investment in foreign securities by Japanese institutions. However the paper also discusses the internationalisation of the yen as well as financial liberalisation and capital market efficiency in Japan. My comments are primarily on the capital export portion of the paper. In that context, I would like to reiterate some of what Mr Okumura has said, but with a different perspective and emphasis.

First, I think it is worth emphasising that we are talking about very large amounts of money. From Table 4.1 we can calculate that Japan's cumulative capital account balance for 1985 through to the first half of 1988 was slightly in excess of $200 billion equivalent. Within the capital account, Japanese net purchases of foreign securities for the same period were almost $290 billion equivalent, whereas Japanese foreign direct investment was a relatively modest $54 billion equivalent. Short-term capital exhibited a large net inflow for Japan during that period, financing part of the foreign security investments. There was also a non-trivial amount of intervention by the Central Bank – the cumulative amount for that period indicated in Table 4.1 is $61 billion.[1] Turning to Table 4.2, we see some even larger amounts. Total external assets at the end of 1987 were almost $1.1 trillion dollars, and net external assets are projected to be $435.6 billion by the end of 1990.

A large portion (on the order of $600 billion) of the gross external asset position is commercial bank lending, whereas the external net asset accumulation is accounted for by security purchases. The latter can be seen in Table 4.5, which gives total foreign security holdings by investor category at the end of 1987. If we include investment trusts and use 125 yen/dollar for translation purposes, total foreign security holdings approach $300 billion.[2] I think it is important for us to recognise that we are looking at a consequence of Japanese trade surpluses and that trade surpluses cannot exist (by definition) without offsetting financial flows.

It should also be noted that the projections of net external asset positions in Table 4.2 are based on 'the strong assumption that the trade imbalances in both Japan and the United States narrow to almost zero by the end of 1990'.[3] I would not want to place a high probability on that event. Consequently, I think we should view the situation as follows: Japanese investors have built up large external asset positions (mostly in foreign securities); these positions are growing very rapidly; and this growth will probably continue to be very substantial.

In that context, it clearly behoves us to have better information on questions such as: Who is providing this financing and why? What kind of securities do they wish to hold? What kind of security trading strategies are they apt to utilise? In this regard, I feel that Mr Okumura's paper does an excellent job of identifying the major institutional investors providing funds to the market, and some of their motivations. However I feel we should be somewhat concerned about the potential ability of these investors to influence market prices. For discussion purposes, I will follow Mr Okumura's approach of separating capital exports into three categories: foreign direct investment, portfolio investment and commercial bank lending.

I concur that foreign direct investment (FDI) is not likely suddenly to become the dominant channel for offsetting the trade imbalance. However I would like to point out that much of Mr Okumura's discussion revolves around a comparison of 1986 surveys for German versus Japanese manufacturing firms. The situation in Japan now appears somewhat different from what it was in the autumn of 1986, when those surveys were conducted. At that time, the yen was rising strongly and Japanese manufacturers were exceedingly concerned about how they were going to compete at exchange rates of 150 or 140 yen/dollar. There was considerable discussion about shifting portions of their manufacturing operations overseas in an attempt to reduce costs, subject to maintaining the firms' employment commitments in Japan. That talk appears to have died down, because many of the major manufacturers now feel relatively comfortable with their ability to compete at 125 yen (or even less) to the dollar.

While there has been some overseas investment for cost reduction reasons, it appears that a great deal of foreign direct investment is actually a defence against potential protectionist trade barriers. Presumably this will continue; but these are very long-term commitments and are not likely to increase enough to provide the kind of financial flows that appear to be necessary to offset the trade imbalance. Also, buried in the FDI numbers are real estate investments, which are motivated somewhat differently. The appreciation of the yen has presumably been a very significant factor in the attractiveness of Los Angeles office buildings, Hawaiian hotels and so on. However real estate investment is also unlikely to overtake the role of the portfolio investment in financing the trade imbalance.

Turning to commercial bank lending, Mr Okumura emphasises the relative lack of internationalisation for the yen as inhibiting Japanese banks from undertaking large net lending positions. However it appears that these banks are increasingly capable of lending in foreign currencies and using swap or forward markets to effectively translate those loans into yen-denominated assets with which to balance their domestically generated yen liabilities. This suggests that we may see commercial banks assume a larger role in providing the financial offsetting to the trade imbalance.

Let us now focus on portfolio investment. Most of the investment in foreign securities has been coming from a relatively small number of major institutions. In part, this is because the Japanese financial system is highly concentrated, with relatively few major banks, life insurance companies and so on. However, in addition, most of the foreign security investment is coming from the life insurance companies and 'trust accounts of all banks' (see Table 4.5). These two categories represent roughly half of foreign security holdings as of March 1988. Since we are dealing with a small number of institutions, it is important for us to consider the kind of behaviour we might expect from these institutions over the longer run.

As a first step, it is useful to understand why these institutions have been rapidly building up their foreign security positions. Part of the answer comes from regulatory changes. It was not until 1986 that the proportion of foreign securities in the portfolios of life insurance firms, pension funds and trust accounts was allowed to exceed 10 per cent. I believe the limit for life insurance companies is now 30 per cent, and these firms have been quite aggressive in moving towards that limit. This build-up appears to have been partially motivated by an underlying concern that a natural disaster in Japan could cause a very large flow of claims, with life as well as non-life insurance companies seeking to diversify their assets away from the source of those potential claims.

In addition, pension accounts have been growing very rapidly, owing to the shift away from lump-sum retirement payments towards funded pension plans. This growth, coupled with increasing longevity and 'greying' in Japanese society, has resulted in a need for long-term assets to match those long-term liabilities. There is a dearth of long-term bonds available in the Japanese market, and a natural response is to seek assets with the desired maturity structure in foreign markets. Both the desire to diversify away from Japan and the need for long-term assets have tended to push Japanese institutional investors towards US government bonds, where there is a large and highly liquid market with maturities out to 30 years. Indeed something like 90 per cent of Japanese foreign security holdings are in the form of bonds, with the vast majority being US government securities.

There has also been a strong desire by Japanese insurance companies to provide attractive dividend yields (the figure of 8 per cent has been frequently mentioned) to policy purchasers. Since such yields have not been readily attainable in the Japanese bond markets, this has also been a strong motivation for going overseas. Early on, most of the foreign bond purchases were not hedged. As a consequence, there were some high-interest yields coupled with substantial exchange losses: however those losses apparently did not directly enter into the official dividend calculation. Although these institutions are becoming increasingly sophisticated about hedging, I understand that they are still essentially 'playing the yield curve' by hedging short-term while holding long-term securities. One assumes that they will eventually recognise that a fully-hedged position will provide a yield similar to that found in the Japanese market. That may alter their investment strategy.

Japanese institutional investors have also recently used a 'dividend capture' strategy on equity trading in the US markets. The procedure is basically to buy the stock just before it goes ex-dividend and sell it just afterwards. Since this activity is motivated by restrictions on the way these firms calculate their dividend yield in Japan, a relaxation of those restrictions is again likely to change their behaviour.

Given the large sums of money concentrated with relatively few Japanese institutions, these firms have the potential capability to 'move markets'. Thus a portfolio 're-balancing' decision could result in major security price adjustments and perhaps even exchange rate movements. Consequently it is particularly significant that these institutions have previously tended to follow a buy-and-hold strategy.

Mr Okumura attributes this buy-and-hold behaviour to a preoccupation with investing new funds as Japanese institutions built up their foreign security positions. That situation is apparently changing. There is also a long tradition in Japan of financial institutions following buy-and-hold strategies regarding domestic investments; however the motivation is somewhat different in the domestic case, where the institutions often have business tie-ups with the firms involved. In Japan, financial institutions have often followed relatively similar strategies. This has sometimes been attributed to firms learning and emulating each other's 'better' ideas. In part, such behaviour may also have been due to the regulatory process that Dr Suzuki has mentioned. He has also suggested that, as some of these regulations are relaxed, we may see differing strategies across financial institutions in Japan.

Thus there are several reasons to question the strength of motivations for a buy-and-hold policy. As these firms become increasingly involved in portfolio strategies, it seems quite plausible that we may observe some relatively rapid adjustments in portfolio positions. Regardless of the underlying rationale, such adjustments could have disruptive effects in the financial markets. In a slightly different context, Mr Okumura alluded to a similar situation. According to his account, when these institutions are nervous about the exchange rate situation they become relatively reluctant to invest additional funds. Given the nature of the trade imbalance, that puts a great deal of pressure on a Central Bank if it wishes to 'smooth' exchange rate movements.

In conclusion, I think that Mr Okumura has made an admirable job of identifying an area about which we need to be concerned and better informed. We have a situation where a relatively small number of Japanese financial institutions are holding large and rapidly growing foreign security positions. These firms can have a substantial impact on market prices, and I think it behoves us to develop a much better understanding of these institutions' characteristics and motivations.

Notes

1. It is my understanding that this amount represents only the change in the Bank of Japan's short-term positions and that some of the 'long-term' foreign security purchases mentioned above were by government agencies.
2. This exceeds the net external position due in part to activities such as Japanese banks acquiring floating rate notes with funds borrowed in the Euro-dollar markets.
3. H. Okumura, this volume, Table 4.2, note 2.

COMMENT

Robin Webster

First I should like to offer some comments about what one might call the 'external aspects' of Mr Okumura's thought-provoking paper. With regard to Japanese financial institutions in the international markets and the *intermediary* role they play there, I would agree with Okumura that in the next few years we will not see a fall-off in that role. The growth of Japanese banking and securities business in international markets is not surprising, given Japan's economic strength, but it also reflects their competitive approach to business. The Japanese securities houses form a powerful force in international capital markets with great placing power and increasing technical and market skills. Obviously there will be deregulation and liberalisation in Tokyo markets which will gradually make the markets back home more attractive. However, while it is cheaper to raise funds in overseas markets and easier to do so, Japanese borrowers will continue to take advantage of these markets and the arbitrage and other opportunities available to them. And there is, of course, a ready supply of Japanese investors.

I think Okumura has provided a useful run-through of the main types of private sector institutional investing in foreign securities markets (though if we were to include the public sector, the Post Office Savings System would also be highlighted).

One interesting question arising from the paper is whether Japan's cash-rich companies can be expected to increase their *productive investment* in Japan. If so, they are likely to have smaller funds available for Zaitech-type investments abroad. Having experienced how profitable Zaitech can be and having built up fairly sophisticated Treasury operations, they are unlikely to dismantle such operations altogether. Zaitech-type activity is likely to become more restrained and, in the longer term, deregulation of Tokyo markets may make domestic borrowing more attractive for Japanese companies. This year (1988) there has been no clear trend to suggest a fall-off in new borrowing. In the second quarter of 1988, for example, new issues of equity-related fixed-rate bonds approached the higher levels we witnessed before the October market crash of 1987. Many of these issues were bond issues with attached equity warrants, most of which were issued by Japanese entities. Clearly the strong Japanese stock market in this period was an attraction. An increasing part of the yen funding, which is obtained from these issues by way of currency swaps, seems likely to be earmarked for productive rather than financial investment. As is known, Japanese investors have been major purchasers of such issues.

Investment strategies are likely to become more sophisticated, to avoid speculation and to be less inclined to take risks with the dollar. Overall, private sector flows may be reduced by a combination of falling current account surpluses and by the growing availability of instruments in the Tokyo market, less Zaitech, more productive investment and a slow-down in corporations' and financial institutions' asset growth.

Another relevant question is the extent to which Japanese money will continue to *flow to the United States* (and to the US dollar, including of course, Euro-dollars). Okumura mentioned several reasons why Japanese are basically 'buy and hold' types of investors. A crucial factor behind their US investment is the sheer size (and liquidity) of the US markets, in particular the US treasury bond market, relative to other markets. Improved hedging techniques, including the increasingly sophisticated use of futures markets to limit exchange rate risks, should in many cases enable Japanese investors to pass on some of the risks of continuing to invest in the world's largest debtor nation. The fact is that at present there are no other markets capable of absorbing the volume of funds which the Japanese economy has available for overseas investment, as a result of its tremendous industrial success. Nevertheless, although the greatest single investment flow will continue to be to the United States, Japanese corporate and financial investors will surely seek to extend further their portfolio diversification into non-US (and non-dollar) markets where they can identify suitable opportunities.

Okumura rightly notes the growing importance of *the yen as an international currency* for portfolio investment. Indeed in 1987 yen-denominated fixed-rate Euro-bond issues accounted for 19 per cent of all issues in all currencies. And the share of the yen in new external lending by banks in the Bank for International Settlements (BIS) area rose from 3 per cent in 1982 to 29 per cent in 1987.

Obviously the yen has, as Okumura says, a long way to go before it has the same standing as the US dollar as an *international currency* and it will certainly be interesting to see how quickly and how far the Japanese authorities are prepared to allow the yen to develop. Some further increase in the use of the yen for international banking and capital market transactions does seem inevitable. Indeed senior Japanese officials have talked publicly of the need to move away from a dollar-based world economy system to one based more on the yen and European currencies. At the September 1988 International Monetary Fund (IMF) meetings in Berlin, Governor Sumita said that Japan is removing barriers to the yen's use as a reserve currency and suggested that studies were needed on the role of Special Drawing Rights (SDR) in 'international liquidity management' and how to make it an easily usable international reserve currency.

Not directly related to securities markets, though of increasing significance and relevance in the light of recent announcements from Berlin, it should be noted that the capital account outflows from Japan include *substantial and growing amounts of aid.* I make this point because the growth of external 'loans', which Okumura refers to as possibly 'lacklustre', may be significantly boosted by the aid element. Not so long ago people were talking about the need for Japan to increase its contribution. Such comment appears to have fallen on willing ears and Japan has an increasingly cohesive and coherent aid policy, particularly arising from ex-Prime Minister Nakasone's $20 billion initiative, but now backed up by new plans for greater Export-Import Bank lending. However I am sure that Okumura is right in highlighting the portfolio investment in foreign securities as being the future mainstay of Japanese capital exports, and I agree with him also that overseas direct investment will continue to expand.

I should now like to turn to the *domestic Japanese securities markets* to pick up one or two points arising from Okumura's paper and in particular his thoughts about the prospects for development of Tokyo markets to a level where they are fully equipped to handle a wide range of international financial transactions. He says that Japan's financial markets trail New York and London in several respects. I think, however, that the progress made in Tokyo in recent years has been remarkable in many aspects of deregulation and liberalisation. Not all the experiments have been successful – for example the bankers' acceptance market has not really got off the ground and I do not think it will do so while the cost of borrowing through this market is more expensive than direct borrowing from banks – but there has been considerable progress in other areas, such as, for example, the setting up of the commercial paper markets, the development of certificates of deposit and other market instruments, the new offshore market and the futures markets, quite apart from all the measures in the Euro-yen markets. Of course there is still much to do, for example in the areas of further interest rate de-control, and further improvements in the domestic yen bond markets are necessary. However in these and other areas the Japanese authorities are thinking about what might be possible, though understandably they have to take account of representations from quarters where vested interests may only be overcome by the offer of suitable *quid pro quos.* Such considerations dictate the rate of progress that can be made.

Okumura calls for improvement in the method of issue of *government bonds* and notes that the authorities have now decided to increase the amount sold through auctions to about 40 per cent of ten-year bond issues. This will no doubt please foreign houses, particularly, I believe, US-owned institutions and the US authorities who have lobbied hard for concessions in this area.

I found Okumura's comments on *Japanese bond markets* struck a chord with those who have watched the rather disappointing performance of new issues of Samurai bonds, where a familiar comment is that the issuing procedures remain cumbersome and difficult. Yen financing in the Euro-bond markets certainly seems easier and more attractive for borrowers. In the domestic bond market Okumura calls for a drastic revision of the trustee role performed by the commissioned bank, a function which certainly seems unusual to those in Western markets. As someone once said, 'There is a right way, a wrong way, and a Japanese way.' He also calls for greater use of rating classifications and this too is an area to which the Japanese authorities are addressing themselves. The Ministry of Finance has gradually relaxed eligibility requirements in a number of ways. In fact, the number of companies that can float unsecured bonds has increased from 50 in 1985 to about 400. One important measure recently introduced was a system of competitive negotiation between issuer and prospective lead managers. Another shot in the arm for the flagging Samurai and domestic corporate bond markets will be the beginnings of Japan's own 'shelf registration system' which will allow much of the paperwork for bond issues to be done in advance, ready for the issues to be 'taken off the shelf' when the market conditions are right.

One of the changes which Okumura calls for is for *international standardisation of the tax system.* Objectively this may be a splendid idea, but I think in practice we have to recognise that such days are a long way off. In fact, the development of some financial centres may have been helped by what one might call 'competition in fiscal laxity', a trend which in principle central bankers would want to discourage from going too far. Nevertheless I would certainly agree that tax considerations are of primary importance and that unnecessarily restrictive tax rules in a particular market do need to be ironed out if they are not to be damaging to natural growth of that capital market.

I should just like to say a few words about the sometimes politically sensitive question of *market access for foreign institutions into Tokyo.* Here I should immediately acknowledge the fact that markets in Tokyo today are unrecognisable from just a few years ago. I believe there are now 45 foreign houses licensed to deal in securities in Tokyo. These include the securities subsidiaries of foreign banks with branches in

Japan. These subsidiaries have been allowed licences, admittedly by a rather roundabout route involving a 50 per cent non-bank commercial partner, providing a concession to foreign institutions which is not available to Japanese institutions which are still caught by Article 65. Applications for securities licences now seem to be dealt with on far more of a routine basis than previously. This is very welcome. Of course, once in the markets, foreign institutions will not find the going easy. It is a sobering thought that, in the year to March 1987, 37 foreign houses with securities licences in Tokyo enjoyed a combined operating profit of only $10 million and an overall after-tax loss of $37 million. Competition is intense and a combination of long-standing practice, custom, cultural and historical relationships makes it difficult to attract domestic business. But there are no laws or regulations which discriminate against foreign houses.

So foreign institutions will certainly find the going tough, but, except in one area, which I will come back to briefly in just a moment, there are no longer problems of access to Tokyo markets in terms of licences. Indeed the new law on registration and licensing of investment management companies has been implemented very smoothly and, from the point of view of British firms, with no problems at all.

A key area for foreign firms is *the Tokyo Stock Exchange*. A total of 22 foreign securities houses now have membership and this represents very considerable progress which the authorities in the United Kingdom welcome. However the UK government would want to see the Tokyo Stock Exchange open to all qualified applicants, including firms who were unsuccessful in the round of memberships at the end of last year. We would like to see Japan and other international centres grant the same freedom of access to their markets as exists in the United Kingdom.

Finally, I would just like to add the thought that, as we move towards the next century, I would expect to see, in no particular order, London, Tokyo and New York increasingly prominent as the main three international financial centres in the world. In many major respects, the Tokyo capital markets – and I must not forget Osaka – are already large, influential and important. I have little doubt that this importance will increase. At the same time the need for *international co-operation between securities regulators* is widely recognised and has been emphasised by the growing international activity in securities markets. Securities exchanges are establishing formal information, trading and settlement links across national boundaries. International securities regulators already have informal meetings and there are growing contacts between officials. But many would think that some form of wider international harmonisation is needed on a multilateral basis with a global forum for consultation and co-operation. I have little doubt that this too will emerge.

5 The Role of Japanese Financial Institutions Abroad

Gunter Dufey

INTRODUCTION

Over the last decade, the ranking of the 10 largest commercial banks in the world has changed drastically. Once dominated by institutions headquartered in the United States and France, by 1988 Japanese banks occupy the top five ranks of global banking, as measured by assets. Using the same measure, 12 of the 20 largest banks in the world are Japanese and a total of 82 Japanese banks rank among the top 500. Ranked by value of deposits, seven of the 10 largest banks are Japanese. Tables 5A.1, 5A.2 and 5A.3 in the Appendix list the respective ranking of the top banks in the world by the specified criteria for the year 1986. Further, Table 5.1 indicates the prominence that Japanese banks have gained in international lending and deposit-taking.

To some observers such evidence suggests that Japanese financial institutions can repeat the feat that manufacturers have performed internationally. The mixture of excellence in process technology, new product development, hard work, persistence and the ability to adapt has enabled Japanese manufacturers to make considerable inroads in the global market place.

The underlying issue of this discussion paper is whether the well-documented international expansion of the Japanese financial service industry, represented primarily by commercial banks,[1] securities companies and other financial service providers, parallels the success of the Japanese manufacturing industry not only in terms of the observed phenomenon *per se* but also in terms of the underlying determinants. The crucial question is whether this success is based on special skills or whether it is based on the rapid growth of the monetary sector of Japan's economy, and is particularly due to that country's external

132

surpluses. In this respect, the ancillary question is whether these external surpluses will persist.[2]

During the 1980s, there have been many reports, articles and speeches on the subject of the growth of Japanese financial institutions in international markets. While much of this literature is quite superficial, tending to be purely descriptive at best, it often has an alarming undertone: that Japanese financial institutions, in mysterious, inscrutable ways, are able to underprice their services, exploiting unfair advantages never quite precisely defined, by which they make life difficult for their competitors in international and domestic markets alike. With financial service, and especially banking, being a particularly 'political' industry, the issue of sources and future of Japanese expansion is of special interest, not only for their unfortunate competitors.

Unfortunately, the number of analytical papers on the subject of Japanese expansion in international financial markets dwarfs the volume of publications on this subject in general. In part, this may well be a function of the complexity of the issues that defies an easy explanation. One should be very much aware of this possibility. Still, the issues remain and demand to be addressed. In addition, Japanese manufacturing enterprises, focusing on medium and high technology products, have taught the world valuable lessons regarding the combination of dynamic manufacturing technology and human resource management. And while the success rate of Japanese firms outside Japan has been accompanied by some spectacular failures, it is undeniable that Japanese management succeeded in many areas of manufactured products where Western firms were less successful.[3]

With respect to financial services, particularly banking and investment banking, similar arguments have been put forth. Apart from a large number of casual articles and press reports, a recent book is representative of that view:[4] the authors advance the argument that Japanese financial institutions, based on advantages in a regulated and, therefore, profitable home market are penetrating foreign markets in a patient and prudent manner, buying market share through aggressive pricing, acquiring the necessary skills through strategic alliances, and simply buying foreign talent whenever necessary.

While the focus of this paper is clearly on the external activities of Japanese financial institutions, it must be recognised that the international role of financial institutions in general cannot be insulated from their domestic market activities. As Aliber puts it: 'There are few uniquely international institutions: rather international banks are a subset of domestic banks with significant numbers of foreign branches and subsidiaries.'[5]

Table 5.1 Total cross-border bank lending and deposit-taking (billion US dollars; change in period)[1]

	1984	1985	1986	First half 1986	First half 1987
Lending[2] to world	**189**	**248**	**510**	**111**	**299**
Industrial countries	129	188	401	86	239
of which: United States	36	54	93	24	17
Japan	20	40	153	32	110
Developing countries	37	46	90	18	50
Offshore centres[3]	22	39	92	24	47
Other developing countries[4]	13	8	−1	−7	3
Other transactors[5]	6	11	−7	−7	7
Unidentified non-bank borrowers[6]	17	3	25	14	3
Memorandum items					
Capital importing developing countries[7]	16	9	—	−6	3
15 heavily indebted developing countries[8]	5	−1	−2	−2	—
Oil exporting countries[9]	−2	1	−1	—	—
Deposit-taking[10] from world	**197**	**274**	**561**	**115**	**266**
Industrial countries	118	186	416	103	215
of which: United States	7	22	82	19	6
Japan	12	42	114	24	64
Developing countries	43	77	127	11	43
Offshore centres[3]	19	54	132	29	24
Other developing countries[4]	23	22	−4	−18	18
Other transactors[5]	2	8	−8	−3	4
Unidentified non-bank depositors[6]	34	3	25	4	6

135

Memorandum items

Capital importing developing countries[7]	25	20	10	−5	16
15 heavily indebted developing countries[8]	14	5	−5	−3	2
Oil exporting countries[9]	1	7	−22	−17	1

Notes:

1. Data on lending and deposit-taking are derived from stock data on the reporting countries' liabilities and assets and are adjusted for changes attributed to exchange rate movements.

2. As measured by changes in the outstanding liabilities of borrowing countries defined as cross-border interbank accounts by residence of borrowing bank plus international bank credit to non-banks by residency of borrower.

3. Consisting of The Bahamas, Bahrain, the Cayman Islands, Hong Kong, the Netherlands Antilles, Panama and Singapore.

4. Includes some accumulations of interest arrears and reductions in debt that have been converted to equity or sold to non-banks.

5. Transactors included in IFS measures for the world, to enhance global symmetry, but excluded from IFS measures for 'All countries'. The data comprise changes in identified cross-border bank accounts of centrally planned economies (excluding Fund members) and of international organisations.

6. Calculated as the difference between the amount that countries report as their banks' positions with non-resident non-banks in their monetary statistics and the amount that banks in major financial centres report as their positions with non-banks in each country.

7. Consisting of all developing countries except offshore centres and the eight Middle Eastern oil exporters (Islamic Republic of Iran, Iraq, Kuwait, Libyan Arab Jamahiriya, Oman, Qatar, Saudi Arabia and the United Arab Emirates).

8. Consisting of Argentina, Bolivia, Brazil, Chile, Colombia, Côte d'Ivoire, Ecuador, Mexico, Morocco, Nigeria, Peru, Philippines, Uruguay, Venezuela and Yugoslavia.

9. Consisting of the eight Middle Eastern oil exporters (see footnote 6 above), Algeria, Indonesia, Nigeria and Venezuela.

10. As measured by changes in the outstanding assets of depositing countries, defined as cross-border interbank accounts by residence of lending bank plus cross-border bank deposits of non-banks by residence of depositor.

Data: IMF *International Financial Statistics;* Bank for International Settlements; and IMF Staff estimates.

Source: *IMF Survey,* 30 Nov. 1987, p. 360.

Thus, in the first part of this analysis, we dispose of the distinction between (a) traditional cross-border financial activities in either domestic or foreign currency on one hand, and (b) the so-called offshore or Euromarket activities, where transactions are carried out from entities chartered in jurisdictions using third-country currencies.[6] While this distinction is important for many reasons, especially regulation, from a managerial perspective, it is less so. Funds are fungible and the market for forward foreign exchange and its modern extension, the currency swap market, has blurred this distinction between the markets considerably: a yen loan funded out of Japan covered with a time-congruent sale of yen against US dollars forward is *de facto* a dollar loan!

Given the complexity of the subject, our first goal is quite modest; we will simply review and analyse some descriptive statistics about changes in the relative size of banks, always measured strictly by the magnitude of assets. Particularly, we want to ascertain to what extent changes in relative market shares in terms of assets as represented in popular competitive populations,[7] that is, the largest 300–500 banks as published annually in *The Banker*, can be explained by 'obvious' factors, such as changes in exchange rates and change in monetary aggregates. Particularly, we want to recast the data, focusing on the growth of assets measured in real terms, and eliminating inflation and exchange rate changes.

In the following section, we put our findings in perspective, in part by comparing them with recent work published by the Board of Governors of the Federal Reserve System.[8] In the third part of the paper we intend to engage in what might be classified as 'educated speculation'. Borrowing concepts from economics, foreign direct investment theory, and the theory of industrial organisation, we develop some tentative hypotheses about the international expansion and specific strategies of Japanese financial institutions. Finally, we present a research agenda that can be pursued by us and others to penetrate more deeply into possible reasons and explanations that allow us to forecast some of the trends in the dynamic global competitive environment for financial services.

FACTORS INFLUENCING INTERNATIONAL EXPANSION OF FINANCIAL INTERMEDIARIES

The following analysis documents some recent developments in the relative positions of banks in selected countries, namely the United

States, Japan, Germany, the United Kingdom and France. The focus is on recording the relatively rapid rise of banks headquartered in Japan as a major force in global bank competition. To this end, the paper presents some statistics regarding the assets of major banking entities with the objective of separating the effects of exchange rate fluctuations and inflation from 'real' measures.

The first section records the relative position of the Japanese and US banks as reported in *The Banker*'s top 300–500 banks. The second section focuses on the top ten leading banks of the five countries listed above. The Appendix records some of the basic data used in compiling the analysis.

Japanese v. US Banks

This section reviews the relative position of Japanese and US banks, as reported in *The Banker*'s annual ranking of the top 300–500 banks world-wide.

In current dollar terms (using current yen/dollar exchange rate), the assets of the top Japanese banks exceed those of the US banks. The assets of the top Japanese banks at current exchange rates have been increasingly consistently relative to those of the US banks (Table 5.2, column 8). The conclusion is the same when current *real* exchange rates are used (Table 5.2, column 10). In 1979 the number of US banks making it into *The Banker*'s top 500 was 2.1 times that of the Japanese banks; by 1986 this ratio declined to 1.27.

If we use a constant yen/dollar exchange rate, the growth in Japanese bank assets relative to those of US banks is not as strong as when we use the current foreign exchange rate to value assets of Japanese banks (Table 5.2, column 9). When looking at the *level* of this ratio (not the change), there is a certain arbitrariness in selecting a particular yen/dollar exchange rate. We have used the 1975 year-end yen/dollar exchange rate to compute Japanese bank assets in constant dollars. If we used an exchange rate from another year, say 1980, then the ratio of assets of US banks to assets of Japanese banks in constant dollars would be lower.

In 1980 US banks had assets 1.25 times those of Japanese banks in constant dollars. In 1983, this ratio declined to 1.03. Since then, this ratio has hovered around 1 (Table 5.2, column 9). During the period 1980–4 the dollar appreciated relative to the yen. However, during these years, the ratio of assets of American banks to those of Japanese

Table 5.2 Relative positions of leading US and Japanese banks[1]

Year	US banks		Japanese banks Assets (mill. $)				Ratio of US assets to Japanese				Year end	
	No. of banks	Assets (mill. $)	At current FX rate	At 1975 FX rate	At current real FX rate	No. of banks	At current FX rate	At 1975 FX rate	At current real FX rate	No. of US to Japanese banks	¥/$ exchange rate[2]	$\left(\dfrac{P_j}{P_{us}}\right)^2$
1975	80	574 385	454 940	454 940	506 343	52	1.27	1.27	1.13	1.54	302.7	1.11
1976	79	627 604	548 638	520 998	624 607	55	1.14	1.21	1.05	1.44	287.45	1.14
1978	56	760 162	1 078 013	673 625	1 203 042	58	0.71	1.13	0.63	0.97	189.15	1.12
1979	124	1 027 566	1 085 820	801 003	1 147 328	59	0.95	1.28	0.90	2.10	223.3	1.06
1980	118	1 104 128	1 258 779	882 434	1 273 669	61	0.88	1.25	0.87	1.93	212.2	1.01
1981	114	1 176 526	1 344 968	1 033 941	1 246 250	61	0.88	1.14	0.94	1.87	232.7	0.93
1982	117	1 298 170	1 399 844	1 246 399	1 257 435	61	0.93	1.04	1.03	1.92	269.5	0.90
1983	119	1 393 307	1 739 844	1 357 044	1 511 220	66	0.80	1.03	0.92	1.80	236.1	0.87
1984	114	1 518 856	1 964 120	1 592 968	1 648 680	75	0.77	0.95	0.92	1.52	245.5	0.84
1985	110	1 703 542	2 466 454	1 768 155	2 061 061	77	0.69	0.96	0.82	1.42	217.0	0.84
1986	104	1 909 158	3 815 648	1 928 623	3 168 783	82	0.50	0.99	0.60	1.27	153.6	0.83

Notes: 1. The banks are from the list of top 300/500 banks in the world; until 1978 assets are of the banks in the top 300. Assets of US banks are as of 31 December, while those of Japanese banks are as of 30 September, converted to dollar figures, using the 30 September dollar/ yen exchange rate. Note that, since the above dates do not match, comparisons are suggestive, not exact.

2. Rounded to the nearest two decimal places. P_j and P_{us} are third quarter 'implicit price levels' for Japan and the US respectively, used in computing the real exchange rate.

Source: *Banker*, June/July issues.

banks in constant dollars was declining. In contrast, the appreciation of the yen, starting in 1985, has not resulted in any significant decrease in the ratio of assets of US banks relative to those of the Japanese banks, in constant dollar terms. Thus the increase in relative position of Japanese banks *vis-à-vis* US banks cannot be attributed to the currency changes. This may be due to the fact that, in a global market, banks compete in a number of currencies, not only their home currency.

To obtain a measure of changes in assets of Japanese banks due to changes in exchange rates, we undertook the following data analysis: Let A_t be the assets of Japanese banks in current dollars at end of time t; let X_t be the ratio of current dollar/yen exchange rate to dollar/yen exchange rate in a particular year (our base year). We chose the base year exchange rate to be that at the end of 1978. This year was chosen because it seems to lie in the middle range of the present exchange rate and that at the end of 1975. Then the change in assets in current dollars of Japanese banks converted to constant dollars

$$\frac{A_t - A_{t-1}}{X_t} \tag{5.1}$$

can be decomposed as (a) the sum of change in total assets in constant dollars of Japanese banks:

$$\frac{A_t}{X_t} - \frac{A_{t-1}}{X_{t-1}} \tag{5.2}$$

and (b) the change in assets due to exchange rate changes:

$$\left[\frac{X_t - X_{t-1}}{X_t}\right] \left[\frac{A_{t-1}}{X_{t-1}}\right] \tag{5.3}$$

In equation form, this becomes

$$\frac{A_t - A_{t-1}}{X_t} = \frac{A_t}{X_t} - \frac{A_{t-1}}{X_{t-1}} + \left[\frac{X_t - X_{t-1}}{X_t}\right] \left[\frac{A_{t-1}}{X_{t-1}}\right] \tag{5.4}$$

The left- and right-hand terms for this equation are presented in Table 5.3, along with changes in assets of US banks starting in 1980. This year was chosen because, starting in 1979, we have data for the top 500 banks; prior to 1979 the data set comprises the top 300 banks. Comparing columns 2 and 3, we find that Japanese banks, starting in

Table 5.3   Yearly changes in assets of US and Japanese banks

Year	Change in US bank assets	Change in Japanese bank assets		
		$\dfrac{A_t - A_{t-1}}{X_t}$	$\dfrac{A_t}{X_t} - \dfrac{A_{t-1}}{X_{t-1}}$	$(\dfrac{X_t - X_{t-1}}{X_t})\,(\dfrac{A_{t-1}}{X_{t-1}})$
1980	76 562.00	154 130.81	202 229.44	− 48 098.93
1981	72 398.00	70 040.13	− 28 782.00	98 821.69
1982	121 644.00	38 575.02	− 110 668.00	149 243.63
1983	95 137.00	272 236.69	411 197.00	− 138 960.69
1984	125 549.00	172 752.00	119 397.00	53 355.05
1985	184 686.00	437 748.50	636 447.00	− 198 698.06
1986	205 616.00	1 661 019.00	2 548 179.00	− 887 160.19

Notes: 1. The values in $ millions are derived from data in Table 5.2.
2. See text for explanation of symbols.

year 1983, have been increasing their assets faster than US banks, even when corrected for yen/dollar exchange rate changes.

Relative Positions of Leading Banks of Major Banking Countries

This section complements the previous section by focusing on the top ten leading banks in each of the following countries: United States, Japan, Germany, United Kingdom and France. By narrowing attention to the major banks in these countries, a more meaningful comparison of the relative position of each country as a banking entity can be expected, since it is these leading banks that compete most intensively at the global level. Various measures of growth in assets of these banks are given below.

The available published data only record the assets of the banks expressed in nominal US dollars at the prevailing exchange rate at the end of the accounting year. Thus such data contain the effects of nominal variables, such as exchange rate and price level changes; or more precisely, differing rates of US and foreign inflation with no corresponding movements in the exchange rate. A scheme for decomposing the assets expressed in dollars into real and nominal effects is presented below.

The growth rate in assets expressed in current US dollars, of leading non-US banks, can be decomposed approximately as the sum of growth rate in real assets of foreign banks (expressed in constant units of banks' home currency), depreciation rate of the dollar, and the inflation rate in the banks' home country. For example, the growth rate in assets of Japanese banks measured in US dollars can be decomposed roughly as the sum of growth rate in real assets (expressed in constant yen), depreciation of the US dollar *vis-à-vis* the Japanese yen, and the Japanese inflation rate.

Formally, let A be assets measured in US dollars, R be real assets, P be the relevant non-US price level and E the exchange rate, expressed as US dollars per unit of the relevant foreign currency. Then

$$\frac{\Delta A_t}{A_{t-1}} \simeq \frac{\Delta R_t}{R_{t-1}} + \frac{\Delta E_t}{E_{t-1}} + \frac{\Delta P_t}{P_{t-1}} \qquad (5.5)$$

where

$$\Delta Y_t = Y_t - Y_{t-1}$$

Table 5.4 presents information regarding the variables on both the left- and right-hand side of the above equation for the top ten leading banks of select countries. Data in this table suggest that, during the late 1970s and 1980s, leading Japanese banks, on average, have grown in real assets three times as fast as US banks, roughly twice as fast as the German and British banks, and one and a half times as fast as the French banks. In terms of real assets, the growth of Japanese banks is more pronounced in the 1980s than in the late 1970s.

The growth in US dollar assets of leading Japanese banks is as much due to the depreciation of the US dollar *vis-à-vis* the yen as it is due to growth in real assets of leading Japanese banks. The same can be said about the German banks. On the other hand, the growth in dollar assets of French and British leading banks seems to owe as much to the growth in real assets as it does to inflation; on average the US dollar has depreciated very little *vis-à-vis* the British pound and the French franc.

Work done concurrent with our research has provided results very similar to our statistics (see Table 5.5).[9] In our study, instead of basing findings on only the top 100 banks in the world, we have extended the population to the top 500 banks (with the exception of 1975, 1976 and 1978 where the top 300 banks are used). As these comparative data show, only the average growth rate of bank assets in France presented a large discrepancy with our results. This was apparently owing to the fact that we included data for 1978, when major accounting changes affected data for French banks.

Table 5.4 Growth measures of leading banks, by country

Year	US $\frac{\Delta A_t}{A_{t-1}}$	$\frac{\Delta R_t}{R_{t-1}}$	$\frac{\Delta P_t}{P_{t-1}}$	Japan $\frac{\Delta A_t}{A_{t-1}}$	$\frac{\Delta R_t}{R_{t-1}}$	$\frac{\Delta P_t}{P_{t-1}}$	$\frac{\Delta E_t}{E_{t-1}}$	Germany $\frac{\Delta A_t}{A_{t-1}}$	$\frac{\Delta R_t}{R_{t-1}}$	$\frac{\Delta P_t}{P_{t-1}}$	$\frac{\Delta E_t}{E_{t-1}}$	UK $\frac{\Delta E_t}{E_{t-1}}$	$\frac{\Delta A_t}{A_{t-1}}$	$\frac{\Delta R_t}{R_{t-1}}$	$\frac{\Delta P_t}{P_{t-1}}$	France $\frac{\Delta A_t}{A_{t-1}}$	$\frac{\Delta R_t}{R_{t-1}}$	$\frac{\Delta P_t}{P_{t-1}}$	$\frac{\Delta E_t}{E_{t-1}}$
1976	22	16	5	17	3	7	5	24	8	4	11	-16	-1	6	11	13	14	10	-10
1978	29	12	15	85	9	12	52	72	24	8	29	20	39	-4	21	78	25	20	19
1979	16	7	8	0	15	3	-15	18	7	4	6	9	43	12	17	32	15	11	4
1980	9	0	10	15	4	5	5	-5	2	5	-12	7	28	2	18	9	8	14	-11
1981	5	-4	10	11	21	1	-9	-8	2	4	-13	-20	8	18	14	-4	8	14	-21
1982	5	1	4	6	20	2	-14	0	1	5	-5	-15	5	16	7	2	9	9	-15
1983	2	-1	4	21	6	0	-14	-5	6	3	-13	-10	0	6	4	-3	10	10	-19
1984	8	4	4	10	13	1	-4	-7	7	1	-13	-20	-7	11	5	0	8	7	-13
1985	8	5	3	25	8	3	13	35	3	3	28	25	20	-11	7	26	-5	5	27
1986	8	5	2	53	6	2	42	36	4	3	27	2	14	9	2	26	2	2	17
1987	3	0	3	18	13	0	5	30	5	1	23	27	29	-3	5	31	5	3	21
Average	10	4	6	24	11	3	9	17	6	4	6	1	16	6	10	19	9	10	0

Notes:

1. $\frac{\Delta Y_t}{Y_{t-1}}$ is the percentage change in Y_t, where $\Delta Y_t = Y_t - Y_{t-1}$.

2. A is assets expressed in current US dollars; R is assets expressed in constant domestic currency units; P is the GNP deflator, that is, R is assets expressed in domestic currency deflated by the GNP deflator, with the exception of France where it is the CPI; and E is the exchange rate of dollars per unit of domestic currency.

3. A and E are end of the year figures, except for Japan, where they are as on 30 Sept. P is the fourth quarter price level, except for Japan, where it is the third quarter price level.

4. The 1978 figures represent percentage change from 1976 to 1978, since data for 1977 are missing.

Table 5.5   Growth rates of assets of leading banks by country

	US	Japan	Germany	France
Present study				
Average growth rate (per cent)	10	24	17	19
Standard deviation of growth rate	8	24	25	24
Coefficient of variation	0.8	1.0	1.5	1.3
Dohner & Terrell				
Average growth rate (per cent)	16	19	15	12
Standard deviation of growth rate	6	17	17	13
Coefficient of variation	0.6	0.9	1.1	1.1

Dohner and Terrell went beyond the scope of our analysis and examined also the share of large banks in terms of domestic bank assets, data usually referred to as concentration ratios. The underlying idea is that two countries, equal in every other respect, but different in terms of the concentration of banking assets, would obviously show a larger number of banks for the country with a higher concentration in the top banks' ranking. By the same token, *changes* in concentration ratio should lead to changes in the number of banks included in any international ranking of top banks. Looking at the statistics of the Dohner and Terrell study, there are no significant changes in the concentration ratio for the top banks in Japan, Germany and the United States. This eliminates changes in concentration ratios as a possible explanation of the observed shift.

Dohner and Terrell also confirmed the general notion that growth in bank assets is closely related to growth in nominal GNP. The exception to this is the United States, and we shall come back to this fact later.

Dohner and Terrell then proceeded to construct a model relating bank asset growth to five independent variables, including a dummy variable to capture the effects due to bank mergers, divestments and major accounting changes. We have not proceeded along the same line, however. Instead, as a preliminary step, we break down bank asset growth into (a) real growth in bank assets, (b) asset growth due to price changes, and (c) asset growth due to exchange rate changes. More sophisticated analysis and modelling will be the agenda for future research.

SOURCES OF COMPETITIVE ADVANTAGE FOR JAPANESE FINANCIAL INSTITUTIONS ABROAD

Traditionally, bankers have a reputation as being conservative. They have usually left the honour of first entry into hostile foreign territories to others, playing a supportive role as camp followers. The Japanese bank expansion abroad has been no exception. Some of the earliest branches of Japanese banks have been in California, following the Japanese immigrants who settled there in the late nineteenth and early twentieth century.[10]

The more recent expansion followed corporate customers who began to establish distribution, service and manufacturing facilities abroad, beginning in the 1960s. Japan's foreign direct investment activities were originally rather timid and cautious, concentrating on relatively small operations in Asia, particularly Taiwan, Korea and the countries of South-east Asia. The foreign investment boom in the industrialised countries followed in the 1970s and 1980s, often as a reaction to threats against their export markets that the Japanese companies had developed with diligent, long-term efforts. In this respect it is noteworthy that the bulk of Japanese foreign direct investment occurred after the heyday of US corporate expansion abroad.

There is a great deal of parallelism between the expansion pattern of US and European banks on one hand and Japanese banks on the other. However, one might speculate about even stronger ties between Japanese banks and their industrial customers. The pronounced sense of mutual obligation in Japanese culture would make for an even greater 'captivity' factor with respect to Japanese enterprises operating outside Japan; and, vice versa, the same sense of mutual obligation has probably induced Japanese banks to follow their customers more promptly, even in markets where they might not have developed an interest otherwise. Clearly, supportive data on this phenomenon will be hard to come by and the evidence remains anecdotal. As an additional differentiating factor, one might cite the tight regulation of expansion at home and abroad by Japanese supervisory authorities that explain the observed 'lock-step' pattern of expansion of Japanese institutions abroad.

What goes for foreign direct investment applies even more to trade. While an argument can be made that the foreign trade activities, both imports and exports of a country, can be financed by institutions outside that country, ultimately trade finance requires the intermediation of banks with whom a (credit) relationship is established. To illustrate this point: for many years a considerable proportion of Japan's commodity trade, particularly the oil trade, has been financed in the New York acceptance market, where this type of business accounted for a large part of the so-called 'third-country acceptances' which comprised, at times, a volume of 20–30 per cent of the acceptance market in total.[11] However, particularly in the early years, all those bankers' acceptances were also endorsed ('guaranteed') by Japanese branches in New York.

With respect to Japan, another special factor is significant: a considerable part of exports and virtually all imports are financed in non-yen currencies, mostly in dollars. Thus Japanese banks are torn between the disadvantage of having to fund themselves in a foreign currency and the advantage of having the relationship with customers. We believe it is for that reason that the major Japanese banks, particularly the city banks and the long-term credit banks, established funding vehicles in the major offshore centres and in New York early in order to gain access to non-yen currencies, primarily US dollars. As far as the dynamics of this situation are concerned, we would argue that, in the efficient international money market, particularly in the Eurocurrency markets where interbank transactions dominate, funding capabilities become, over time, less important in comparison to relationships with clients, where credit analysis, that is, an understanding of the company's future cash-flows and ability to make payments under stress, are of essence. Thus we would expect Japanese international bank expansion to be highly correlated with the growth of the international trade of that country in general, and increasingly so.

Data in Table 5.6 show that the affinity of growth in Japanese bank assets exceeds that of the United States relative to the growth of trade. Further, the lower elasticity of US asset growth with respect to trade may well be due to the fact that foreign banks recaptured a part of the trade financing that US banks had originally obtained as a result of their strength in the dollar-denominated credit market. While we have not found sufficiently conclusive data to present here, anecdotal evidence suggests strongly that Japanese banks have not remained merely guarantors of their companies' trade obligations, but do the financing now in a dollar market themselves, both offshore and onshore.

Along the same lines, there is evidence on the role of Japanese banks serving as conduits for the export of financial capital from Japan. Over the last decade, Japan has changed from a capital importing to a capital exporting country. Table 5.7 gives the correlations between quarterly

Table 5.6   Major bank asset growth rates and implied elasticities, 1972–86

Country	Bank asset growth rate	Total trade growth rate	Implied elasticity with respect to $ trade
Canada	11.7	10.9	1.07
France	12.2	11.9	1.03
Germany	15.0	12.1	1.24
Japan	20.9	19.1	1.09
Switzerland	16.4	12.3	1.33
United Kingdom	13.1	11.5	1.13
United States	10.1	13.2	0.77

Source: Robert S. Dohner and Henry S. Terrell, 'The Determinants of the Growth of Multinational Banking Organizations: 1972–86', *International Finance Discussion Papers*, No. 326, June 1988, p. 17.

Table 5.7   Correlations, gross external assets and capital flows, 1977–87

	US external assets	Japanese external assets
US capital flow	0.68	0.57
Japanese capital flow	− 0.74	− 0.62

capital account and the quarterly external asset positions of both Japanese and US banks.

There seems to be a strong association (-0.62) between Japanese capital flows and the growth in external asset position of Japanese banks; the capital account of Japan in the late 1970s was positive (Japan was a net importer of capital) and, starting in 1982, it was almost all the time increasingly negative (Japan was a net exporter of capital).

The external assets of US banks and Japanese banks have grown during the 1977–87 period, but the growth in gross external assets of Japanese banks has been very rapid compared to the growth in gross external assets of US banks. In the last quarter of 1987 the gross external assets, expressed in US dollars, of Japanese banks was about 16 times what they were in the first quarter of 1977, while the US banks saw only about a six and a half times increase in their gross external assets during the corresponding period. (See Table 5A.4 in the Appendix.) While the above comparison does not correct for movements in the yen/dollar exchange rate, the positive correlation between US capital account and the gross external asset position of US banks suggests that the US banks were able to withstand the adverse effects of capital imports; the positive correlation suggests that the US banks (at least the leading ones) are highly global in their operations and can cater to a more diverse clientele, rather than to US-related customers only.

Japanese entry strategies into the wholesale market in the United States and other open financial markets, such as London, have been influenced further by differences in terms of cross-border lending, largely exposure to sovereign borrowers. Much has been made about cross-border lending into developing countries and I shall assume that the reader is familiar with the various aspects of this phenomenon. Relevant for the rapid growth of Japanese financial institutions in the 1980s, however, is the fact that, while all banks from developed countries engaged to almost the same extent in acquiring bank assets abroad, it turned out that the concentration of such assets was not the same. European banks, for example, had loans to Latin American countries as well as Asian countries. However, quite naturally, 'loans follow trade' and thus a large proportion of those loans went to Eastern bloc countries.

By the same token, Japanese city banks and others had their books full of LDC loans, but the Japanese banks had concentrated their lending to countries like South Korea, The People's Republic of China and countries further along the Asian side of the Pacific Rim. It turned out that none of these countries, with the notable exception of the Philippines, had the same difficulties that bedevilled virtually all the Latin American countries. It is not surprising, therefore, that we should find Japanese banks making considerable inroads in national markets in those areas of the banking business where 'quality', as perceived by the market, is important. We are referring here to the stand-by letter of credit business where Japanese banks have gained a considerable market share, particularly in the US market.

This brings us to a related further point: While the previous considerations can be summarised under the motto 'following customers', banks in general have quickly recognised the advantage of spreading overheads and have pursued local customers once they had a presence established in a local market. With respect to this strategy, Japanese banks have probably some disadvantages in terms of building

organisations that can effectively establish relations with local customers – disadvantages germane to all banks headquartered abroad.
This can be overcome either by: (1) training or hiring local personnel
that can develop these relationships or (2) aggressive pricing. It appears
that, at least from the experience in the US markets, Japanese financial
institutions have emphasised the second path more than have, say,
European headquartered banking institutions.

Japanese entry strategies, at least in the United States, were also
motivated by another consideration: the need to gain access to foreign
currency funds. For Japanese banks this must be a significant factor,
given the nature of Japanese trade financing. And, while the offshore
markets have provided an ample supply of funds at competitive rates,
Japanese institutions have felt a need to open up an alternative source
of dollar deposits, from a market considered to be safer.[12] It is difficult
to explain otherwise the expansion of Japanese banks into the California consumer banking market where other competitive advantages are
hard to find and the immigrant base has long been dispersed and/or
become totally integrated into the American melting-pot.

Japanese financial institutions have not only been making considerable advances in terms of growth of assets abroad, they have also made
great strides in the securities business. Table 5.8 shows the advance of
Japanese institutions in the Euro-bond underwriting tables over the
past decade.

By the same token, since the mid-1980s, Japanese institutions have
begun to play significant roles in the US Treasury market and are
gearing up to become active participants in the markets for government
securities in several industrialised countries, such as the United Kingdom, West Germany and France. Observations of transactions in the
market show, however, that these activities have in the past been closely
related to the Japanese customer base. What the Japanese securities
firms have done is to forwardly integrate into the market channels by
which Japan's surpluses are laid off in international fixed-income
markets. There is very little evidence that the Japanese securities
houses, either in London or in New York, have made any significant
inroads into serving non-Japanese portfolio managers (with paper
other than Japanese securities).

So far, at least, this expansion has been directly related to a defensive
action by the Japanese houses to recapture market share that Western
institutions had previously usurped. Wall Street and Lombard Street
are full of stories of the good old days, back in the 1970s, when Western
financial institutions made good money by selling non-Japanese secur-

Table 5.8 Shifts in Euro-bond league tables, 1969–87

	(Jan–June) 1969	Position in league table 1977	1981	1985	1987
Crédit Suisse First Boston (A)	3	2	1	1	2
Merrill Lynch		23	6	2	21
Morgan Guaranty			8	3	8
Salomon Brothers International		45	5	4	9
Morgan Stanley International (B)	4		3	5	7
Deutsche Bank AG	1	1	4	6	3
Goldman, Sachs International		16	9	7	17
Nomura International Group		17	16	8	1
U.B.S. (Securities) Limited		3	13	9	13
Banque Paribas				10	12
Orion Royal Bank Limited		8	15	11	37
Daiwa		19	17	12	5
S.G. Warburg	5	4	2	13	11
Swiss Bank Corp. International		10	12	14	16
Bankers Trust				15	40
County NatWest				16	23
Lloyds Merchant Bank				17	—
Commerzbank				18	14
Yamaichi			14	19	6
Shearson, Lehman Brothers				20	25
Nikko Securities					4
Industrial Bank of Japan					10
Dresdner Bank					15
Baring Brothers					18
Long-Term Credit Bank of Japan					19
Bank of Tokyo					20

Notes: (A) White Weld & Co. in 1969, Crédit Suisse White Weld in 1977 and Crédit Suisse First Boston in 1981 and 1985.

(B) Morgan et Cie International in 1969 and 1977, Morgan Stanley in 1981 and 1985.

Sources: *Euromoney*, Annual Financing Report, March 1988, for 1987; IFR book manager full credit league table for 1981 and 1985; *Euromoney* lead manager league table for 1977; *The Banker*, 1970, p. 777, for 1969.

ities to institutional investors in Japan. Now, of course, it is painful for these houses as the market goes through a process where the Japanese financial intermediaries and securities houses capture that business. As it turns out once again, client relationships are more important than relationships or skills in the transactional securities markets.

The securities business is different from the banking business also in terms of regulation. Not only had Japan inherited from its US occupation forces a version of the Glass-Steagall Act in the form of

Article 65 of the Banking Law, Japanese securities markets were relatively 'over-regulated' at home. For many years, beginning in the second half of the 1970s, Japanese corporations found that they could raise debt as well as equity in the offshore markets cheaper and faster than at home. The Japanese warrant issues are particularly good examples of this phenomenon as they can only be understood as an elegant way – given their structure with very low coupons and near-money equity options – to raise additional risk capital, avoiding costs and restrictions in the home market. By the same token, an increasingly large part of this paper has been placed directly with Japanese institutional investors, after brief warehousing to get around the 90-day rule. When considerations such as these are combined with the fact that, outside Japan, Article 65 applied, but less stringently, it is not surprising to see that both banks and securities houses developed a considerable range of activities abroad.

While the offshore markets gave the Japanese banks and securities houses more freedom, the domestic market provided other advantages. Relevant here is, in particular, the incidence of domestic interest rate control, especially in the money markets, together with the well-known tax treatment of consumer savings that has, in the past, not only given Japanese banks advantages in certain market segments (which of course were, in part, offset by disadvantages in other segments of the domestic market), but has allowed them to arbitrage either on price or with respect to availability risk. To illustrate: Japanese banks and institutions have a competitive advantage with respect to offshore yen bank loans and deposits as well as yen-denominated bonds (Euro-yen bonds). This is because they can make commitments in terms of liquidity risks as they can expect to have preferred access to the domestic market when necessary. Such differential market conditions are important not only with respect to risk arbitrage but also with respect to rate arbitrage: one of the few markets where swap spreads are still significant is that involving yen funds. As arbitrage operations, currency swaps are dependent on the existence of a comparative advantage. In a partially regulated market, such advantages abound.

So far, our discussion has focused on macroeconomic and regulatory determinants. However the success or failure of a group of financial institutions in a global competitive market depends ultimately on the individual institution. Thus enterprise-specific factors have to be considered. And while the former variables can sometimes be captured by available data and evidence that is consistent with theory, with respect to the microeconomic factors evidence is scarce and data are few and far between. Nevertheless our discussion would be incomplete, were it not to address these issues.

The success factors of individual banks in a global market have been identified as risk capital, information technology and human resources.[13]

We have few original insights to add to the current debate on the attempt by regulators world-wide to impose strengthened and standardised bank capital adequacy rules on the industry. We accept the prevailing wisdom that Japanese banks will be rather pressed, but because of their access to the Tokyo equity market and their undervalued holdings of equities, they will be able to overcome these constraints. In any case, we believe the role of bank capital as a competitive weapon can be overstated, owing to the implicit governmental guarantee behind large banking institutions of major industrialised countries. Thus the role of equity capital is not the same as it would be with respect to ordinary corporations that are permitted to fail.

An important dimension of competition in international banking is the ability to process information cheaply and efficiently. This goes far beyond pure computer technology. Ultimately, banking in virtually all its manifestations is a service industry that requires the co-ordination of a large number of people in complex organisations. The emphasis on effective internal communication in Japanese organisations is definitely a factor of strength. A relatively rich literature from the theory of organisational behaviour emphasises and documents this fact quite well. Much has been made of the ability of Japanese institutions to substitute informal oral communications for voluminous and formalistic paper reports that may fail to capture the essential aspects of relevant information. Thus Japanese institutions may have an advantage that is culturally based – as long as everybody is Japanese! In terms of pure information technology, few serious observers will deny that the Japanese possess both the technology and the distribution of skills to use information technology successfully.

If one pushes information technology further, one comes very quickly to the third and most difficult factor: human resources. The nature of the financial service industry requires a few brilliant and ambitious people, a large structure of well educated middle managers to manage the myriad of customer relationships and analytical tasks that are to be done, and a fair number of clerical personnel for 'the factory', involving transaction processing. It is with respect to these crucial aspects that research is almost completely lacking. Even at the risk of walking on thin ice, we would suggest that Japanese clerical productivity is lagging behind Japanese factory productivity. This is clear to anyone who has ever spent time in a Japanese office and has looked into a Japanese manufacturing plant.[14]

By the same token, Japanese financial institutions have, in our view, great strength, stemming from a broad cadre of middle managers whose compensation, by international standards, is modest. They are recruited from the top universities, having performed best in the traditional Japanese education system and tending to be also the most conservative segment of their cohorts. They are dedicated and broadly trained. This group of employees is one of the distinct sources of strengths of Japanese financial institutions – but also one of their weaknesses.

Where questions about the strength of Japanese financial institutions outside Japan emerge is in their ability to compete successfully in the new capital markets products, beginning with mergers and acquisitions to the trading in securities and, particularly, the derivative products, for example, option products and swaps. In this respect, Japanese institutions seem to suffer from two handicaps:

1. To maintain a structure that puts great emphasis on monetary incentives and a star system where people are richly rewarded on a short-term performance basis goes counter to traditional Japanese personnel policies.
2. While foreign talent can be bought, the integration of this kind of professional employee into a Japanese structure that is different in terms of a culture and language is very difficult to manage.

Over the long run, the costs of maintaining such a structure promise to be excessive, as the relationship between turnover, quality and the concomitant costs will not add up to the revenues required. In our view this is the Achilles' heel of Japanese financial institutions.

However we make this statement with considerable trepidation and humility, as Japanese institutions have proved to be adaptable in the past. It is not yet clear to what extent the new products can stand by themselves and to what extent they are linked to other aspects of business, such as the availability of risk capital, global communication and information capabilities, and so on, which will be sufficient to overcome a handicap in one dimension of what is really a multidimensional problem.

FUTURE RESEARCH AGENDA

Our discussion now turns to the research agenda. Much needs to be done to gain a better understanding of the sources of competitiveness of Japanese banks world-wide.

A logical starting-point would be to expand and improve on existing data for measuring 'success' in the financial service industry. There are considerable measurement problems. Footings are not a very good indicator. In fact, quite to the contrary, as big footings suggest big balance sheets, which in today's market is not where the value-added in the financial service industry is found. Big footings are typical for low margin businesses where people live 'on other people's deposits rather than their wits', to quote a statement that has been made in the UK market in a slightly different context, but which would be applicable here. Big footings are, in other words, representative of the 'stuffees' of the international market-place, rather than the value-added business of origination, packaging and trading.

A second major research concern is to build a data bank that would allow for a breakdown of banks' assets by domestic banking activities and international banking activities. For a start, effort should be focused on collecting data for banks of the major industrialised countries, such as the United States, Japan, Germany, France and the United Kingdom.

Further, we need refined theories explaining international banking activities. Preliminary work cited earlier would serve as a useful foundation on which to build. Special attention needs to be given to an explanation as to how banks can exploit their competitive advantage in their expansion abroad and to what extent they must alter it as they expand.

The next research agenda is to construct econometric models relating banks' asset growth with salient economic variables. This will, it is hoped, enable us meaningfully to identify the key determinants of banks' asset growth. Our own and Dohner and Terrell's (1988) work in this area will serve as a good starting-point.

The fourth research agenda that we have identified centres on the need to understand better the competitive advantage of banks in relation to their international competitors. Courtadon's (1985) work on 'The Competitive Structure of the Eurobond Underwriting Industry' can be extended and/or modified to address our concern. In particular, we would like to document evidence showing to what extent financial institutions are capable of capturing business where there is no national affiliation between investors/depositors and borrowers/ issuers.

Last, but not least, there is a need systematically to identify the role of human capital as a strategic resource in the performance of banks internationally. In this regard, we foresee the need to employ research methods from a number of fields outside finance and economics.

Do Japanese institutions have systematic weaknesses in their personnel practices as they apply to the global market-place? (Japanese banks' personnel practices may well be very good for a relatively protected, static domestic market-place.) In particular, can apparent difficulties of integration of *gaijin* professionals be overcome?

As the financial service industry has moved toward increased specialisation, the rotation policy of Japanese institutions may not be conducive to creating the specialists that this complex, high technology business requires. While it does inspire loyalty in people, allowing the surplus value to be captured by the employing institutions, it definitely has disadvantages. This is not to say that the alternative, namely to attract high-powered specialists at 'exorbitant' salaries, is not without problems. History has provided many examples where the company's assets can and do 'walk out of the door'. The issue of an appropriate personnel policy for multinational financial institutions is a fascinating and interesting question. Indeed, it appears to be one of the key competitive dimensions of a service business that deals basically in homogeneous commodities, where the ability to differentiate depends very much on people and their interaction with the organisation as determined by management. While time will tell how well Japanese financial institutions perform in this game over the longer run, many people will not have sufficient time to await the outcome.

Appendix

Table 5A.1 Ranking of top 50 banks in the world (1986)

Rank 86	85	Bank and head office	Assets less contra accounts	Total deposits	Capital and reserves	Pre-tax profits	Pre-tax on assets (%)	profits on capital (%)	Capital assets ratio (%)	Net interest on assets (%)
1	2	Dai-Ichi Kangyo Bank	240 742	186 032	5 825	991	0.43	17.98	2.39	0.22
		Tokyo	8.1	6.6	8.1	9.1	0.44	18.04	2.38	—
2	3	Fuji Bank	213 471	167 355	6 165	1 095	0.53	18.51	2.89	—
		Tokyo	6.3	8.4	8.8	11.6	0.51	18.05	2.82	—
3	4	Sumitomo Bank	206 120	165 305	6 074	1 249	0.63	21.68	2.95	—
		Osaka	7.8	8.1	11.6	16.4	0.58	20.77	2.85	—
4	5	Mitsubishi Bank	204 794	159 441	6 117	976	0.50	16.93	2.99	—
		Tokyo	9.0	10.2	12.9	12.9	0.47	16.54	2.88	—
5	7									
		Osaka	10.7	9.5	6.8	10.9	0.52	19.29	2.70	—
6	1	Citicorp	191 355	114 689	9 060	1 700	0.95	20.21	4.73	3.42
		New York	14.4	9.3	16.7	-0.9	1.11	24.18	4.64	3.51
7	11	Norinchukin Bank	162 353	146 192	762	298	—	—	0.47	—
		Tokyo	7.6	9.8	6.5	-6.2	—	—	0.47	—
8	13	Industrial Bank Japan	161 617	138 091	4 531	888	0.58	20.51	2.80	1.87
		Tokyo	11.3	9.3	9.8	62.5	0.40	15.10	2.84	1.98
9	8	Crédit Agricole	154 407	131 712	6 725	529	0.36	8.19	4.36	3.03
		Paris	8.0	7.8	8.6	7.8	0.35	8.29	4.33	—
10	6	Banque Nationale de Paris	141 871	120 292	4 471	772	0.54	21.07	3.15	2.45
		Paris	0.1	2.8	56.4	31.7	0.41	21.88	2.02	2.37
11	17	Tokai Bank	138 458	113 810	3 605	528	0.40	15.08	2.60	—
		Nagoya	8.4	9.3	6.3	2.1	0.41	16.03	2.65	—
12	10	Crédit Lyonnais	132 076	113 780	2 518	629	0.48	30.46	1.91	2.46
		Paris	1.2	2.0	56.5	23.1	0.39	32.55	1.23	2.28

Table 5A.1   Ranking of top 50 banks in the world (1986)

Rank 86 85	Bank and head office	Assets less contra accounts	Total deposits	Capital and reserves	Pre-tax profits	Pre-tax on assets (%)	profits on capital (%)	Capital assets ratio (%)	Net interest on assets (%)
13 18	Mitsui Bank Tokyo	132 043 / 5.6	104 858 / 4.3	3 325 / 12.7	633 / 37.1	0.49 / 0.38	20.17 / 16.19	2.52 / 2.36	— / —
14 15	Deutsche Bank Frankfurt	131 808 / 8.5	81 356 / 6.8	5 175 / 6.9	1 387 / 5.4	1.10 / 1.09	27.70 / 29.90	3.93 / 3.99	2.80 / 2.44
15 21	Mitsubishi Trust & Banking Tokyo	127 372 / 11.9	111 065 / 11.0	2 822 / 20.1	719 / 79.6	0.60 / 0.38	27.82 / 17.81	2.22 / 2.06	— / —
16 22	Sumitomo Trust & Banking Osaka	125 157 / 11.9	110 671 / 11.8	2 870 / 19.1	734 / 75.9	0.62 / 0.41	27.80 / 18.22	2.29 / 2.15	— / —
17 12	National Westminster Bank London	122 862 / 14.8	107 285 / 12.4	6 808 / 55.4	1 491 / 25.7	1.30 / 1.12	26.65 / 28.68	5.54 / 4.09	2.86 / 2.66
18 16	Barclays London	116 380 / 21.1	96 275 / 18.5	5 483 / 12.5	1 319 / 4.8	1.24 / 1.29	25.47 / 28.91	4.71 / 5.07	3.43 / 3.55
19 36	Mitsui Trust & Banking Tokyo	116 056 / 12.8	99 399 / 13.4	2 467 / 19.9	510 / 92.7	0.47 / 0.27	22.56 / 13.17	2.13 / 2.00	5 859 / 6.5
20 14	Société Générale Paris	116 013 / 3.2	3 367 / 3.7	3 367 / 32.0	624 / 42.3	0.55 / 0.36	21.08 / 20.37	2.90 / 2.27	3.53 / 3.08
21 23	Long-Term Credit Bank of Japan Tokyo	115 529 / 3.7	99 124 / 3.3	2 435 / 6.4	520 / 27.1	0.46 / 0.38	22.03 / 18.34	2.11 / 2.05	0.76 / 0.65
22 24	Bank of Tokyo Tokyo	111 996 / 1.4	87 285 / -0.7	3 695 / 53.7	620 / 9.1	0.56 / 0.53	20.32 / 22.89	3.30 / 2.18	1.12 / 1.06
23 34	Daiwa Bank Osaka	102 835 / 8.9	88 724 / 8.8	2 290 / 7.0	304 / -35.3	0.31 / 0.53	13.74 / 24.57	2.23 / 2.27	— / —
24 9	Bank America Corp San Francisco	102 204 / -10.9	82 205 / -12.7	4 038 / -11.2	-350 / 58.0	-0.32 / -0.37	-8.15 / -0.83	3.39 / 3.96	3.50 / 3.54
25 36	Yasuda Trust & Banking Tokyo	101 342 / 14.4	86 318 / 14.5	1 900 / 14.0	395 / 83.5	0.42 / 0.26	22.14 / 13.91	1.87 / 1.88	— / —

26	25	Dresdner Bank Frankfurt	101 185	62 161	3 276	550	0.55	18.28	3.24	2.09
			4.4	1.8	19.7	11.9	0.53	19.16	2.82	2.05
27	26	Taiyo Kobe Bank Kobe	95 663	75 924	1 670	251	0.28	16.22	1.75	5.91
			11.2	8.7	17.6	-10.0	0.33	19.85	1.65	6.68
28	33	Union Bank of Switzerland Zurich	93 728	81 079	5 352	700	0.78	13.56	5.71	1.07
			9.1	10.2	7.8	8.9	0.77	14.16	5.78	1.10
29	29	Compagnie Financière de Paribas Paris	93 240	60 329	2 072	779	0.87	44.91	2.22	1.87
			9.2	7.9	48.2	11.3	0.83	34.09	1.64	1.93
30	19	Chase Manhattan Corp New York	92 147	66 003	4 944	844	0.95	17.95	5.37	3.39
			8.6	7.6	10.9	-6.0	1.08	21.16	5.25	3.30
31	30	Hong Kong and Shanghai Bank Hong Kong	90 771	81 837	3 403	—	—	—	3.75	—
			31.6	32.5	21.2	—	—	—	4.07	—
32	37	Swiss Bank Corp Basle	84 896	65 353	5 220	579	0.71	11.84	6.15	0.36
			7.7	6.6	14.7	6.0	0.72	13.33	5.77	0.24
33	54	Tokyo Trust and Banking Tokyo	81 889	71 862	1 501	344	0.46	24.44	1.83	—
			20.9	17.8	14.2	88.3	0.30	14.91	1.94	—
34	20	Midland Bank London	78 397	67 948	2 980	640	0.78	22.44	3.80	3.00
			-8.4	-12.2	9.4	23.6	0.59	19.88	3.18	2.98
35	49	Nippon Credit Bank Tokyo	78 261	69 135	1 514	276	0.37	18.77	1.93	0.67
			11.1	13.1	5.9	-2.0	0.42	20.15	2.03	0.55
36	38	Westdeutsche Landesbank Girozentrale Dusseldorf	76 243	70 846	2 123	164	0.22	7.79	2.78	1.25
			4.3	4.1	2.2	94.6	0.12	4.06	2.84	1.25
37	42	Commerzbank Frankfurt	75 430	50 695	2 509	373	0.51	16.69	3.33	1.95
			8.0	7.6	27.9	10.2	0.51	18.98	2.81	2.00
38	31	J.P. Morgan New York	74 643	42 960	5 130	1 166	1.64	24.49	6.87	2.19
			10.4	7.8	16.8	27.3	1.42	22.54	6.50	2.20
39	51	Kyowa Bank Tokyo	73 338	58 797	1 401	323	0.46	24.26	1.91	1.24
			8.0	6.6	11.2	15.5	0.44	22.84	1.85	1.36
40	27	Manufacturers Hanover Corp New York	72 918	45 544	3 766	443	0.60	12.13	5.16	2.76
			-1.9	-1.5	6.2	-25.8	0.81	17.48	4.77	2.87

Table 5A.1 Ranking of top 50 banks in the world (1986)

Rank 86	85	Bank and head office	Assets less contra accounts	Total deposits	Capital and reserves	Pre-tax profits	Pre-tax on assets (%)	profits on capital (%)	Capital assets ratio (%)	Net interest on assets (%)
41	39	Banca Nazionale del Lavoro	72 695	38 567	3 916	373	0.52	10.29	5.39	1.81
		Rome	2.5	−33.8	17.5	4.6	0.52	11.85	4.70	1.54
42	45	Bayerische Vereinsbank	72 125	67 547	1 763	331	0.47	20.19	2.44	1.36
		Munich	5.8	5.6	16.4	19.8	0.42	19.56	2.22	1.39
43	72	Shoko Chukin Bank	71 538	64 571	1 599	70	0.10	4.54	2.24	2.18
		Tokyo	12.0	11.9	7.8	18.9	0.10	4.12	2.32	2.35
44	34	Lloyds Bank	70 523	62 852	4 049	1 032	1.53	27.73	5.74	3.60
		London	9.2	8.6	19.3	24.8	1.28	25.77	5.25	3.49
45	32	Royal Bank of Canada	67 743	60 609	3 354	480	0.72	15.10	4.95	2.96
		Montreal	2.5	0.8	11.9	−3.4	0.78	17.45	4.54	2.77
46	44	Banco do Brasil	67 017	26 459	5 447	317	0.60	7.46	8.13	5.20
		Brasilia	70.2	71.6	78.8	−69.9	4.29	54.40	7.74	8.06
47	48	Algemene Bank Nederland	66 908	58 571	2 346	358	0.54	16.92	3.51	1.87
		Amsterdam	3.1	0.5	24.3	7.2	0.51	18.18	2.91	1.88
48	61	Crédit Suisse	63 900	56 812	3 759	469	0.79	13.25	5.88	0.49
		Zurich	17.0	17.6	13.4	10.6	0.80	13.13	6.07	0.58
49	55	Rabobank	63 727	60 203	3 523	417	0.67	12.36	5.53	2.67
		Utrecht	6.0	5.8	9.6	0.2	0.70	13.55	5.35	2.70
50	50	Amsterdam-Rotterdam Bank	63 438	58 343	2 141	269	0.43	13.71	3.37	1.77
		Amsterdam	3.9	4.1	19.9	17.3	0.39	13.97	2.92	1.83

Notes: Figures on first line in $ million (columns 1–4) or percentages (columns 5–8); second line shows percentage growth in local currency in past 12 months (columns 1–4) or previous year's ratios (columns 5–8).

Source: *The Banker*, July 1987, p. 115.

Table 5A.2   Ranking of top 35 banks by capital reserve, capital assets ratio and deposits (1986)

	Capital and reserves	$m	Capital–assets ratio	%	Deposits	$m
1	Citicorp	9 060	Oversea-Chinese	14.26	Dai-Ichi Kangyo	186 932
2	National Westminster	6 808	Provincia de Buenos Aires	14.05	Fuji Bank	167 355
3	Crédit Agricole	6 725	DBS Bank	12.73	Sumitomo Bank	165 305
4	Fuji Bank	6 165	Riyad Bank	12.20	Mitsubishi Bank	159 441
5	Mitsubishi Bank	6 117	United Overseas Bank	11.91	Sanwa Bank	152 608
6	Sumitomo Bank	6 074	National Bank of Dubai	11.90	Norinchukin Bank	146 192
7	Dai-Ichi Kangyo	5 725	Dela Nacion Argentina	11.56	Industrial Bank of Japan	138 091
8	Barclays	5 483	TSB Group	11.49	Crédit Agricole	134 712
9	Banco do Brasil	5 447	Brasileiro de Descontos	11.18	Banque Nationale de Paris	120 292
10	Union Bank of Switzerland	5 352	Caja de Madrid	10.49	Citicorp	114 689
11	Swiss Bank Corp	5 220	Jyske Bank	10.37	Tokai Bank	113 810
12	Deutsche Bank	5 175	Saudi American Bank	10.37	Crédit Lyonnais	113 780
13	J. P. Morgan	5 130	Banque du Caire	9.84	Mitsubishi Trust	111 065
14	Sanwa Bank	5 011	National Bank of Abu Dhabi	9.53	Sumitomo Trust	110 671
15	Chase Manhattan	4 944	Banco di Sardegna	9.50	National Westminster	107 285
16	Industrial Bank of Japan	4 531	Banco Itau	9.50	Mitsui Bank	104 858
17	Banque Nationale de Paris	4 471	Banque Nationale d'Algérie	9.40	Mitsui Trust	99 399
18	Lloyds	4 049	Gulf International	9.32	Long-Term Credit Bank	99 124
19	Bank America	4 039	Alahli Bank of Kuwait	9.24	Société Générale	97 834
20	Bank of China	3 976	First Alabama	8.81	Barclays	96 275
21	Banca Nazionale del Lavoro	3 916	Industrial Devpt of India	8.78	Daiwa	88 724
22	Manufacturers Hanover	3 766	Schroders	8.70	Bank of Tokyo	87 285
23	Crédit Suisse	3 759	Arab Banking	8.65	Yasuda Trust	86 318
24	Bank of Tokyo	3 695	Gulf Bank	8.57	Bank America	82 205
25	Tokai Bank	3 605	Commercial Bank of Kuwait	8.13	Hongkong and Shanghai	81 837

Table 5A.2   Ranking of top 35 banks by capital reserve, capital assets ratio and deposits (1986)

Capital and reserves		$m	Capital–assets ratio	%	Deposits	$m
26	Rabobank	3 523	Banco do Brasil	8.13	Deutsche Bank	81 356
27	Hongkong and Shanghai	3 403	Banco del Estado de Chile	8.09	Union Bank of Switzerland	81 079
28	Société Générale	3 367	Banco Espanol de Credito	8.07	Taiyo Kobe Bank	75 924
29	Royal Bank of Canada	3 354	First Pennsylvania	7.91	Toyo Trust	71 862
30	Mitsui Bank	3 325	Unibanco	7.88	Westdeutsche Landesbank	70 846
31	Dresdner Bank	3 276	Den Danske Bank	7.68	Nippon Credit Bank	69 135
32	Cariplo	3 150	S. G. Warburg	7.66	Midland	67 948
33	Monte del Paschi di Siena	3 146	Ameritrust	7.50	Bayerische Vereinsbank	67 547
34	Chemical New York	3 120	First Virginia	7.47	Chase Manhattan	66 003
35	Midland Bank	2 980	First National Cincinnati	7.42	Swiss Bank Corp	65 353

Source: The Banker, July 1987, p. 153.

Table 5A.3 Ranking of top 35 banks by profitability (1986)

Pre-tax profits	$m	Pre-tax profits on assets	%	Net interest income on assets	%
1 Citicorp	1 700	Provincia de Buenos Aires	1.99	Provincia de Buenos Aires	36.23
2 National Westminster	1 191	Bancomer	3.57	Banco de Nacion Argentina	21.98
3 Deutsche Bank	1 387	Brasileiro de Descontos	3.50	Unibanco	16.12
4 Barclays	1 319	Extérieur d'Algérie	3.31	Canara	9.19
5 Sumitomo	1 219	Banco Itan	3.25	Banco Real	8.91
6 J. P. Morgan	1 166	Banamex	3.09	Bank of Baroda	8.81
7 Fuji	1 095	Ratidain	2.99	Central Bank of India	8.79
8 Lloyds	1 032	Espanal de Credito	2.82	Estado de Sao Paulo	7.22
9 Dai Ichi Kangyo	991	Vojvodjanska	2.78	Banco Itau	6.99
10 Mitsubishi	976	Cassa di Verona	2.55	Sovae	6.68
11 Sanwa	952	Nationale d'Algérie	2.47	Ljubljanska Banka	6.67
12 Rafidain	933	Sovae	2.37	Chugoku Bank	6.10
13 Industrial Bank of Japan	888	Crédit Populaire d'Algérie	2.34	Banco de Chile	6.08
14 Chase Manhattan	844	Banca Serlin	2.29	Taiyo Kobe	5.94
15 Bank of China	840	Credito Romagnola	2.22	Bank of Fukuoka	5.90
16 Cariplo	790	Cassa in Bologna	2.18	Bank of New Zealand	5.86
17 Paribas	779	Cassa di Torino	2.18	Banco de Sabadell	5.75
18 Istituto San Paolo	777	Frankfurter Sparkasse	2.17	Bancomer	5.73
19 BNP	772	Svenska Handelsbanken	2.16	Chiba Kogyo	5.67
20 Aumiromo Trust & Banking	734	S. E. Banken	2.16	Citizens National	5.67
21 Mitsubishi Trust & Banking	719	Popular Espanol	2.11	Popular Espanol	5.45
22 Union Bank of Switzerland	700	Banco Real	2.07	Caja de Madrid	5.44
23 Banco Espanol de Credito	687	Banespa	1.96	Bank of Hiroshima	5.36
24 Midland	640	Cassa di Padova	1.92	Fidelcor	5.31
25 Mitsui	633	National Bank of Dubai	1.92	Banco do Brasil	5.20

Table 5A.3   Ranking of top 35 banks by profitability (1986)

Pre-tax profits		$m	Pre-tax profits on assets	%	Net interest income on assets	%
26	Crédit Lyonnais	629	Central Bancorp	1.87	TSB Group	5.20
27	Société Générale	624	First Virginia	1.87	Banco de Santander	5.05
28	Bank of Tokyo	620	Banca Popolare di Novara	1.86	L'Afrique Occidentale	4.97
29	S. E. Banken	580	First American Corp	1.85	Banco de Vizcaya	4.88
30	Swiss Bank Corp	579	Unibanco	1.81	Fédérative du Crédit	4.81
31	Dresdner	550	Estado de Chile	1.81	First Virginia	4.74
32	Crédit Agricole	529	Morgan Grenfell	1.80	CTC Group	4.74
33	Tokai	528	Fleet Financial	1.79	Compagnie Bancaire	4.68
34	Bankers Trust	520	United Bank for Africa	1.79	United Bank for Africa	4.63
35	Long-Term Credit Bank	520	Bank of New Zealand	1.76	Caja Zaragoza	4.59

Source: *The Banker*, July 1987, p. 159.

Date (year and quarter)	US capital flow	Japanese capital flow	Gross external assets US banks	Gross external assets Japanese banks
1977 1	−3.93	−0.29	77.40	22.00
1977 2	−1.51	−1.90	81.90	19.20
1977 3	−0.41	−2.75	83.70	19.40
1977 4	−9.93	−0.13	92.60	21.70
1978 1	−12.34	1.98	98.80	23.40
1978 2	0.34	−6.31	101.50	25.80
1978 3	0.68	−3.13	107.40	30.60
1978 4	−19.21	−0.31	119.20	33.70
1979 1	3.81	−4.45	110.00	36.60
1979 2	−0.30	−3.77	117.70	37.10
1979 3	−8.79	3.35	129.90	45.00
1979 4	−12.30	−2.36	136.30	45.50
1980 1	3.73	5.35	134.60	49.80
1980 2	−24.08	9.47	152.60	51.30
1980 3	−12.89	2.12	164.80	60.10
1980 4	−6.16	1.94	176.80	65.70
1981 1	−15.85	2.86	183.70	74.80
1981 2	−4.37	0.14	201.60	70.30
1981 3	5.56	−3.93	215.30	82.40
1981 4	−16.44	−0.63	256.30	84.60
1982 1	−2.61	−2.54	283.30	90.40
1982 2	−8.69	−5.63	322.10	81.30
1982 3	−10.56	−5.98	346.10	90.40
1982 4	−9.92	−1.37	363.40	90.90
1983 1	−11.52	−2.54	384.50	99.30
1983 2	12.83	−5.96	383.40	95.80
1983 3	12.09	−7.06	386.50	108.40
1983 4	11.89	−6.14	396.60	109.10
1984 1	21.23	−4.28	394.00	121.10
1984 2	22.81	−8.82	417.20	115.10
1984 3	20.61	−10.59	403.00	124.10
1984 4	15.08	−12.87	409.60	126.90
1985 1	24.69	−8.31	411.60	139.60
1985 2	15.37	−14.19	411.50	146.00
1985 3	25.88	−12.98	406.20	166.00
1985 4	38.44	−18.05	417.80	194.60
1986 1	20.49	−13.23	414.40	225.10
1986 2	9.18	−20.01	425.40	244.60
1986 3	28.79	−19.63	441.20	292.70
1986 4	31.04	−20.61	471.20	345.30
1987 1	26.45	−10.23	452.00	400.40
1987 2	11.04	−12.65	469.80	441.60
1987 3	47.83	−17.55	488.10	508.80
1987 4	−5.07	−3.92	508.90	576.90

Note: 1. In billions of US dollars.

Sources: Capital flows: sum of direct investment, portfolio investment-nie, other long-term capital-nie and other short-term capital: *International Financial Statistics*, various issues, IMF. Gross External Assets: *International Banking Developments*, various issues, *Bank for International Settlements*.

Notes

+ Gautham Nookala and Pheng-Lui Chng provided research assistance. Dr K. Ito provided valuable comments. The author benefited considerably from discussions with Dr A. Tschoegl, Swiss Bank Corporation International, Tokyo.

1. Bank Lending During First Half 1987 is Triple the Year-Earlier Level', *IMF Survey*, 30 November 1987.
2. *Midland Bank Review*, 'The World's Largest Creditor – How Long Can Japan's Surplus Last?', Summer 1987, p. 16.
3. For a thorough review of the experience of Japanese manufacturing firms in the United States see: Chalmers Johnson, 'Japanese-Style Management in America', *California Management Review*, Summer 1988, pp. 34–45.
4. Richard W. Wright and Gunter A. Pauli, *The Second Wave: Japan's Global Assault of Financial Services* (New York: St. Martin's Press, 1987).
5. Robert Z. Aliber, 'International Banking: A Survey', *Journal of Money, Credit, and Banking*, vol. 16, no. 4, November 1984, part 2, p. 661.
6. Gunter Dufey and Ian H. Giddy, *International Money Market*, ch. 1 (Englewood Cliffs, NJ: Prentice-Hall, 1978); and Aliber, 'International Banking', p. 662.
7. It is not clear, for purposes of an analysis of global competition in the financial service industry, what the appropriate competitive tiering is. It probably requires in-depth analysis of various submarkets.
8. Robert S. Dohner and Henry S. Terrell, 'The Determinants of the Growth of Multinational Banking Organizations: 1972–86', *International Finance Discussion Papers*, Number 326 (Board of Governors of the Federal Reserve System, June 1988).
9. See ibid.
10. Adrian E. Tschoegl, 'Foreign Direct Investment in Banking in California', *Working Paper 1058–79* (Cambridge, Mass.: MIT, March 1979).
11. Eric Hill, 'Banker's Acceptances', in T. Q. Cook and T. D. Rowe (eds) *Instruments of the Money Market*, 6th edn (Federal Reserve Bank of Richmond, 1986).
12. Gunter Dufey and Ian H. Giddy, 'Eurocurrency Deposit Risk', *Journal of Banking and Finance* 8, 1984, pp. 567–89.
13. George Volta, Vice Chairman, Bankers Trust, address at the Pacific Rim Bankers Seminar, Seattle, 1 September 1988. See also Ingo Walter, *Global Competition in Financial Services: Market Structure, Protection, and Trade Liberalization* (Cambridge, Mass.: Ballinger Publishing Company, 1988) especially ch. 4.
14. Ikujiro Nonaka, 'Japanese Methodology of Knowledge Creation and Production System', *Organizational Science*, vol. 22, no. 1, Spring 1988, pp. 21–9.

References

Aliber, Robert Z. (1984) 'International Banking; A Survey', *Journal of Money, Credit, and Banking*, vol. 16, no. 4, November, pt 2, pp. 661–78.

Aliber, Robert Z. (1987) 'Financial Innovation and the Boundaries of Banking', *Managerial and Decision Economics*, vol. 8, pp. 67–73.

Courtadon, Carol L. (1985) 'The Competitive Structure of the Eurobond Underwriting Industry', *Monograph Series in Finance and Economics 1985–1* (Salomon Brothers Center for the Study of Financial Institutions, New York University, 1985).

DeCecco, Marcello (ed.) (1987) *Changing Money: Financial Innovation in Developed Countries* (Oxford: Basil Blackwell, in co-operation with the European University Institute, Florence).

Dohner, Robert S. and Henry S. Terrell (1988) 'The Determinants of the Growth of Multinational Banking Organizations: 1972–86', International Finance Discussion Papers, no. 326, Board of Governors of the Federal Reserve System, June.

Dufey, Gunter and Ian H. Giddy (1978) *The International Money Market* (Englewood Cliffs, NJ: Prentice-Hall).

Dufey, Gunter and Ian H. Giddy (1984) 'Eurocurrency Deposit Risk', *Journal of Banking and Finance* 8, pp. 567–89.

Dufey, Gunter and Adrian E. Tschoegl (1986) 'International Competition in the Services Industries: Institutional and Structural Characteristics of Financial Services – With Specific Reference to Banking', a research report prepared for the Office of Technology Assessment, US Congress.

The Economist, 'A Survey of the City of London', 25 June 1988.

The Economist, 'Eurobonds Out of Warranty', 16 July 1988, p. 73.

Goldberg, Lawrence G. and Denise Johnson (1987) 'The Determinants of U.S. Banking Activity Abroad', International Business and Banking Discussion Paper Series, 87–6, International Business & Banking Institute, University of Miami, October.

Hanley, Thomas H., John D. Leonard, Carla A. D'Arista and Dina I. Oddis (1987) 'European Bank Equity Conference: The Competitive Position of U.S. Multinational Banks in a Global Marketplace', Salomon Brothers Inc. Stock Research, November.

Hill, Eric (1986) 'Bankers' Acceptances', in T. Q. Cook and T. D. Rowe (eds), *Instruments of the Money Market*, 6th edn (Federal Reserve Bank of Richmond).

IMF Survey (1987) 'Bank Lending During First Half of 1987 is Triple the Year-Earlier Level', 30 Nov., pp. 353, 360–1.

International Financial Review (1987) 'Japan's Securities Houses', issue 703, 12 December, pp. 000–000.

International Financial Review (1988) 'Japan's Investment', issue 716, 19 March, pp. 000–000.

Iwami, Toru (1988) 'Internationalization of Japanese Banking; Factors Affecting its Rapid Growth', discussion paper, Research Institute for the Japanese Economy, University of Tokyo, January.

166 *Comment*

Jeffries, Francis M. (1988) 'Japanese Foreign Direct Investment in U.S. Banking and Financial Services' (Poolesville, MD: Jeffries & Associates, Inc.).

Johnson, Chalmers (1988) 'Japanese-Style Management in America', *California Management Review*, Summer, pp. 34–45.

Jones, Rosamund and Matthew Barrett (1988) 'The Best of Times, The Worst of Times', *Euromoney*, Annual Financing Report, March.

Midland Bank Review (1987) 'The World's Largest Creditor. How Long Can Japan's Surplus Last?', Summer, pp. 16–23.

Nonaka, Ikujiro (1988) 'Japanese Methodology of Knowledge Creation and Production System', *Organizational Science*, vol. 22, no. 1, Spring, pp. 21–9.

Rugman, Alan M. (1987) 'Multinationals and Trade in Services: A Transaction Cost Approach', *Weltwirtschaftliches Archiv – Review of World Economics*, vol. 123, no. 4, pp. 651–67.

Tschoegl, Adrian E. (1979) 'Foreign Direct Investment in Banking in California', working paper 1058–79 (Cambridge, Mass.: MIT, March).

Tschoegl, Adrian E. (1988) 'Foreign Banks in Japan', *Bank of Japan Monetary and Economic Studies*, vol. 6, no. 1, May, pp. 93–118.

Walter, Ingo (1988) *Global Competition in Financial Services: Market Structure, Protection, and Trade Liberalization* (Cambridge, Mass.: Ballinger Publishing Company).

Woodworth, Richard (1988) 'An Analysis of Japanese International Investment Patterns: Part I', *Currency & Bond Market Trends*, vol. 4, no. 25, Merrill Lynch Capital Markets, 1 July.

Wright, Richard W. and Gunter A. Pauli (1987) *The Second Wave: Japan's Global Assault on Financial Services* (New York: St. Martin's Press).

COMMENT

Robert Z. Aliber

The Dufey paper is in three parts. The first part seeks to answer whether Japanese bank assets have grown more rapidly than the assets of banks headquartered in other countries, or whether instead the growth in Japanese bank assets in US dollars in an artifact of the appreciation of the yen. The analysis largely involves measuring the impact of the changes in the exchange rates on the size of banks headquartered in different countries. The second part seeks to explain why the overseas presence of Japanese banks increased at such a rapid rate in the 1980s. Finally, there are some brief comments on future research in the concluding section.

To understand the growth in the share of Japanese banks in the world market for deposits and loans, a model that incorporates four or five different phenomena is needed. The first phenomenon to be explained is the rapid growth in the external assets of Japanese banks. Moreover the external assets of all Japanese banks have increased at about the same rate, as if they were a drum and bugle corps. The question here is whether there is a director to the drum and bugle corps, or whether each bank looks over its shoulders and emulates the other banks.

The third factor to be explained is the profitability – or lack thereof – associated with the external expansion of Japanese firms. The argument implicit in low profitability on external assets is that initially Japanese firms capture market share abroad by cutting price – a practice that conforms with the observation that firms that produce an unbranded commodity capture market share by offering it to customers at a lower price than that of their competitors. If this price-cutting phenomenon is generalised, the conclusion is that these firms are less profitable than the cartels that previously supported the price, or else the price-cutters have a compensating advantage.

The fourth factor requiring explanation is that the market valuation of individual Japanese banks is very high. Consider the relation of market value to book value of banks headquartered in different countries. The market value of *any one* bank in the top group of Japanese banks is greater than the *sum* of the market value of the eight largest British banks. The ratios of market to book value for Japanese banks are between six to one and twelve to one (the Bank of Tokyo has a ratio of market to book value of six to one and the Industrial Bank of Japan has a ratio of market value to book value of twelve to one). The comparable ratios for British banks are less than unity. A fifth element is that the cost of capital to Japanese firms in general and Japanese banks in particular is substantially less than the cost of capital to non-Japanese banks.

We need a theory that explains the behaviour of Japanese banks and their rapid external penetration in the 1980s. This theory should provide insights into lock-step behaviour, the low profitability on the new foreign business, the high market valuation of individual institutions and the low cost of capital of Japanese firms. Dufey ignores these financial phenomena, and follows the gravitational approach to the foreign expansion of banks. Japanese banks follow their customers abroad.

The alternative explanation is that the penetration of Japanese banks abroad and the penetration of Japanese firms abroad is that these firms have a cost-of-capital advantage. And this argument explains why

Japanese capital is going abroad, namely that interest rates on bonds and anticipated yields on equities in the United States are substantially higher than interest rates on bonds and anticipated yields on equities in Japan. The follow-the-leader behaviour of the gravitational pull hypothesis, the same economic forces that explain Japanese investment in real estate in Los Angeles, hotels in New York and tyre firms in Ohio, explains the growing presence of Japanese banks: with price–earnings ratios of between 20 and 30 to one in Japan compared to price–earnings ratios in the United States one-half that size, it becomes advantageous to the maintenance of the price of the shares of Japanese firms trading on the Tokyo Stock Exchange to incorporate foreign earnings with their own earnings. Consider Bridgestone Tire's purchase of Firestone. Bridgestone, a firm with a price–earnings ratio of 50 to one, purchases Firestone, a firm with a price–earnings ratio of 10 to one. This transaction initially reduces the price–earnings ratio of Bridgestone; if investors then bid up the price of Bridgestone shares, Bridgestone shareholders do quite nicely.

The rapid Japanese expansion in terms of foreign ownership is a 1980s phenomenon. The timing of this expansion is more or less congruent with a significant reduction in the costs of capital of Japanese firms.

The question of how rapidly Japanese financial firms will continue to expand in the foreign markets can be answered only after determining how long there will be a significant disequilibrium in interest rates and equity prices between Tokyo and foreign financial centres.

COMMENT

Dietmar K. R. Klein

The paper by Professor Dufey provides us with a very good basis for a discussion on the role of Japanese financial institutions abroad. In fact, I do not have any serious or essential objections to the findings and tentative conclusions drawn from the evidence, but I may offer a few complementary observations.

In the introductory section the structure of the paper is laid out and the underlying issue defined, namely to come to a clearer perception about the determinants of the international expansion of the Japanese financial service industry. In terms of *descriptive statistics*, Table 5.1

provides an overview of total cross-border bank lending and deposit taking on the basis of IMF and BIS data, which are collected on a resident basis. One might add a table showing the changes in the relative positions of international financial centres. Even more relevant would be the presentation of data on international banking classified by the nationality of banks as collected and published from time to time by the Bank for International Settlements in Basle.

The second section mainly reviews the relative position of Japanese and US banks as reported in *The Banker*'s annual ranking of the top 500 banks world-wide. This is followed by a comparative analysis of the expansion of assets of the top ten banks of the five major countries. The main emphasis is to present a scheme to decompose the growth of assets expressed in dollars into real and nominal effects, but not yet to present an analysis of the factors influencing the international expansion of financial intermediaries. Apart from the impact of exchange rate movements, this topic is actually treated later, though with the special emphasis of identifying thereby the particular sources of competitive advantage which Japanese financial institutions enjoy abroad.

At any rate there seems to me too much emphasis on finding out to what extent the growth in assets expressed in US dollars (not the growth in US dollar assets!) of leading Japanese banks is as much due to the depreciation of the US dollar *vis-à-vis* the yen as it is to the growth in real assets of leading Japanese banks.

I think that, in the long run, there should not be much of an identification problem, because any inflation differential will be translated into exchange rate changes. One should only be careful about the choice of the beginning and the end of the time-span investigated. It is then of secondary importance whether one compares asset growth rates per annum in current dollar terms or in price-adjusted real dollar terms.

However, in the short to medium term, it is one of the main points of the paper that the impact of large exchange rate changes on deviations from the trend change in the purchasing power parity is highly significant. But then there is a complementary remark that the analysis should not just stop with the impact on recorded asset growth but rather be extended to the effect on capital adequacy. The own capital positions of Japanese as well as European banks have substantially improved in the last three years, owing to the exchange rate-related shortening of their balance sheets.

In the third section, we find a comprehensive and systematic discussion of the sets of factors influencing the international expansion of financial intermediaries in general and Japanese institutions in particular:

1. a set of macroeconomic determinants;
2. regulatory determinants; and
3. enterprise-specific, that is, microeconomic factors, such as risk capital, information technology and human resources.

I may be forgiven for pointing out that this topic was also systematically treated some time ago in the OECD study on 'The Internationalisation of Banking: The Policy Issues'. That monograph was written by Rinaldo Pecchioli, with the active assistance of official experts in the Committee on Financial Markets and its Experts Group on Banking. Here Professor Dufey tries – successfully I think – to answer the intriguing question of where to locate the specific competitive advantages which can explain why Japanese financial institutions as a group have fared so much better than other banks and securities houses.

Just two remarks concerning *regulatory* factors:

1. The fact that there have been domestic regulatory constraints and market rigidities in combination with free access to financial markets abroad has led not only to large cross-border flows in securities, but also to the internationalisation of banking operations denominated in yen as well as in US dollars. I think I should draw attention to the amazing fact that, although Japan is in a strong current account position, the gross inflow of funds, mainly through the Japanese banking system, has been bigger than the gross outflow via this system (the bulk of the outflow was brought about through portfolio transactions).
2. As to risk capital and capital adequacy rules, I do not concur with the sweeping statement, made by Professor Dufey, that the role of bank capital as a competitive weapon could be overstated owing to the implicit government guarantee behind large banking institutions from major industrialised countries. While it is quite likely that large banks with a systemic risk potential will somehow be saved from outright default, supervisory authorities are determined to raise the level of liable capital in order to limit the problem of 'moral hazard'. It is equally likely that, in the case of a looming default, shareholders will lose their share capital, board members will lose their jobs, and unprotected creditors such as other banks will lose their money.

Finally, let me emphasise the considerable change which has taken place in the international roles of Japanese banks in recent years by looking at the changes in the nationality structure of international banking, which is relevant to our topic. For this purpose we should not look at international banking data classified along geographical borderlines on the basis of resident/non-resident criteria. Instead, we ought to look at international bank assets of banks in seventeen countries reporting to the BIS according to their home countries. In this case the available BIS statistics include foreign currency claims on residents. Excluded are domestic currency claims on residents, which are usually by and large financed by domestic currency funds. Included are all international claims of banks and subsidiaries located in other countries inside the reporting area, though allocated according to the home country or nationality-of-lending-bank principle. In dollar terms, about half of total reported growth in 1986 as well as in 1987 was accounted for by Japanese banks. Less strong, but equally above the average, was the growth of international assets owned by European banks, in particular by French, Swiss, German and Italian banks. In contrast, international assets growth of US banks was quite modest.

As a result, the market share of Japanese banks in total international banking had reached more than one-third by the end of 1987. US banks which, in 1982, at the beginning of the international debt crisis in Latin America, still had a leading position in international banking, with a share of more than one-third of the world total, had fallen back to a share of about 15 per cent by the end of 1987. The change was even more dramatic if one tries to refine the figures somewhat – though this can only be done *grosso modo*. The statistical data on gross international banking claims are inflated by *intra*-bank group relations between headquarters and foreign branches and other affiliates or between foreign affiliates of the same banking group. Excluding them (not, however, truly interbank claims), the share of US banks by the end of 1987 had declined even further, to about 11 per cent, not very far ahead of the respective market shares of French banks (10 per cent), German banks (9 per cent), Swiss banks (about 8 to 9 per cent if one includes fiduciary assets) or British banks ($6\frac{1}{2}$ per cent).

It might also be mentioned that the US banks include in their reporting the international business of their branches in five major non-reporting offshore financial centres, whereas banks of other nationality or origin in these centres, especially Japanese banks, have to remain uncovered. This leaves a considerable statistical gap for Japanese banks operating especially through Hong Kong and Singapore, and doing business with other banks and non-banks.

Disregarding the domestic business denominated in local currencies outside does not provide a complete framework for the competitive strength of Japanese banks, and in any case the picture is incomplete in so far as the securities houses, which are statistically largely uncovered, are concerned. However it shows that, in international banking proper, the relative shift in market shares in favour of Japanese financial institutions has been much larger than can be shown merely by comparing complete balance-sheet data.

COMMENT

Hiroshi Nakaso

First of all, the paper is most valuable in its presentation of (a) recent developments in the relative positions of banks in major countries; (b) sources of competitive advantage for Japanese financial institutions abroad; and (c) future research agenda. Here, I would like to make three brief comments, each relating to the three respective points presented in the paper.

The first is with regard to the growth rate of Japanese banks' assets. As pointed out in the paper, during the late 1970s and through most of the 1980s, asset size of Japanese banks kept growing at a considerable rate. However there seems to have been at least some signs of slow-down recently in the pace of expansion. This is now being observed among Japanese banks in the London market and could perhaps be regarded as one of the basic and initial strategies adopted by Japanese banks to meet the international convergence of capital adequacy requirements.

Looking at the Japanese banks in London, it seems that the initial steps are reflected in squeezing the size of 'deposits' on their balance sheets. The deposits held by Japanese banks in London are mostly interbank transactions (the major part in dollars), therefore with very narrow margins. Profit-maximising incentives led, only naturally, to a rapid piling up of such deposits until around mid-1987. However, subsequently, as the need to prepare for the introduction of international capital adequacy requirements was perceived as more imminent, the banks started to cut down the size of such deposits. This was justified in their basic strategy to restrain rapid asset expansion as well as to improve return on assets (ROA) by removing less profitable assets.

Thus the total outstanding deposits held by 23 operating Japanese banks in London, measured in terms of pounds sterling at the end of March 1988, stood at £76.3 billion, down 16 per cent from the previous years' figure of £90.3 billion. Consequently, the whole asset size of these 23 banks, which had kept expanding throughout the previous decade, for the first time came virtually to a stand-still at £235 billion as of the end of March 1988.

However, the figures I have mentioned are nominal ones, expressed in terms of pounds calculated at current exchange rates. Calculations to separate the effects of exchange rate fluctuations, as shown in Dufey's paper, would be required for further in-depth analysis.

My second comment is with regard to the points that the paper seems to suggest in noting that control or regulation over Japanese domestic money market interest rates might have provided Japanese banks with some competitive advantage in financial markets abroad. Such arguments could have been justified in the late 1970s, but increasingly less so in recent years. Today no interest rate control remains in the domestic interbank money market (call market and bills market). Meanwhile, in the so-called open market, where non-banks, including individuals, also participate, various measures to liberalise interest rates have been implemented, including the reduction of minimum denomination of CDs and large denomination time deposits which bear market interest rates. In fact, the minimum denomination of large denomination time deposits is expected to be further reduced, step by step, to ¥10 million in the autumn of 1989. In addition, negotiations are being conducted by the people concerned on the liberalisation of interest rates on small denomination deposits at the earliest possible stage.

Under such circumstances, and where no exchange control exists, short-term capital would move freely between domestic and foreign money markets. So if, for example, money rates in foreign markets exceed those of the domestic market for some reason or other, such interest rate differential would generally diminish sooner or later through interest arbitrage. Any bank, therefore, might have the opportunity to take advantage of such interest-rate differential and find itself engaged in, for example, temporarily profitable Euro-yen transactions. But such transactions would not guarantee permanent advantage and would prove to be no longer profitable, given free movement of funds between domestic and foreign markets.

My third and last point is with regard to the integration of non-

Japanese talent into the structure of Japanese banks. The apparent difficulty is referred to in the paper as one of the Achilles' heels of Japanese banks and is also pointed to as one of the crucial factors that might affect the competitiveness of Japanese banks abroad in the coming years.

The Japanese banks seem to be fully aware of the significance of this. As a matter of fact, Japanese banks' officers often stress that the hiring and training of talented local personnel is essential, not only to maintain each bank's status as one of the key players in the international banking circle, but also for it to compete successfully in the new capital market products and establish relations with local customers.

Although the paper points out some possible difficulties, including cultural or language problems, Japanese banks in London seem already to have embarked on the process. Here, again, data collected by the Bank of Japan's London office with respect to this problem might provide some indications. According to the data, the total number of personnel hired in 23 Japanese banks in London was 2284, as of end of March 1988, out of which 1766 were local personnel whose numbers had increased by 37 per cent over a two-year period. This exceeds both the number and growth rate of Japanese personnel, which stood at 518 at the end of March 1988 and had increased by 11 per cent during the same period.

What these figures imply, we still have to see. But the amazing thing is that 93 per cent of newly hired personnel during the six-month period to March 1988 were non-Japanese. However, to what extent the integration of non-Japanese professionals has been achieved or will be achieved successfully still remains to be seen through individual banks' experience, as well as through further research and analysis.

6 The Future of Japanese Financial Development

COMMENT

John Forsyth

The rapid growth of the Japanese financial sector both within the domestic economy and within the international financial markets is a fact. If we are seeking an explanation we need to examine whether the growth is due to competitive advantage gained through superior technology and skills, regulatory advantage, or comparative advantage derived from the overall performance and structure of the Japanese economy.

The first explanation, competitive advantage derived through superior technology and skills, has provided the source of Japanese expansion in many industries; superior productivity and superior ability to introduce new products have been central to market success in many industries. However, while Japanese financial institutions have been efficient and effective operators in the markets, there is no real evidence that in the financial sector their skills and technology give them a clear competitive edge over their international competitors.

There is no parallel to the nineteenth-century expansion of the British financial system which did depend on exploiting internationally distinctive institutional arrangements and techniques; the Hong Kong and Shanghai Bank's prospectus said that it was their intention to establish in the Far East a bank run and organised on sound Scottish principles. In the case of Japan, there is no such simple and confident belief in the superiority of Japanese companies and their way of doing business underlying the expansion of their institutions in the international market.

The second explanation of Japan's financial growth, regulatory advantage, is one that has found considerable support. There has been a widespread feeling that Japanese institutions, in particular Japanese banks, have been able to expand their activities in the international markets because they enjoyed a more favourable regulatory environment, in particular with respect to capital requirements. Japanese financial growth therefore has been attributed to the fact that Japanese institutions have not been competing on a level playing-field, but one one which gives them an unfair competitive advantage. It now seems axiomatic that no playing-field is described as level by any group unless they derive positive advantage from it, and on that basis it is certainly possible to argue that elements of the regulatory structure favour Japanese institutions. The introduction of the new BIS guidelines on capital adequacy will end this distortion and so will remove some of the regulatory advantage enjoyed by Japanese banks. I would be surprised if this brought an end to Japan's relatively strong growth in the financial area, although I believe that it will change patterns of intermediation significantly.

However it should be remembered that Japanese financial institutions have also been constrained to operate under a regulatory system based on Glass-Steagall, even though Glass-Steagall was entirely contrary to Japanese financial traditions. This latter point is particularly important and leads me to consider that Japanese financial institutions have been disadvantaged by Glass-Steagall in a way which outweighs any advantage derived from capital adequacy requirements.

If the first two explanations of Japanese financial growth are rejected we must seek an explanation of the rapid growth of Japanese financial institutions in the international markets which relates to the overall development of the Japanese economy. The rapid growth of the Japanese economy in the postwar period has obviously presented a huge opportunity for Japanese financial institutions and provided scope for very rapid expansion. It should not, however, be regarded as a simple benefit for the Japanese financial sector.

Earlier in this volume reference was made to the fact that Japanese banks were having to pay a significant margin over the London Interbank Offer Rate (LIBOR) on their deposits up to the mid-1970s. That related directly to the fact that Japan's share of the world trade had been expanding very rapidly, generating a demand for trade finance which posed real problems in the Japanese financial system. Between 1961 and 1971, Japan's market share in world trade grew at 7.9 per cent while the only other major country to increase its market share in the face of this Japanese expansion was Germany, which managed a mere 1 per cent growth rate.

The present expansion and strength of the Japanese financial sector cannot be explained in terms of the growth of Japanese trade, for during the period when Japan's trade was expanding most rapidly its financial institutions were under significant strain in their international operations. The growth of the Japanese financial sector and its emergence as a major force has been a phenomenon of the 1980s which gives a convincing indication as to its source. For it is only in the 1980s that Japan has emerged with a major structural balance of payments surplus and begun to accumulate a large external asset position. The critical factor in Japanese financial growth has been its emergence as a major creditor nation. The growth of Japan's net external asset position provides the best indicator of its emergence as a major financial power and its likely future development in the financial sector.

In 1981, Japan's net external assets were under 1 per cent of gross domestic product (GDP): by 1987, the figure had risen to 12 per cent of GDP despite the huge currency loss on their holdings of international bonds, in particular US treasuries. In 1989, net external assets are projected to reach 15.8 per cent of GDP and it seems reasonable to anticipate that, by the late 1990s, Japan's net external assets will mount to over 30 per cent of GDP and that they may eventually reach 40 per cent of GDP.

In the context of a national economy, this is by no means unprecedented. As recently as 1986 the United Kingdom's external assets amounted to 29 per cent of GDP and Holland's external asset position is well over 30 per cent of GDP. However the scale of the Japanese economy does create a qualitative as well as a quantitative difference. A small country such as Holland can have net external assets at a very high proportion of GDP without having a great impact on the rest of the world, but for a large economy such as Japan a high level of external assets does have major implications world-wide. In the case of the United States a net external asset position which was built up in the 1960s, which was not very substantial as a proportion of GDP, was sufficiently significant in relation to the rest of the world to cause a strong political reaction. The Jean-Jacques Servan-Schreiber of the 1990s will indubitably be writing about the 'défi japonais' and, while present concerns centre around Japanese export penetration, concern in the future is bound to shift to Japanese investment penetration. This has not yet occurred because the Japanese structural surplus is a very recent phenomenon, so that neither the stock position nor the institutional mechanisms for capital outflow have developed fully.

In retrospect it is clear that the current account surplus and capital export by the OPEC countries in the 1970s initially flowed almost exclusively through the banking system, as it took time for them to develop the mechanisms required to deploy their funds in a more complex manner. Indeed, in the case of many OPEC countries, the mechanisms only began to develop after the surplus position had disappeared. However, in the case of the Middle Eastern oil producers, their surplus reflected the economic rents arising from oil production rather than domestic value-added, so that they had no particular advantage as direct investors in the international economy, and in that sense the range of their asset choices was limited.

The case of Japan is quite different, as Japanese growth has depended on the generation of value-added within their own economy, so that it has been associated with the emergency of supremely exportable skills. However this potential was not exploited initially, as in the early years the preponderance of funds was directed into the international bond market, with some diversification into equities in recent years. Latterly direct investment which allows Japanese companies to exploit their technology and management skills outside Japan has begun to grow very rapidly and may in time account for the largest proportion of Japanese capital export.

The mechanisms thus exist for generating large and diversified capital outflows from Japan, but they are as yet rather poorly developed and they have not been sufficient to prevent the large valuation difference emerging as between the Tokyo market and the other international markets. This has manifested itself in a very strong performance in the Tokyo stock market, which is not in itself an incentive to Japanese institutions to accelerate their international investments.

It is interesting to compare the development of the Japanese surplus and its financing with that of the United Kingdom earlier in the 1980s. The United Kingdom, whose surplus had derived from oil, has been the other great surplus country in the 1980s; but in her case the institutional mechanisms for exporting capital were much more fully developed. The United Kingdom had abolished exchange control in 1979 and still had in place many of the institutional mechanisms which were developed during the great period of British capital export in the nineteenth century. The result was a very rapid development of diversified international portfolio investment by British institutions, which enabled the British economy to be a major beneficiary of the great bull phase in world stock markets. The British corporate sector also began exporting capital on a substantial scale at an early stage and has continued aggressively as its financial position has strengthened. UK companies were perfectly used to having a high proportion of their assets overseas and had few cultural or linguistic difficulties in expanding their overseas operations at a rapid pace. The consequence was that, once valuation levels became slightly expensive by international standards, very large capital outflows were stimulated from institutional investors and the corporate sector.

To take a specific example, if an aggregate business in the United Kingdom saw that its price–earnings ratio had moved higher than those of similar companies in other industrial countries, it was relatively simple to increase earnings per share by acquiring such companies and financing the purchase by issue of new shares in the domestic market.

While in Japan such institutional mechanisms existed, they were not significant enough to affect the valuation level in the domestic market and therefore to prevent a valuation level being sustained in Tokyo at a significant premium to that in the other international markets.

In the longer term it seems likely that the institutional mechanisms will develop within the Japanese economy to a point where the capital outflows will be sufficient to begin influencing the valuation level. In this respect the critical point will be when Japanese companies begin to recognise that they can increase their earnings per share growth by using their highly-rated paper to acquire cheaper trading assets outside Japan. The opportunities for doing so at the present time are extraordinary, even though there are still significant barriers in terms of language, culture and experience. The rewards, however, are such that the barriers will be overcome, and by the end of the century a number of Japanese chief executives will look back at present relative valuation levels and say, as Clive did of his early years in Bengal, 'When I look back I am astonished at my own moderation.'

Once this happens it is clear that direct investment will begin to supplement financial investment and, as this occurs, the financial sector may benefit less from Japanese capital exports than it does at the moment. One should never forget that the financial sector is the capital exporter of both first and last resort. This means that the sudden emergence of a structural surplus is bound to favour the financial sector in the short term, but in the longer term the reaction of the corporate sector will lead to a contraction in the financial sector's role.

It is now common ground that Japan is going to become a major creditor economy, but the implication of this is that it will have an external asset position producing a rising flow of investment income which will in time, through the workings of the market, lead to a deficit on trade. That is what happened in the United Kingdom and there is no reason to suppose that it will not in time happen in Japan.

The emergence of Japan as a major international creditor does not necessarily imply that Tokyo is bound to become a global financial entrepôt. It is evident that within Europe the role of international financial centre and the role of capital exporter are not synonymous. Germany remains the great capital exporter within Europe, but it has for a number of reasons rejected the idea of developing a great financial entrepôt in Frankfurt. The idea has not been without attractions, but it carries with it implications which are not acceptable to the German community. London has always been eager to develop and maintain its entrepôt role and in the 1960s and 1970s demonstrated that such a role could be developed even in an economy with a chronically weak current account position. In the case of Japan, its future position as a capital exporter is assured, but it is not yet clear how far that will be associated with the development of an entrepôt role.

What is certain is that Japan has the opportunity to develop an entrepôt role in association with that of a capital exporter, but this must involve a significant degree of liberalisation of the Japanese market. In this context the future role of the yen is likely to prove critical.

There is now evidence of the emergence of trade and currency blocs in both Europe and North America: in Europe the 1992 process is moving the individual countries into a closer economic union, despite concerns about sovereignty, and in North America a parallel process is under way. A consequence of this may well be the emergence, as a response to common pressures, of an Asian trade and currency bloc. If this is the case there would seem to be no real competitor to the yen as the central currency or to Tokyo as the dominant market.

In this respect the separation of the role of regional entrepôt from that of major capital exporter in Europe does not provide a complete analogy, for two reasons. First, the position of West Germany within Europe, as the largest of four major powers, is a far less predominant one than that of Japan in Asia. Second, in Europe, London and the sterling markets represent, despite historic mismanagement, a strong competitor in the international markets.

The yen's internationalisation may well be driven by its emergence as the central currency in its own region with a consequent emergence of a regional entrepôt role. Whether that process will ultimately lead on to a global entrepôt role, only time will tell, but the decisive factor is likely to be Japan's willingness to open up its markets.

COMMENT

Ariyoshi Okumura

Recent financial issues in Japan may be characterised by the following points:

1. Challenges and responses *vis-à-vis* BIS capital adequacy rulings;
2. The US Glass-Steagall climate and its impact on Japanese financial system;
3. The Japanese style of insider trading prohibition and its implications; and
4. Internationalisation of the yen and its appraisal.

BIS Rulings

BIS rulings on the capital adequacy ratio of banks are certainly having a very meaningful impact on the management culture of Japanese banks. Quantitatively they now have to control the expansion rate of assets *pari passu* with capital increase, and qualitatively they now have to shift the strategic target from market share to return on assets.

More precisely, when banks set the ratio of annual asset increase at 8 per cent, which is considered to be the most realistic criterion for a model bank under the present financial environment in Japan, then they obviously have to modulate their current cruising speed (12 per cent); this could mean a decline of money flow in the market by ¥13 trillion (or $100 billion) a year. Eventually, non-BIS ruling institutions such as savings and loan associations, insurance companies and agricultural co-operatives will expand their market share, and also place much more reliance on direct financing via bonds and commercial paper. This kind of money-flow shift will of course have the effect of unintentionally increasing monetary stringency.

In the international arena, the results will be, as expected, a mitigation of the Japanese 'over-presence'. It is already happening. If we compare the ranking list of the top twenty syndicated loan lead managers for 1987 and 1988 (January to June), 11 banks were Japanese in 1987 but this figure has dropped to only two in 1988. The falling-off of Japanese banks' presence implies a partial deterioration of their role of recycling the Japanese $100 billion surplus to other parts of the world.

In addition to this, I am afraid that the final amendments of the BIS risk evaluation criteria will eventually choke their muddling efforts and capacity for recycling money to the third-world debtor governments.

Glass-Steagall

Traditionally, Japanese banks had always taken the 'universal banking' practice for granted until General MacArthur forcefully introduced the US-type Glass-Steagall framework. For this reason Japan is closely watching what is happening in the US Congress, where a set of new bills is being considered, indicating a strong possibility that universal banking will be realised. A compromise between the Financial Modernization Act of the Senate and the Depository Institution Act of the House of Representatives will eventually be reached. It is important to note that these two bills have in common the idea that they should allow banks to conduct securities business through bank holding companies. Japanese Glass-Steagall does not allow the establishment of any holding companies by banks; therefore, unless the holding company concept is accepted and honoured, the Japanese financial system will be unable to catch up with US developments. Accordingly a future reform of the Japanese system will be a somewhat complicated process.

The amalgamation of banking and securities business, however, is steadily going on. Banks now sell and deal in government bonds. Foreign-owned banks are even permitted preferentially to conduct the full range of securities business by the establishment of Tokyo branches, of which there are now 25. There is no reason why the MOF should leave this state of unfair counter-discrimination against Japanese banks for long.

BIS rulings may have an accelerating impact upon quicker reform, since, if an international standardisation of banking practice is to be sought, European, American and Japanese banks have to be given a 'level playing-field'. The real 'bottom line' issue is that Japanese banks will have to be given equitable access to the securities as well as to the trust business.

In addition, the aim of a unified Europe for 1992 is another factor that is moving the financial system towards universal banking.

Insider Trading

The Hollywood movie, *Wall Street*, was very interesting, for its key message is that only insiders will win and the outsiders will always fail.

Insider trading regulations in Japan have a long way to go, since ethical standards regarding this type of behaviour have not yet been properly rooted. However several incidents have apparently evoked public sentiment against unjust trading by the insiders.

Three steps for correcting the situation are now conceived by the authorities:

1. measures for voluntary prevention of insider trading by issuing companies, stock exchanges and financial institutions;
2. more active interventions by MOF through use of their interrogatory power; and
3. incorporation of criminal penalty clauses in the Security Transaction Act.

As a first step, the Transaction Act of the Securities and Exchange Law was recently amended and now the MOF has a more powerful right of investigation in order to 'prevent' illegal insider tradings. The incorporation of criminal penalty clauses, however, is a delicate issue, for the MOF is, after all, the supervisor as well as doctor of the securities industry. Therefore prevention should be its main objective. In order to have more meaningful judicial procedures in the future, we will need a more sophisticated system for indictment.

The Tokyo stock market is now the biggest in the world; its capitalisation value was $2.7 trillion in 1987. Trading by non-residents in Tokyo grew very rapidly, and reached $3.5 trillion during 1987. It follows that international standardisation of insider trading regulations is urgently needed in Japan. The Tokyo financial market will never reach its full potential as a world market unless Japan is successful in introducing an acceptable degree of transparency, both in insider trading regulations and in the practice of stock price formation.

The Yen

Now, last but not least, internationalisation of the yen is probably the most interesting and important, yet the most invisible issue of Japan's financial developments. It is certain, however, that internationalisation of the yen has been proceeding steadily in the mid-1980s. The policy stance of the government has clearly changed since 1980. The interest rate structure has been substantially deregulated. Access by foreign banks to the Tokyo market has been liberalised. And the issuance of Euro-yen bonds and the extension of Euro-yen loans have also been liberalised substantially. For the benefit of non-resident borrowers particularly, issuance of Samurai bonds (yen-denominated bonds issued in the Tokyo market) was also liberalised.

In consequence the yen bonds issued in the international market reached ¥3.5 trillion during 1987, which amounted to almost 15 per cent of all international issues; this means that the yen is quickly becoming 'internationalised', as a capital transaction currency at least.

However, if one looks at the yen from a different angle, it is not yet clear whether it is really becoming internationalised. For instance, although the ratio is creeping up, only 40 per cent of Japanese exports and only 10 per cent of imports are settled in yen, and the vast majority are settled in dollars. Needless to say, these ratios reflect the way Japanese trade partners evaluate the utilisation value of the yen. Trade customers' appraisal of the yen as a settlement currency should, in turn, define the future magnitude of the utilisation of the yen as a capital transaction currency.

It is my impression that the yen as a capital transaction currency is proceeding too far ahead of its real needs as a means of settlement. Probably this could be explained by the fact that, for instance, most of the yen bond issuers in the international market swap the yen proceeds, mostly into US dollars, for settlement purposes.

Much depends on how one perceives the internationalisation of the yen. Although one must admit that the importance of the yen as an international means of settlement is steadily growing, there still remains the question of how this is perceived. Will the yen be a co-key currency, together with the US dollar? I would not perceive the situation in that way. Whether a currency is defined as a key currency is decided not by a single function but by multiple functions; not simply by economic performance, but also by military power, political voice and even cultural affinity. Realistically, I do not see any international consensus to accept a hegemony of the yen, even as a regional key currency in Pacific Asia.

However I do think that a triangle setting of the US dollar, European currency unit (ECU) and the yen should be a type of future currency reform. If this comes about, the Japanese monetary authorities will eventually have to take on substantial responsibilities in order to devote themselves to the noble cause of 'policy convergence'. It is important to note that they are gradually becoming prepared for this. Also it is worth considering a theoretical concept of the standard drawing right (SDR) as the sole key currency in the future, which would reduce the burdens placed on the US dollar. There are various alternatives and steps. If the SDR as the key currency is a little far ahead, we might create a transitional menu, such as a triangle setting of the US dollar, the ECU based on the Deutschmark and a Pacific Currency Unit based on the yen, for instance.

In the meantime, the utilisation of the yen in the international market continues to progress steadily without any clear vision of the future landing-place. But one thing is very clear, and that is that the Japanese financial community is well versed in the yen financial business and will be prepared to better service the international economy in the future.

COMMENT

Kumiharu Shigehara

Japan's rapid economic and financial development in the postwar period has been associated with a remarkably high saving rate. It is therefore important to examine, first of all, how Japan's saving rate may develop in the future. This issue was discussed briefly earlier in this volume. It was pointed out that Japan is projected to experience significant population aging. Indeed, according to the OECD work, the proportion of the population aged 65 and older is projected to double between 1980 and 2010. It was also argued that such a demographic change will reduce Japan's saving rate.

The important question here concerns the time profile of the projected decline in the saving rate. The life cycle theory suggests that the expected rise in the numbers of the elderly in the total population by itself will reduce the savings rate. However a projected fall in the fertility rate in Japan may reduce the proportion of young dependents who consume and do not save and the total dependency ratio, that is to say the ratio of both young and elderly dependents to the working population, may remain practically unchanged for some time to come, while the age group of, say, 30 to 55 with a high saving rate may represent a higher proportion of total population. Thus demographic changes may not reduce Japan's savings rate significantly in the near future. A recent study by the OECD, based on a simulation model incorporating the life cycle assumption, suggests that Japan's national saving rate, which stood at around 20 per cent in 1985, may stay at about that level until 2010 and then start to decline sharply to half that level by 2020.

If Japan's saving rate remains high in the foreseeable future, the next important question would be whether the savings can be invested in such forms and in such places that the highest returns will be realised over the long term in the interests of not only the Japanese economy but also of the world economy as a whole. It is hoped in this context that Japan's direct investment abroad will grow further as a major component of the outlet of Japanese savings. Here I agree with Mr Watson, who in his remarks stressed the importance of recipient countries' more flexible policy with regard to foreign direct investment in securing the better world-wide allocation of financial resources. Perhaps I may add another point. The long-term relationship between Japanese banks and their domestic non-bank clients has been previously stressed as an essential feature of the Japanese financial system. A real challenge to Japanese banks in a new economic environment would be the establishment and deepening of their long-term relationships with their clients abroad so as to help them achieve higher growth potential.

This leads me to more specific issues relating to the future international roles of the Japanese banks and the Tokyo financial market. They cannot be discussed without regard to the growing importance of Asian economies, in particular those in East Asia. Some of these countries have extremely high saving rates while others do not. But they all have high growth potential. More flexible cross-border intermediations of domestic savings will become an essential part of the process of their integration into the world economy. The liberalisation of capital controls in these economies would permit their banks and business firms to have greater access to the Japanese banking system and more generally to the Tokyo financial market, which is geographically close to their business bases. This move would be expedited by further actions of the Japanese authorities to make the Tokyo market more market-oriented. It is important to note in this context that the Governor of the Bank of Japan representing the Japanese government at the IMF/IBRD (International Bank for Reconstruction and Development) annual meetings in Berlin in September 1988 indicated that Japan would facilitate the development of the Tokyo market as a world financial centre and that the yen should play a greater role as an international currency.

The role of foreign banks in Tokyo also merits our attention. They are actually at a crossroads. In Japan's high growth period, when Japanese interest rates were persistently higher than those in the western financial centres, foreign banks in Tokyo benefited from this pattern of international interest rate differentials by borrowing funds directly from the Euromarket or through their inter-office accounts, switching then into the yen and then lending the proceeds to the Japanese money markets and to Japanese non-bank enterprises whose access to the international credit markets was limited by exchange controls. This type of wholesale banking business by foreign banks in Tokyo became less profitable in more recent years, as the pattern of international interest rate differentials changed with the fall of interest rates in Japan to levels below those elsewhere and as exchange controls were abolished in Japan, allowing Japanese enterprises to have free access to foreign money and capital markets. In a new situation, most of the foreign banks in Tokyo have been placing greater emphasis on such operations as foreign exchange and Japanese government bond dealings, as well as swap options and forward exchange contracts. There have also been changes in foreign banks' business operations with Japanese corporations overseas. As leading Western banks have much wider networks of information and operations than their Japanese counterparts for conducting business, for example in the Middle East and in African countries, Japanese companies' interest appears to have shifted to business transactions with Western banks which have established strong positions there. In short, the basic strategy of foreign banks in Tokyo now appears to be geared to the achievement of economies of scale by providing a wider range of financial services to customers.

The Japanese banks are also changing their strategy. Under the earlier system of regulated interest rates, they typically competed for deposits from the household sector at administratively fixed low-interest rates and used most of the funds thus obtained for lending to the corporate sector and for the purchase of Japanese government bonds. In other words, they tried to maximise profits through economies of scale in a world of regulated interest rates. However the recent liberalisation of rates on banks' deposits of large denominations has tended to narrow spreads between lending and deposit rates and the planned further liberalisation of rates on bank deposits of smaller denominations will accelerate this process. Reduced profit margins on conventional banking business and the introduction of the Basle Agreement on risk asset ratios have prompted the Japanese banks to review their strategy based on economies of scale and to attach greater importance to economies of scope in their efforts to maximise profits. In this context, the Japanese banks now show a growing interest in the revision of the current legal arrangements distinguishing banking and securities business, which are applied to Japanese banks but not to foreign banks in Tokyo.

Before concluding, let me add a couple of brief comments on this issue. First, the greater the freedom accorded to financial institutions operating in Tokyo in realising economies of scope, the greater would be the attraction of the Tokyo market as an efficient international financial centre. But hasty institutional changes in this direction could impair the soundness of Japanese banking and the payments system, and undermine the confidence of participants in the Tokyo market, which is the *sine qua non* for the development of the Tokyo market as an international financial centre. The process of financial restructuring should involve a careful and constant review of the authorities' supervisory practices and the appropriate adjustment needed to achieve a higher degree of efficiency in the financial system and to secure its soundness.

Second, maintenance of the stability of the yen's domestic value is the key to its position in the international monetary system and also to the role of the Tokyo market as an international financial centre. In this regard, the need to preserve and enhance the effectiveness of the Bank of Japan's monetary policy should be duly taken into account in the restructuring of the Japanese financial system.

COMMENT

Alexander K. Swoboda

My comparative advantage in discussing future Japanese financial developments is a blissful ignorance of the details of Japanese financial markets. This ignorance will give me the opportunity to raise a number of broader, more macroeconomic issues about the future development of the Japanese financial market. I hope that my remarks will help stimulate some discussion of these broader issues.

One recurring point of discussion contained within this volume has been to seek an explanation for the rapid growth of the Japanese banking system over the past few years. The most straightforward explanation, it would seem to me, is that this growth simply reflects the importance Japan has acquired in the world economy; that this growth has only occurred in the past five years and not earlier reflects a catching-up process that was prevented from occurring earlier for a variety of reasons, including delayed liberalisation and integration in the world financial system. That being said, the main questions I want to address are whether and to what extent one can expect Tokyo to play the same type of role as New York or London as an international financial centre (IFC) and whether and to what extent one can expect the yen to come to play the same role as the dollar as an international currency.

To try and provide a first answer to these questions I will take up three issues in turn. The first concerns the general conditions required for a country's financial market to evolve into an international financial centre and for its currency to become an important international currency, that is, a reserve and vehicle currency (among other roles). The second concerns the extent to which Japan fulfills these conditions today. The third concerns the implications for the future role of Japan as a financial centre and of the yen as an international currency.

Conditions for an International Financial Centre

An important requirement for a country or city seeking to become an international financial centre is freedom of capital movements, and freedom of capital outflows in particular, since, once you are in, you want to be sure you can get out. What is at stake here is not just freedom today but also the expectation that such freedom will prevail tomorrow and thereafter; that is, credibility of the commitment of the centre to freedom of capital movements.

There are many factors that underlie such credibility. There is, first, political and social stability. Such stability is required if a stable legal framework defining property rights credibly and permanently is to exist. There is, second, economic stability, without which existing property rights may be called into question. A stable fiscal and monetary environment is particularly important here. The likelihood that freedom of capital movements will be maintained and exchange controls and arbitrary taxation avoided in the future depends crucially on a tradition of fiscal and monetary conservatism lest one expect the government to have recourse to the inflation tax to finance budget deficits and to the imposition of exchange controls to protect the inflation tax base.

There are additional requirements for a country to become an important financial centre and for its currency to be used as an international reserve asset by foreign central banks and as a vehicle for private transactions. One is that the country be economically important enough for a broad internal market for securities denominated in its currency to exist. Another is that the country should not have persistent current account deficits (or have had sizable surpluses over an extended period of time) so that one does not, again, expect the country to impose capital controls in order to protect its balance of payments. The important thing here is not that a current account surplus enables the country to accumulate net assets on the rest of the world but that the surplus diminishes the likelihood of exchange controls in the future and thus allows for the building-up of sizable gross assets on, and liabilities to, the rest of the world. That is, it is not so much net transfers of resources abroad as an important role in international financial markets in terms of gross assets and liabilities that matters here.

Does Japan Meet the Requirements for Becoming an IFC?

Obviously, Japan and the yen are increasingly fulfilling the preconditions for becoming an international financial centre and an international currency, respectively. The rapid growth of the Japanese economy has implied that its relative economic size has increased substantially over the past two decades, with Japanese GNP reaching roughly 60 per cent of that of the United States in 1987 at current prices and exchange rates. The economic importance of Japan in the world economy is not just a matter of relative GNP size; high per capita income, high saving rates, developing capital markets and a large value of exports and imports in absolute terms have all contributed to making Japan the second most important industrialised country (if one does not lump the European Community (EC) economies together). Macroeconomic policy has been quite stable over the past two decades and Japanese financial markets have begun to broaden. In addition, liberalisation of capital markets, both internal and external, has been significant. Finally, the large current account surplus makes it unlikely that exchange controls (at least additional restrictions) should be imposed. Most of the conditions for becoming an IFC thus seem to have been gradually fulfilled.

Nevertheless Japan is not yet a dominant international financial centre, nor is the yen yet a dominant international currency; (even if the yen is increasingly used on capital markets, less than 50 per cent of

Japanese exports and only some 10 per cent of Japanese imports are invoiced in yen). One reason is perhaps that the stability of property rights mentioned above has, in one sense, not yet been achieved. For most foreigners there is not yet a full understanding of what is going on in Japan and there remain questions as to whether access to various financial transactions is and will be on equal terms for everybody or as to whether there are not risks of future (implicit) expropriation of at least part of property rights by local groups. This factor is diminishing in importance, however, as transparency increases and the question becomes how far and how fast Japan is likely to become a dominant financial centre.

Prospects for the Future

Although the preconditions mentioned above are increasingly being fulfilled, neither history nor present circumstances suggests that the yen will rapidly become an international currency of the importance of the dollar, nor that Tokyo is likely to become the dominant financial centre that New York still is. A first reason for this conclusion is that currencies gain (and lose) international status only slowly. The evolution of the world currency system into a sterling era and from a sterling to a dollar standard and area (or era) took well over a century. Sterling lost its status as the dominant currency only long after its relative economic power had declined significantly; similarly, the dollar is likely to remain the most used international currency for a while, even though the relative economic power of the United States has declined steadily over the past two or three decades. The 'depth, breadth, and resiliency' of the United States internal securities market is one reason why it is likely to take some time for the dominance of the dollar to wane, though the process might accelerate.

Second, today's world is not one in which one can expect the hegemony of a single power. Even if Japan manages to catch up in economic size with the United States over the next 20 years, it will not be the single dominant economic power; the United States will still exist and the European Community, if it manages to get its act together, will dominate both in terms of economic size (not to mention the Eastern bloc or Asia outside of Japan). In short, we are moving to a multipolar world where the yen cannot play the role that the dollar used to play (and to some extent still does). This being said, there is little doubt that

Japan and the yen will be one of the major poles of that world and will come to play an increasingly important role, reflecting not only the size but also the high growth rate of Japan.

Third, the future role of Tokyo and the yen will depend crucially on whether the relationship between Japan, the EC and the United States will be a protectionist or an open one. The outcome here is partly a matter of international political economy and politics, but will depend also on whether and how contemporary current account imbalances are dealt with. Initially, I had planned to concentrate my remarks on that last topic and on the role of policy co-ordination, but then shifted the emphasis onto the international financial centre issue. However the policy co-ordination and imbalances topic does have some relevance to the IFC issue. Let me conclude with a few brief comments on the subject.

The main concern, it seems to me, is, or should be, a reduction in the current account deficit of the United States, whether the counterpart is a reduction in the Japanese surplus and/or a redirection of the latter towards other regions, notably the less developed world. The crucial matter here is to achieve an increase in the US national saving rate and the policies to be co-ordinated are primarily fiscal policies, not monetary and exchange-rate policies. I would thus enter a plea for de-emphasising the role of exchange-rate arrangements in the correction of current account imbalances, lest their failure in the absence of more fundamental fiscal correction kindle the very protectionist actions exchange-rate policy was seeking to avoid in the first place. Once again, correction of the US fiscal deficit would seem to be the first obvious step in bringing that country's saving rate up and its current account deficit down. Improvement in the external deficit would in turn seem necessary if the United States is to maintain its status as an IFC, with an important, if not the dominant, currency for years to come – and if Tokyo and the yen are to come to play a role commensurate with Japan's economic size and performance. For a decline in US status brought about by failure to resolve macroeconomic imbalances and accompanied by rising protectionism would benefit neither Japan nor the rest of the world.

Name Index

Subject Index

Note: All entries refer to Japan unless otherwise indicated.